Tick...Ti

Hear that clock ticking? It's the coun........................gy Ecology/Molecular Subject Test, which will be here before you know it. Whether you have a year to go or just one day, this is the time to start maximizing your score.

The Test Is Just a Few Months Away!

Don't worry—you're still ahead of the game. However, it is important that you stop delaying and begin preparing now. Follow **The Big Picture: How to Prepare Year-Round** (page 253) to make the most of your time so you'll be ready on test day. This section gives you strategies to put into place up to a year before you actually take the test.

Actually, I Only Have a Few Weeks!

Even if you're down to the last few weeks before the test, you still have plenty of time for a full review. To make the best use of your time, turn to **The Main Course: Comprehensive Strategies and Review** (page 19), where you'll find **Strategies for Multiple-Choice Questions** (page 21) to help you ace the multiple-choice questions. This section also includes **The Diagnosis: How Ready Are You?** (page 31). This diagnostic test allows you to identify areas of weakness that you should address. You should also review all of the **in-depth subject review chapters** (beginning on page 101) for an overview of the big topics usually covered on the SAT Biology E/M Subject Test. As you work through this information, keep track of the concepts, facts, and ideas that seem confusing or unfamiliar so you can get more information about them. Use the **Practice Tests** (beginning on page 263) to increase your comfort with both the format and content of the test.

WITHDRAWN

Let's Be Honest. The Test Is Tomorrow and I'm Freaking Out!

No problem! Review the **Introduction** (page ix), with information **About the Test** (page x), and **The Essentials: A Last-Minute Study Guide** (page 1), so you know what to expect when you arrive to take the test and have some ideas as to how to approach the test questions. Then, take at least one of the **Practice Tests** (beginning on page 263). Don't worry about your score—just focus on getting familiar with the test. Before you go to bed, review the **Quick Test-Taking Tips** (page 7) once more. They'll walk you through the day ahead.

Relax. Make the most of the tools and resources in this review guide, and you'll be ready to earn a top score.

My Max Score

SAT BIOLOGY E/M SUBJECT TEST

Maximize Your Score in Less Time

Maria Malzone

sourcebooks **edu**

This publication is designed to provide accurate and authoritative information in regard to the subject matter covered. It is sold with the understanding that the publisher is not engaged in rendering legal, accounting, or other professional service. If legal advice or other expert assistance is required, the services of a competent professional person should be sought.—*From a Declaration of Principles Jointly Adopted by a Committee of the American Bar Association and a Committee of Publishers and Associations*

All brand names and product names used in this book are trademarks, registered trade-marks, or trade names of their respective holders. Sourcebooks, Inc., is not associated with any product or vendor in this book.

Published by Sourcebooks, Inc.
P.O. Box 4410, Naperville, Illinois 60567-4410
(630) 961-3900
Fax: (630) 961-2168
www.sourcebooks.com

CIP data is on file with the publisher.

Printed and bound in the United States of America.
VP 10 9 8 7 6 5 4 3 2 1

Also Available in the My Max Score Series

AP Exam Study Aids

AP Biology
AP Calculus AB/BC
AP English Language and Composition
AP English Literature and Composition
AP European History
AP Statistics
AP U.S. Government and Politics
AP U.S. History
AP World History

SAT Subject Test Study Aids

SAT Literature Subject Test
SAT Math 1 and 2 Subject Test
SAT U.S. History Subject Test
SAT World History Subject Test

ASVAB Study Aids

ASVAB: Armed Services Vocational Aptitude Battery

Contents

Introduction

Everyone comes to the SAT Biology E/M Subject Test from a different place. For some, it's the one SAT subject test of their high school career; for others, it's just one test of many. Some students have focused on it all year, supplementing their classwork with extra study and practice at home. Other students haven't been able to devote the time they would like—perhaps other classes, extracurricular activities, after-school jobs, or family obligations have gotten in the way. But wherever you're coming from, this book can help! It's been designed to provide maximum assistance no matter where you are on your study path.

You'll find that this book has been divided into three sections: a last-minute study guide to use in the days before the test, a comprehensive review for those with more than a week to prepare, and a long-term study plan for students preparing well in advance.

Think of each section as full of suggestions rather than as being a rigid prescription. Feel free to pick and choose the most helpful pieces from each section. Of course, if you have time, we recommend that you review *everything*—and take as many practice tests as you can, as many times as you can.

Whether you have a day to cram or a year to study at leisure, here are some things you should know before diving into the test.

For starters: What is the SAT Biology E/M Subject Test, and what does it cover?

About the Test

The SAT Biology E/M Subject Test is used nationally to assess student readiness for college-level work in this discipline. Some colleges require potential students to take particular SAT subject tests in order to qualify for admission to the school itself or to a particular major or course of study. Some schools may even award you college credit if you score high enough—talk to your school guidance counselor about the requirements and possibilities for the schools in which you're interested.

The SAT Biology E/M Subject Test is designed to measure students' knowledge and skills in the biological sciences; specifically, it

- assesses understanding of core biological principles and
- analyzes the ability to recognize and apply basic concepts of the discipline.

Additionally, depending upon the emphasis you choose, the examination also tests either your knowledge of biological communities, populations, and energy flow (ecology), *or* your knowledge of biochemistry and cellular structures and processes (molecular biology).

The hour-long tests consist of a total of 80 multiple-choice questions. The first 60 multiple-choice questions cover core principles in biology. Then, you will choose an additional 20 multiple-choice questions on *either* ecological (E) *or* molecular (M) subject matter.

What's Covered

The concepts covered on the SAT Biology E/M Subject Test break down as follows:

TOPIC AREA	BIOLOGY-E ESTIMATED %	BIOLOGY-M ESTIMATED %
Cellular and molecular biology	15%	27%
Ecology	23%	13%
Genetics	15%	20%
Organismal biology	25%	25%
Evolution and diversity	22%	15%

Help! How Do I Pick Which Test to Take?

On test day, you will have to choose either the Biology-E or the Biology-M Test. Although you *can* eventually take both tests, you *cannot* take them on the same testing day. You will have to indicate on your answer sheet which test you are taking.

So, how do you choose which test to take? Base your decision on your comfort level with and knowledge of the material. You should choose Biology-E if you feel more knowledgeable about biological communities, populations, and the flow of energy. You should choose Biology-M if you feel more knowledgeable about biochemistry and cell structure and processes.

Test Scoring

As you probably already know, SAT subject tests are graded using a raw score that is later converted to a point-based score between 200 and 800.

Here is how the raw score is calculated.

1. For each question you answer correctly, you are awarded one (1) point.
2. For each question you answer incorrectly, you are docked fractional points. (The amount of fractional points varies depending on the test.) For Biology E/M, you lose 0.25 point for each question you answer incorrectly.

3.   You don't earn or lose any points for those questions you do not answer.

4.   Once your correct answers are totaled and the fractional points deducted, your raw score number is produced. If this number is a fraction, it is rounded up or down accordingly.

5.   A complex process called *equating* is then used to convert the raw score to a scaled score between 200 and 800 (with 800 being the highest score available).

Your score shows college admissions staff how well you performed compared to other students who took the test. For example, the mean or average scores for students who took the Biology E/M Subject Test in 2011 were as follows:

- Biology-E: 604
- Biology-M: 635

So, if you took the test in 2011 and scored close to those numbers, college admissions staff understood that to mean you scored about as well as *half* the students who took the test across the United States.

Naturally, your goal should be to beat this average score by as high a margin as possible. And with this material in hand, you should feel confident about your ability to do just that. Put this material to its intended use so you'll have not only a strong understanding of the key concepts being tested but also ample opportunity to practice tried-and-true testing strategies.

Beyond the material in this book, we make an additional SAT Biology E/M Subject Test Practice Test available to you on our website, mymaxscore.com. That site includes practice tests for other SAT subject tests as well.

Good luck!

THE ESSENTIALS: A LAST-MINUTE STUDY GUIDE

So, it's a night or two before the test and you just don't feel ready. Should you panic? Absolutely not! This is the time to take a deep breath and finish final preparations. If you've been taking a biology class, studying regularly, and preparing in other ways throughout the year, you should be just about at your goal. All you need to do is calm your nerves by breathing deeply, refresh your mind by reviewing a few key strategies, and get your belongings together for test day. It's not too late to maximize your score!

First, remember that being anxious is just a waste of your energy. You can let your nerves paralyze you, or you can get into a better frame of mind by focusing your thoughts and energy on the things you can do now. That approach is more likely to bring you success than worrying about how nervous you feel. Guide your energy into positive activities that leave you feeling prepared.

Second, if you're testing soon, you don't have a lot of time available, so it's important to make the most of the time you do have. Find a location where you have privacy to study in peace, such as your bedroom (good) or the library (even better, if your house is a busy one with a lot of distractions). Tune out the world by turning off your telephone, your computer, and all of your other electronic gadgets. Stop texting, quit surfing the Internet, and turn off the music. Ask your family and friends not to disturb you unless it's really important. Close your door (or park yourself in a library cubicle) and get ready.

Getting Ready

Step 1: Review the Test-Taking Tips

Although you're probably already familiar with the format of this test, if it's been a while since you've considered the test setup or if you're just not sure where to start, take a few minutes to review the first section of the book (that means you should also go back to the **Introduction** on page ix before going forward to the **Quick Test-Taking Tips** on page 7). If you only have a few days until you test, take time to carefully review the **Strategies for Multiple-Choice Questions** (page 21) in **The Main Course: Comprehensive Strategies and Review** (page 19). The strategies are tried and true; they can really give your score a boost if you pay attention and apply them carefully.

Step 2: Examine the Big Ideas

If you don't have time for a full content review, at least take the time to look over the basics. We've compiled these for you in **Big Ideas in Biology E/M** (page 13). This section outlines the concepts, themes, and ideas you'll encounter in all parts of this test. If you have time, continue on to the chapter reviews as well.

Step 3: Take a Practice Test

One of the most effective ways to *really* get to know any exam is to take a practice test, preferably one that has been specifically designed to mimic the test in question. In this book, you'll find not one, not two, but *three* complete practice tests for your use (the diagnostic test and two additional practice tests). *Plus*, a fourth practice test is available to you on the mymaxscore.com website at no extra charge. Make sure you download and take that test, too.

When taking practice tests, it's important to pretend you're really taking the exam. That means you should test in a quiet area with no distractions, avoid looking at any reference material while you're testing, and time yourself carefully. Use the answer keys provided to see how well you're likely to do if similar questions are asked on the actual test. When reviewing your responses, watch for common themes or trends and identify the areas where you can improve. Once you know where you need the most help, review the appropriate sections in this book, or go back to your class notes and textbook for more detail.

The Night Before: Gather Your Materials

The last thing you want to do the morning of the test is rush around try-ing to find everything you need. Therefore, we've included a checklist so that you can make sure you've gathered these items together before-hand. Put these items in a backpack or small bag (along with anything else you think you might need). Have your bag ready so that you can grab it and go in the morning.

- Your admissions ticket is critical, so pack this first. Place your ticket in an easy-to-locate side pocket or zippered compartment so you can get your hands on it quickly when entering the test site.

- You will need photographic proof of identity, so bring your photo identification. Acceptable photo ID includes your photo driver's license, state-issued ID, valid passport, or school ID. You can also bring student ID on school stationery; see your guidance counselor if you need this. Store your ID with your admissions ticket.

- Pack several sharpened No. 2 pencils and a nonsmudging eraser. Note that this test is graded entirely by computer, so any smudging *can* impact your results. That's why it's important to make sure your erasers won't leave any marks. Also, note that while there *should* be a pencil sharpener available in the testing room, it's probably not a bad idea to pack a portable sharpener, just in case. Ink pens are not acceptable for this test.

- A calculator is not allowed for this test, so don't bring one.

- Plan to wear or bring a watch so that you can keep an eye on the clock as you work. A watch will help you to pace yourself appropriately. (Of course, if your watch has alarms, buzzers, or beepers, turn them off!)

- Include a small, easy-to-eat snack. Test day is going to be long, and you may need nourishment. Choose a snack that's high in protein with a low carbohydrate count. Avoid messy items like chocolate bars, as these can melt onto your hands and desk. Also avoid nuts, as they can trigger allergies in other testers. Some good choices might be an energy or protein bar or drink or an easy-to-eat piece of fruit such as a banana.

- Pack a bottle of water. You'll want something to drink at some point, and it's best to avoid substances with a lot of sugar or caffeine. Although you may think they'll give you a boost of energy, they're more likely to contribute to test jitters—and you'll have enough of those on your own!

- Avoid packing items you can't take into the testing room. For example, cell phones, pagers, calculators, and other electronic devices are prohibited in the testing room for a variety of reasons.

- Here's one important tip: Try to pack *only* what you need.

  ○ Admissions ticket

  ○ Photo ID

  ○ Pencils, eraser, and portable sharpener

  ○ Watch/timer

  ○ Snack and bottle of water

Test Day: Tips

Here are some other tips for managing test day.

- The night before your test, *don't* stay up all night studying. At that point, you'll be as ready as ever! Instead, concentrate on getting a good night's sleep. It's more important to feel rested and alert than it is to attempt a last-minute cram session.

- Eat a light but satisfying meal in the morning. Protein-rich foods like eggs, nuts, and yogurt are good choices, as they'll fill you up but won't give you a sugar or caffeine crash later. But don't eat too much—you don't want to be sluggish or uncomfortably full. If you must have coffee or another caffeinated beverage, that's fine. Just try not to overdo it.

- Dress in comfortable layers. The testing room might be hot or cold. You can't control the temperature, so you'll need to be able to adjust to it. Also, make sure your clothes are comfortable. Your newest outfit might be gorgeous, but the last thing you need during the test is to feel annoyed by pants that are too tight or irritated by fabrics that feel itchy.

- Don't forget your backpack! It has all of your important stuff in it.

- Relax! Once you get to the testing room, take a few deep breaths and try to channel some of your energy into relaxation. Try blowing your breath into your hands to rid your body of adrenaline. Remind yourself that you know the material, you understand how the test works, and you are ready. It's natural to be nervous, but it's better to use that energy for the mental task ahead.

- Once the test begins, set everything else in your mind aside and focus on doing your best. Don't worry about things you have to do later or tomorrow or next week. Focus on the test in front of you. You've done all you can to prepare—now it's time to make that preparation pay off.

Quick Test-Taking Tips

The SAT Biology E/M Subject Test is a multiple-choice test with 80 questions. You'll answer 60 multiple-choice questions on core principles in biology; then, depending on the additional subject matter you selected, you'll answer an additional 20 multiple-choice questions on *either* ecological (Biology-E) *or* molecular (Biology-M) subject matter. You'll have one hour (60 minutes) to answer all 80 questions. That means you'll have *less than one minute* to read and answer each question. That's one minute to read and comprehend the question, analyze any associated chart or other data, and review all five answer options in order to select the most appropriate response. Clearly, this test is going to go very quickly. But we aren't pointing that out to make you worry. You can and will be successful. But you do need to recognize that a timed test means time is limited. Therefore, it's important that you understand just how to approach each question to maximize your score.

Here's a tip. The SAT subject tests are intentionally designed to discourage test-takers from guessing at answers. If you go back and reread the **Test Scoring** section in the **Introduction** (page ix) of this book, you'll see that test-takers are actually docked a fractional point (0.25) for answering items incorrectly. That approach is meant to deter you from taking random guesses when you don't have any idea about the answer.

However, if you think that means you should never take a guess when you're unsure of an answer, you'd be wrong! We're going to recommend that you make guesses—*educated* guesses. Read on.

Tip 1: Answer the Easy Questions First

For some timed tests, it doesn't make sense to skim the questions to find those that are easier to answer. However, for the SAT subject tests, this is a valid approach, and you should plan to use it. Because you're awarded a raw score point for every correct answer, it's in your best interest to find the questions you feel are "easy" and answer those first.

Tip 2: Don't Use the Answer Booklet Just Yet

If you're skimming the test for easy questions, you can waste a LOT of precious time locating and recording the answers one by one on your answer sheet. For example, let's say you find questions 1, 6, 9, 12, 17, 22, 26, 37, 41, 42, and 57 to be easy and can answer those right away. How much time do you think it will then take you to carefully locate the correct answer lines on the answer sheet in order to fill in your choices? If you guessed "*A lot!*" you'd be right about that. Instead of wasting that time checking and double-checking for the correct answer slots, develop a system for writing directly on the test booklet.

If you're sure of an answer, write the letter of the correct answer option *clearly* in the margin next to the test number in the test booklet. You might want to circle the letter of the correct answer or place a check mark next to the item so that when you later review your answers to move them to the answer sheet, you will know you were *sure* of this answer. That helps avoid wasting even more time reading, rereading, and trying to remember.

We're going to recommend you mark up your test booklet in other ways as you work your way through the test, so make sure you *clearly work out the mark-up system you want to use* beforehand. In general, the simpler the system, the easier it will be for you to use. There's no need to make it complicated.

Tip 3: Answer the Question in Your Head

Read each question or question stem and answer it in your head before you actually look at any of the answer options. At times, answer choices are written in such a way that they intentionally distract you from the correct answer. (That's why they're called "distracters.") However, if you review the answer options with a good idea of the answer in mind, you'll be less confused by other options.

Tip 4: Pay Attention to the Words

As you read the questions and answer choices, pay attention to the wording. Some questions will include words like *NOT* or *EXCEPT*. The inclusion of these words radically changes the answer to the question. You're looking for the answer that is *not* true or that does *not* apply. This might seem obvious, but it's actually quite easy to overlook these words when you're reading quickly.

Other questions might include qualifiers. A *qualifier* is a word or group of words that limits or modifies the meaning of another word or group of words. When a qualifier appears in a question, the correct response must appropriately reflect that qualifier. For example, a qualifier might indicate that the correct answer option is the one that is *sometimes* but *not always* true. Some commonly used qualifiers include

- likely, unlikely;
- apt to, may, might;
- always, never, often, sometimes;
- some, a few, a majority, many, most, much; and
- frequently, probably, usually, seldom, sometimes.

Additionally, keep an eye out for double negatives, because (just as in math) two negatives make a positive. For example, if a question asks you which answer is *not uncommon*, the question is actually asking you which answer is *common*.

Tip 5: Read *All* the Answer Options

Even when you're pretty sure of your answer, make sure you review all of the answer options before making your selection. Sometimes more than one answer may be correct; however, one choice will always be more correct than the others. Additionally, the answer you choose should completely address all parts of the question and reflect any qualifier that has been included in the question.

Tip 6: Use Elimination Strategies

SAT subject tests do penalize you for guessing, but that doesn't mean you should avoid making guesses. What you want to make instead are *educated* guesses; these are guesses you've made after eliminating the answers you know are wrong.

So how do you eliminate wrong answers? Try the following tips.

- Eliminate any answer you know is wrong. Draw a light line through these in the test booklet.

- Eliminate options that seem unlikely or totally unfamiliar. You might want to circle or underline or otherwise highlight the part of the answer that you believe makes it a wrong choice.

- Eliminate options that don't seem to fit grammatically with the stem/question. This is a little trickier, but if it doesn't seem to really fit in with the question, it's probably not the right answer. Again, circle or underline the part of the answer that seems sketchy.

- Give each answer option the "true–false" test. The true–false test simply involves asking yourself if the answer or some part of the answer is false. Sometimes distracters are written to include wording or specific details that are misstated or that demonstrate faulty reasoning. If some part of the answer is wrong, the whole answer is wrong. Eliminate those answer options that are false.

- Watch for the inclusion of absolutes such as *all*, *only*, *always*, or *never*. These often signify incorrect responses, because an absolute can make a sometimes-correct answer wrong when the absolute is applied. For example, "The moon is never visible during the day," is wrong because although the moon is *usually* invisible during the day, there are times of the month and places on the planet when it can be seen. Draw a line through answer options you can eliminate for this reason.

- Look for paired statements with contradictory answers. For example, if option A says, "The sky is green," and option B says, "The sky is blue," that's a paired contradictory statement. In such a situation, one of the pair is frequently the correct answer.

The more answer choices you eliminate, the better your chances of guessing at the correct answer. If you can eliminate at least two or more of the answer options, you should take a guess.

Once you're ready to commit to an answer, write the letter of your answer choice in the margin of the test booklet next to the question number. Circle it or put a check mark next to it as you did with the questions you answered easily.

Tip 7: Fill Out the Answer Sheet with Care

Make sure you're timing yourself as you work through your examination. Every 15–20 minutes, stop what you're doing and mark your answers in your answer sheet. You will *only* get credit for answers in the answer sheet, so this is a critical step! You should make sure you give yourself enough time to transfer the answers from your booklet to your answer sheet.

The SAT subject tests are graded completely by computer, so it's critical that the answer sheet be kept clean and free from any stray markings. Fill in your answers *carefully*, stopping every few questions to make sure your question and answer numbers match before filling in the oval. Also, be sure you have penciled in the answer space completely and haven't left any stray pencil marks in other spaces.

Big Ideas in Biology

W e're not going to lie to you: the SAT Biology E/M Subject Test is no walk in the park. It's a tough test that requires a significant commitment from you. However, unlike some of the other examinations you'll deal with in your high school career, you'll have more than one opportunity to ace this test (it's offered six times per year!). Of course, the best approach to *any* test is to do your best the first time so you don't have to take it again.

Here are quick summaries of the most important "big ideas" or concepts in the SAT Biology E/M Subject Test. Your study should focus on the following key areas.

Cellular and Molecular Biology

Cellular and molecular biology are intertwined disciplines that involve studying the molecular nature of living organisms. This study attempts to understand biochemical life processes and covers a wide range of topics that address fundamental questions, such as how humans and other organisms live, grow, reproduce, mature, and die.

Cellular biology involves the study of cells, specifically their physiological properties and structure, the organelles they contain, how they interact with the environment, and the cellular life cycle. This study is undertaken on both microscopic and molecular levels. Research in cell biology covers a diversity of organisms, such as single-celled organisms (bacteria and yeast) as well as the many specialized cells in multicellular organisms (humans, among others).

Molecular biology is chiefly concerned with the study of the interactions among various cell systems, such as the interactions among different types of DNA, RNA, and protein biosynthesis, as well as the regulation of such interactions.

Some common topics to study include

- basic atomic structures and bonding (hydrogen bonding and DNA);
- characteristics of water (hydrogen bonding, adhesion, cohesion);
- characteristics of solutions (pH, solute concentration);
- organic compounds, including carbohydrates, lipids, and proteins;
- nucleic acids (DNA and RNA);
- protein synthesis (transcription and translation);
- cellular structure and organization;
- cell membranes and transport;
- cell division (binary fission, mitosis);
- the cell cycle;
- cellular respiration;
- photosynthesis; and
- structure and activity of enzymes.

Ecology

Ecology studies the relationships of organisms to one another as well as to their physical and chemical surroundings. It is also concerned with the interactions of different populations within the environment. Ecology may involve studying a single species or population, the wider community that includes many species, the movement of matter and energy through that community, and/or the larger-scale processes within the biome. As a scientific discipline, ecology is concerned with the evolutionary changes that occur among a population in response to interactions at different levels such as population, community, ecosystem, biome, and biosphere.

Ecology encompasses many types of study, including animal behavior, population interactions, the effects of human interventions and environmental changes, wildlife conservation efforts, and nutrient and energy cycling.

Some common topics to study include

- chemical cycles, such as the water cycle, the carbon cycle, and the nitrogen cycle;
- communities, including structure and interaction of populations;
- energy flow and nutrient cycles;
- ecological succession;
- ecosystems and biomes, such as forests, grasslands, deserts, tundra, and so on;
- food chains, including producers and consumers; and
- population growth, including types of growth and environmental carrying capacity.

Genetics

Genetics is the study of heredity, or how DNA is passed from one generation to the next. Genetics involves learning about the organization and regulation of genes, as well as the way genes function and transmit information from an organism to its offspring. Genetics is based upon principles developed by an Austrian monk, Gregor Mendel, who spent decades studying and analyzing heredity in pea plants. Although the study of genetics existed to some degree before Gregor Mendel, his laws form the basis of the modern understanding of inheritance. Specifically, Mendel's study resulted in the development of three key laws: the law of dominance, the law of segregation, and the law of independent assortment. Of course, many genes also follow non-Mendelian patterns of inheritance, such as gene linkage, codominance, sex linkage, and variable expressivity. Population genetics examines the transmission and frequency of alleles in populations.

In the twentieth century, the study of genetics expanded to include molecular genetics, which examines the role of nucleic acids (DNA and RNA) in inheritance. The molecular nature of the gene, the genetic code linking genes to proteins, and the effects of mutations were discovered. The regulation and expression of genes was studied, and the formation of gametes via meiosis was detailed.

Some common topics to study include

- Mendelian genetics and inheritance patterns;
- Punnett squares, probabilities, and ratios;
- non-Mendelian inheritance patterns (gene linkage, codominance);
- meiosis, crossing over, and recombination;
- codons and the genetic code;
- mutations;
- gene expression and regulation; and
- allele, genotype, and phenotype frequencies.

Organismal Biology

Organismal biology is the study of structure, function, ecology, and evolution at the organismal level. In order to survive, all organisms must coordinate vital life processes, such as the acquisition and circulation of food and oxygen, the elimination of waste, and the continuation of the species via reproduction. Multicellular organisms must also maintain internal homeostasis, which can be accomplished by sensing and responding to internal and external conditions (for example, via negative feedback loops). Over many eons, multicellular organisms have evolved sophisticated organ systems to accomplish these tasks. Each of these systems includes the organs and associated parts that work together to carry out body processes. Organismal biology is concerned with the different systems organisms have evolved over time in order to meet their bodily needs.

Some common topics to study include

- human organ systems, such as digestive, circulatory, nervous, and so on;
- physiology (human and animal);
- reproduction and development (emphasis on plants and animals);
- structure, function, and development of organisms (emphasis on plants and animals);
- animal behavior, including social behavior and learning;
- classification, growth, and evolutionary developments of plants; and
- structure and function of roots, stems, and leaves.

Evolution and Diversity

Biological evolution is a result of the changes that occur in populations over time. Evolution involves genetic rather than nongenetic changes that cannot be passed to the next generation. One process by which this occurs is natural selection. Some inherited characteristics help organisms to better survive or reproduce in the particular environment in which the organism lives; because such characteristics confer an advantage, they tend to increase in frequency in the population. Other characteristics—those that confer disadvantages—tend to decrease in frequency. Other mechanisms that lead to evolutionary change include sexual selection, founder effects, and population bottlenecks.

Speciation is the formation of new species. Over Earth's history, many species have formed, with some becoming extinct. This process has led to the diversity of species that we see today. Taxonomy attempts to sort all living things according to their evolutionary histories.

Life's history began sometime after the formation of Earth, about 4.6 billion years ago. Scientists have tried to re-create the atmospheric conditions of the early Earth to better understand how life formed. The evolution of cyanobacteria, which carry out photosynthesis and release oxygen, led to a massive change in the composition of Earth's atmosphere, paving the road for the evolution of life on Earth.

Some common topics to study include

- origins and early history of life;
- history of life on Earth, including extinctions;
- evidence and patterns of evolution;
- natural selection; and
- diversity and classification of living organisms.

THE MAIN COURSE: COMPREHENSIVE STRATEGIES AND REVIEW

About the Test

The SAT Biology E/M Subject Test is used nationally to assess student readiness for college-level work in the discipline of biology. This test is designed to measure your knowledge and skills in the biological sciences; specifically, it

- assesses understanding of core biological principles and
- analyzes the ability to recognize and apply basic concepts of the discipline.

Additionally, depending upon the emphasis chosen, the examination also tests either your knowledge of biological communities, populations, and energy flow (E Test), *or* your knowledge of biochemistry and cellular structures and processes (M Test).

The examination takes one hour. During this hour, you'll answer a total of 80 multiple-choice questions. First, you'll answer 60 multiple-choice questions on core principles in biology. Then, depending on the subject matter you selected, you'll answer an additional 20 multiple-choice questions in *either* ecological (Biology-E) *or* molecular (Biology-M) subject matter.

For more information on the content of each test, refer back to the **About the Test** section of this book (page x).

How It's Scored

As you probably already know, SAT subject tests are graded using a raw score that is later converted to a point-based score between 200 and 800. The scoring of the examination is covered in detail in the previous **Test Scoring** section. Refer back to page xi for a review.

Strategies for
Multiple-Choice Questions

A ll of the questions on the SAT Biology E/M Subject Test are multiple choice, but there are several different types of multiple-choice questions that you will encounter on this test. To be prepared to tackle these questions, you should take some time to review the specific question types and consider some basic strategies for addressing them successfully.

This section is specially designed to help you prepare for the types of questions asked on this test. It provides some basic strategies to help you answer the different types of questions.

Basic Question-Answering Strategies

As outlined in the **Quick Test-Taking Tips** section on page 7, there are some important general strategies you should keep in mind when answering questions on the SAT Biology E/M Subject Test. Utilizing these basic strategies on test day will help you answer questions as efficiently and accurately as possible. These strategies include the following:

1. Skim the Questions

It is important to remember that the SAT Biology E/M Subject Test is a closely timed 60-minute test. As such, it is critical to monitor the time you spend on each individual question. One way you can cut down on time is to skim through the test questions and answer the easier ones first. Since you receive a raw score point for every correct answer, skimming through the test and answering the easy questions that you are sure of will help ensure you get credit for the information you know.

You can also save time by recording your answers to these questions on the test next to the number of the question or on a separate sheet of paper and then go back and transfer the answers to your answer sheet a little later. Be sure to do this before the end of the test period approaches—you don't want to run out of time!

2. Answer the Question Before Looking at Answer Choices

For each new question, read the stem first and try to answer it in your head before looking at the answer choices. Answer choices may be designed to distract you from the correct answer and may confuse or mislead you. Answering the question in your head before looking at the choices will help you to arrive at the correct answer and prevent you from being confused by the incorrect choices.

3. Read All Answer Choices

Even if you have read the question and answered it in your head, you should still be sure to read all of the answer choices before making your final selection. Keep in mind that there may be more than one plausible answer. In these cases, you may have to choose the *most* correct choice or the choice that most completely answers the question. As a result, it is important that you read through all of the answer choices, even if you think you know which is correct, just to be sure that you are selecting the best possible choice.

4. Read Carefully

When you are reading questions and answer choices, pay careful attention to the wording. Many questions use words like *NOT* or *EXCEPT*, which can have a significant effect on the meaning of the question and can lead to mistakes if the question is misread or misunderstood. Some questions may also include *modifiers*, which are words or phrases that limit or modify the meaning of another word or phrase. In some cases, for example, a modifier may be used to direct you to seek an answer choice that may be correct under certain circumstances but that is not always true. You should also watch out for double negatives, which occur when two negative words are used together to create a phrase with a positive meaning, such as *not uncommon*, which actually means *common*.

5. Use Elimination Strategies

One of the most important things to remember about the SAT Biology E/M Subject Test is that, as with other SAT subject tests, there *is* a penalty for guessing—that means if you answer a question incorrectly, you lose a percentage of a point. Although this doesn't mean that you should *not* take a guess at an answer, it does mean you should be sure that you are making an *educated* guess. To make an educated guess, you need to first eliminate answer choices you know are wrong or suspect are probably wrong.

Start by first eliminating the choices you know are wrong. In many cases, you can also eliminate choices that seem unlikely or appear totally unfamiliar. For questions in which the stem is completed by the answer choice, eliminate choices that would make the completed stem grammatically incorrect.

Another way to eliminate incorrect answer choices is to use the "true–false" test. To do this, simply read the answer choice and ask yourself whether it is true or false on its own. If a particular answer choice is false on its own, you can assume that it is incorrect and eliminate it.

Questions and answer choices that use *absolutes*, such as *all*, *always*, *only*, or *never*, often provide clues to which answer choices can be eliminated, since an absolute can make an answer that is sometimes correct wrong when the absolute is applied. For example, "You can always see the stars shine at night," is wrong because although the stars can *usually* be seen shining at night, there are some instances when they cannot be seen due to, for example, cloud cover or some other circumstance.

Finally, when reading through the answer choices, look for contradictory paired statements. For example, if a set of answer choices includes "the desert is wet" and "the desert is dry," you can usually assume that one of these is likely correct (and often is the answer to the question). You can, at a minimum, eliminate the incorrect paired choice.

6. Choose the Right Section

The SAT Biology E/M Subject Test offers you the option of answering 20 molecular questions or 20 ecological questions. You can choose only one section during the test. You should choose the section on which you are likely to score more highly. That's why you should answer all questions when taking the practice tests in this book. You can compare your scores and determine which section makes the most sense for you to choose.

The Question Types

Though all of the questions on the SAT Biology E/M Subject Test are multiple choice, they are not all the same. The majority of the questions you will encounter are the typical type of multiple-choice questions that appear on most SAT tests, but some are unique to this exam and require specific strategies to be answered correctly. This section will provide you with a brief overview of the different types of questions you will need to be prepared to answer for the SAT Biology E/M Subject Test, as well as helpful tips on how to approach them.

Matched Answer Choice Questions

The first part of the SAT Biology E/M Subject Test is a series of matched-answer questions. For this question type, you are given a set of five answer choices, followed by two to five brief questions or statements. These questions require you to select the answer choice that fits each question. Unlike matching questions you may have encountered in other tests, you can use an answer choice several times, once, or not at all.

Straightforward Questions

The straightforward question is the common, run-of-the-mill multiple-choice question you normally encounter on a wide variety of tests. These questions usually appear in the form of an actual question or a statement that you must complete. An example of a straightforward question that is simply formatted as an actual question would be *"Which molecules are produced during photosynthesis?"* Another straightforward question might require you to complete a statement. For example, *"Birds maintain osmotic balance by…"*

When answering straightforward questions, keep two important strategies in mind:

- **Be certain you know what you are being asked.** Before you try to answer a question, you must be sure that you fully understand exactly the question. Read the question more than once, especially if it uses complex wording. Once you have identified exactly what you are looking for, read through the answer choices. Knowing exactly what to look for before reading the answer choices can help you to get an idea of what the correct answer might be and which incorrect answers you can eliminate.

- **Read each answer choice carefully.** In many cases, more than one answer choice may sound like it could be correct at first. Remember to read through all choices and select the one you think is the *best* answer. Simply selecting the first answer that sounds right without reading the others can easily lead to wrong answers, even when you actually know the correct answer.

Negative Questions

Negative questions are tricky because they actually require you to select the "wrong" answer. Negative questions are easy to identify because they usually contain the word *EXCEPT* or, occasionally, *NOT*. A negative question might look like this: *"Which of the following is NOT a result of ovulation?"* An EXCEPT question, which usually requires you to complete a statement, might look like this: *"All of the following are examples of intraspecific competition EXCEPT..."*

When answering negative questions, keep two important strategies in mind:

- **Remember that you need to find the "wrong" answer.** The answer choices for negative questions usually work differently than those of other types of questions. While you are normally looking for a correct answer choice among a field of wrong choices, with these questions you are looking for the "wrong" choice among a field of "correct" choices. Also, keep in mind that if any part of an answer choice is incorrect, the entire statement is incorrect.

- **Check your answer by using it to complete the statement.** When you are answering a negative question that requires you to complete a statement, you can check your answer by inserting it into the statement and seeing if it makes sense. If the completed statement doesn't make sense, you can probably assume that you have chosen the incorrect answer choice.

Combined-Choice Questions

Some questions include a list of statements or terms designated with Roman numerals (I, II, III...). Each answer choice includes one or more options from the list (for example, I only, II and III). You must determine which options satisfy the question that is being asked and then choose the answer that includes that combination of options.

Systematically work through the list, and cross out any option that you eliminate. Double check that the options that are left do, in fact, answer the question. Then, systematically eliminate any answer choice that includes an incorrect option. Be sure that the answer choice you select includes *all* of the correct Roman-numeral options.

Table-, Diagram-, and Graph-Based Questions

Some questions on the SAT Biology E/M Subject Test will require you to refer to a table, diagram, or graph in order to determine the correct answer. Before you attempt any of these questions, you should be sure that you feel confident in your ability to accurately interpret these types of visual information.

You will likely encounter a few questions that require you to interpret a chart or graph. In order to answer these questions correctly, you will need to know how to read a chart or graph and understand the information it contains. Most commonly, these questions will require you to be familiar with bar graphs, line graphs, and tables.

There are usually two types of chart and graph questions: identifying-trend questions and detail/comparison questions. Identifying-trend questions ask you to analyze the graph or chart you are given and identify a major trend that it represents. Detail/comparison questions ask you to pick out or compare certain details from the graph or chart.

The following table is an example of the type of graph you would likely find on the SAT Biology E/M Subject Test:

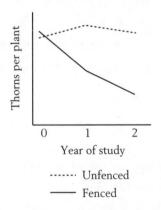

An identifying-trend question for this table might ask you to determine how the number of thorns changed over time. A detail/comparison question, meanwhile, might ask you to determine how fencing in the plants affected the number of thorns that grew on them.

When answering table-, chart-, or graph-based questions, keep three important strategies in mind:

- **Study the table, chart, or graph first.** It's always a good idea to carefully examine the table, chart, or graph before you read the question. Suppose you find yourself faced with a graph-based question. Take a moment to look at the graph and try to determine its meaning before you look at the question. Since you can refer back to the graph at any time, you won't need to remember any specific details, just the big picture. Spending a little time getting familiar with the graph will help you to better understand the question.

- **Watch out for labels.** Most tables, charts, and graphs have labels that are critically important to the meaning of the table, chart, or graph. Pay close attention to labels and remember to take them into consideration when you are trying to interpret the information.

- **If you are stumped by the table, chart, or graph, skip the question and come back later.** Some tables, charts, or graphs may be difficult to understand. If you are having a hard time figuring out what the visual information means, it may be in your best interest to just move on. These questions are often more time consuming than others. Since you only have a limited amount of time in which to work, it may be best to skip over questions you are having trouble with and come back to them later, if you have time remaining.

Research Questions

Some questions on this test are based on the descriptions and results of experiments. These are sometimes based on famous experiments that led to important and fundamental discoveries in science. They may also present research that is not well known and that may be unfamiliar to you. You may be asked to draw conclusions based on the results of the experiment or to predict what would happen if the experiment were conducted differently, or one of many other similar questions.

The following is an example of a typical research-based question.

56. Experimenters labeled the raw materials used in photosynthesis with radioactive isotopes. They then tested the products of photosynthesis for radioactivity. Results are shown in the table.

LABELED REACTANT	RADIOACTIVITY OF PRODUCTS		
	O_2	GLUCOSE	H_2O
$H_2^{18}O$	+	−	−
$C^{18}O_2$	−	+	+
$^{14}CO_2$	−	+	−

Which conclusion can be drawn from the results?

A. Water molecules remain unchanged in photosynthesis.

B. Carbon dioxide is the source of water…

When answering research-based questions, keep two important strategies in mind:

- **Read the description and data carefully.** In order to determine the correct answer to a research-based question, you will need to have a clear understanding of what was done and what the results showed. Take some time to read the information carefully and more than once, if you need to. Make sure that you understand before moving on to the question or answer choices. The better you understand the data, the better your chances of answering the question correctly.

- **Be certain you know what you are being asked.** As with other question types, you should always make certain that you understand the question before moving on to the answer choices. Once you have a clear understanding of the research under review, you'll need to make sure you know what the question is asking. While some research-based questions are fairly straightforward, others may be complicated and require a more careful reading.

The Diagnosis:
How Ready Are You?

Diagnostic Test

This part of your book includes a full-length diagnostic test. This test has been designed to help you identify and correct potential problem areas with this subject test, ultimately helping you to improve your score. When you take the actual SAT Biology E/M Subject Test, you will answer the first 60 questions and then you will choose either the Ecology (E) Test (questions 61–80) or the Molecular (M) Test (questions 81–100). However, you don't have to make that choice right now. Instead, we encourage you to use the diagnostic test to determine which test is likely to result in a higher score. So, for the diagnostic test, take *both* the Biology-E Test and the Biology-M Test. You can then compare your scores for each section and make some decisions about which test you might want to take.

Other areas you should consider as you take the diagnostic test include the amount of time you are spending on each question and whether or not you are reading the questions closely enough. You might discover that you consistently struggle with certain types of questions or with items that address specific topic areas or ideas. All of these issues are resolvable. However, to fix them, you must first identify them. That means it is essential to complete the diagnostic test in an environment that mimics the actual testing environment as closely as possible. Follow these guidelines:

- Block out a full one-hour time period to take the diagnostic test. Stay within this allotted time frame. Time yourself and stop testing when the hour is up.

- Select a quiet environment that has a minimal amount of distraction, such as an unoccupied room in your home, at your school, or in the local library.

- Turn off your cell phone, your computer, and any other electronic device. Ask your family and friends to avoid disturbing you during the testing period.

- While taking the test, have *only* the examination and answer key open. Don't use other resource materials! If you do, the person you're cheating is yourself.

- Again, don't cheat! Even though you may be tempted, looking up the answers will only hinder your progress.

- As you take the test, have a highlighter available. Use it to quickly mark any term or concept that seems unfamiliar to you. Later, you will be able to use this information to decide where to focus your studies.

- Finally, make sure you follow any instructions provided.

In the Biology E/M Subject Test, each question or incomplete statement is followed by five possible answers or completions. Select the one choice that is the best answer and mark it on your answer sheet. At times, the same information is used for a group of questions. This will be indicated. Follow all directions given.

Once you have completed the examination, assess your score by checking your answers against the key provided at the end of this section. More information about assessing your performance is provided in that section.

Good luck!

Diagnostic Test

SAT Biology E/M Subject Test

Time—60 minutes

80 questions

Directions: The set of lettered choices below refers to the numbered questions or statements immediately following it. Select the one lettered choice that best fits each statement. A choice may be used once, more than once, or not at all in the set.

Questions 1–3 refer to the following.

- A. Respiration
- B. Photosynthesis
- C. Decomposition
- D. Nitrogen fixation
- E. Fermentation

1. This process converts electromagnetic energy to chemical potential energy.

2. This process breaks a triple bond.

3. This process produces ammonia.

Questions 4–5 refer to the following.

    A. Carrying capacity
    B. Population density
    C. Limiting factor
    D. *K*-selection
    E. *r*-selection

4. The maximum population that environmental resources in a given area can sustain

5. A factor that confers fitness on those individuals that can reproduce quickly

Questions 6–8 refer to the following diagram.

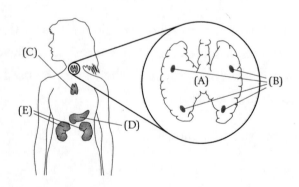

6. Which organ decreases the amount of glycogen stored in the liver?

7. Which organ produces a hormone that decreases the amount of calcium in the bones?

8. Which organ is responsible for the maturation of immune system cells?

Questions 9–11 refer to the following.

    A.   Golgi body

    B.   Mitochondrion

    C.   Ribosome

    D.   Endoplasmic reticulum

    E.   Lysosome

9.   This organelle contains enzymes that synthesize lipids and hormones.

10. This organelle is present in prokaryotes.

11. This organelle is responsible for the production of ATP.

Questions 12–14 refer to the following.

    A.   Artificial selection

    B.   Directional selection

    C.   Disruptive selection

    D.   Neutral selection

    E.   Stabilizing selection

12. The type of selection that results when heterozygous individuals have lower fitness than homozygous individuals

13. The type of selection that reduces the phenotypic variation in a population

14. The type of selection that results in a shift in the mean of a continuous phenotype, such as size or length

Questions 15–17 refer to the following.

    A. Arthropoda
    B. Bryozoa
    C. Chordata
    D. Cnidaria
    E. Mollusca

15. Members of this clade have pharyngeal slits at some point in development.

16. Members of this clade lack differentiated tissues.

17. Members of this clade have radial symmetry.

Questions 18–20 refer to the following.

    A. Enteric nervous system
    B. Somatic nervous system
    C. Peripheral nervous system
    D. Parasympathetic division
    E. Sympathetic division

18. The motor neurons that enervate skeletal muscle are part of this system.

19. Activation of this system slows the heart rate, constricts the pupils, and stimulates pancreatic activity.

20. The human nervous system is divided into two major categories; one is the central nervous system and the other is this.

Directions: Each of the questions or incomplete statements below is followed by five suggested answers or completions. Some questions pertain to a set that refers to a laboratory or experimental situation. For each question, select the one choice that is the best answer to the question.

21. Which of these refers to an individual's ability to pass on its phenotype to future generations?

    A. Fitness
    B. Heritability
    C. Limited environmental resources
    D. Overproduction of offspring
    E. Phenotypic variation

22. Mammals and birds have four-chambered hearts. The other taxa shown in the diagram below have three-chambered hearts.

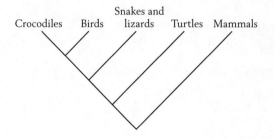

    The hearts of birds and mammals are BEST described as

    A. analogous
    B. homologous
    C. parallel
    D. transitional
    E. vestigial

23. What is the function of endosperm tissue in plants?

    A. Differentiates to form root structures
    B. Provides nutrients to the plant embryo
    C. Gives rise to male gametes that make up pollen
    D. Makes up the photosynthetic cells inside the leaves
    E. Forms the tissues that transport water and nutrients

24. In meiosis, at which stage does crossing over occur?

    A. Prophase I
    B. Prophase II
    C. Metaphase I
    D. Metaphase II
    E. Telophase I

25. Which leaf structure is derived from ground tissue?

    A. Cuticle
    B. Epidermis
    C. Mesophyll
    D. Phloem
    E. Xylem

26. While cooking, you touch the hot edge of the pan and quickly pull your hand away. Which of these are involved in generating this reflex?

I. Brain
II. Spinal cord
III. Sensory neurons
IV. Motor neurons

A. I and IV
B. III and IV
C. I, III, and IV
D. II, III, and IV
E. I, II, III, and IV

27. In cats, the allele resulting in deafness occurs more often in those with white-colored coats. Which is the most likely cause of this association?

A. Gene linkage
B. Sex linkage
C. Crossing over
D. Independent assortment
E. Recombination

28. Which of these factors does NOT determine population size?

   A. Birthrate
   B. Death rate
   C. Emigration
   D. Dimorphism
   E. Immigration

29. A man with blood type A has a child with a woman who has blood type B. Both are homozygous for their blood type alleles. Which of these are possible blood types for the offspring?

   I.   Type A
   II. Type B
   III. Type O
   IV. Type AB

   A. II only
   B. I and II
   C. I, II, and IV
   D. I, II, III, and IV
   E. IV only

30. A dihybrid cross is performed between two fruit flies. What proportion of offspring is expected to express the recessive phenotype for both traits?

    A. 1 in 2
    B. 1 in 4
    C. 1 in 8
    D. 1 in 16
    E. 3 in 16

31. Which of these statements BEST summarizes the competitive exclusion principle?

    A. Predators exert a cyclic effect on the population size of their prey.
    B. Two populations in the same ecosystem cannot occupy the same niche.
    C. Pollutants accumulate in greater concentrations at higher trophic levels.
    D. The trophic structure of ecosystems describes energy flow through a community.
    E. An ecosystem has limited resources and cannot support an unlimited population.

32. Which of these is the last stage of cellular respiration in which the oxidation of organic molecules derived from glucose yields ATP?

   A. Chemiosmosis
   B. Citric acid cycle
   C. Electron transport chain
   D. Glycolysis
   E. Oxidative phosphorylation

33. Which groups of organisms are capable of meiotic recombination?

   I.   Monera
   II. Protista
   III. Fungi
   IV. Plantae
   V.   Animalia

   A. IV and V
   B. I, II, and III
   C. III, IV, and V
   D. I, II, III, and V
   E. II, III, IV, and V

34. Which of these occurs in the Calvin cycle?

    A. Production of ATP
    B. Chemical breakdown of water
    C. Fixation of carbon
    D. Production of oxygen gas
    E. Absorption of light energy

35. The diagram represents the cell cycle.

Compared to a cell in the G1 phase, a cell in the G2 phase has

    A. twice as much DNA
    B. half as much DNA
    C. twice as many centromeres
    D. half as many centromeres
    E. twice as many chromosomes

Questions 36–37 refer to the plant groups below.

    I.   Angiosperms

    II.   Gymnosperms

    III. Horsetails, ferns, club mosses (lycophytes and pterophytes)

    IV. True mosses, liverworts, and hornworts (bryophtyes)

36. Which plants contain tracheid and vessel element cells?

    A. I only

    B. II only

    C. I and II

    D. I, II, and III

    E. I, II, III, and IV

37. Which plants produce spores instead of seeds?

    A. I, II, and III

    B. II, III, and IV

    C. II and IV

    D. III and IV

    E. IV only

38. Which diagram correctly depicts a countercurrent exchange system?

A.
| 15 | 40 | 65 | 100 |
| 5 | 25 | 55 | 90 |

B.
| 15 | 40 | 65 | 100 |
| 5 | 25 | 55 | 90 |

C.
| 15 | 40 | 65 | 100 |
| 90 | 55 | 25 | 5 |

D.
| 15 | 40 | 65 | 100 |
| 90 | 55 | 25 | 5 |

E.
| 90 | 55 | 25 | 5 |
| 90 | 55 | 25 | 5 |

39. Where does chemical digestion of food begin in the digestive system?

A. Mouth
B. Stomach
C. Esophagus
D. Small intestine
E. Large intestine

40. Which of these enzymes are responsible for the digestion of protein?

   I.   Amylase
   II. Lipase
   III. Pepsin
   IV. Trypsin

   A. I and II
   B. I and III
   C. II and III
   D. II and IV
   E. III and IV

41. Which tissue derives from the ectoderm layer formed during embryonic development?

   I.   Brain
   II. Epidermis
   III. Limb bones

   A. I only
   B. II only
   C. I and II
   D. I and III
   E. II and III

42. Which of these describes the cell walls of fungi?

    A. They are composed of cellulose.
    B. They are composed of chitin.
    C. They are composed of a lipid bilayer.
    D. They are composed of peptidoglycan.
    E. Fungi lack cell walls.

43. Which major animal groups are considered amniotes?

    I.   Amphibians
    II. Birds
    III. Mammals
    IV. Reptiles

    A. I, II, and IV
    B. II and III
    C. II, III, and IV
    D. I and IV
    E. IV only

Questions 44–45 refer to the following diagram.

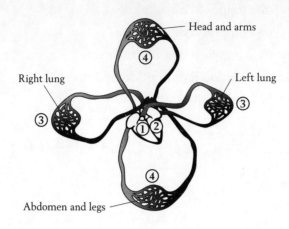

44. The path of blood through the circulatory system is

    A.   1 to 2 to 3 to 4 to 1
    B.   1 to 3 to 2 to 4 to 1
    C.   1 to 4 to 2 to 3 to 1
    D.   2 to 3 to 4 to 1 to 2
    E.   2 to 4 to 3 to 1 to 2

45. The parts of the circulatory system that make up the systemic circulation include

   A.   1 and 2
   B.   1 and 3
   C.   1 and 4
   D.   2 and 3
   E.   2 and 4

46. The human body regulates the concentration of glucose in the bloodstream so that it remains within a narrow range. In response to an increase in blood glucose above this range, the pancreas

   A.   releases insulin, signaling muscle cells to release glucose
   B.   releases glucagon, signaling muscle cells to take up glucose
   C.   releases glucagon, signaling adipose cells to take up glucose
   D.   releases insulin, signaling the liver to convert glucose to glycogen
   E.   releases glucagon, signaling the liver to convert glucose to glycogen

Directions: Each group of statements below concerns a laboratory or experimental situation. In each case, first study the description of the situation. Then choose the one best answer to each question following it.

Questions 47–49 refer to the following.

Researchers measured the beak heights of finches (genus *Geospiza*) on three different islands. *Geospiza fuliginosa* inhabits Island 2, *G. fortis* inhabits Island 3, and both species inhabit Island 1. The graphs below show results.

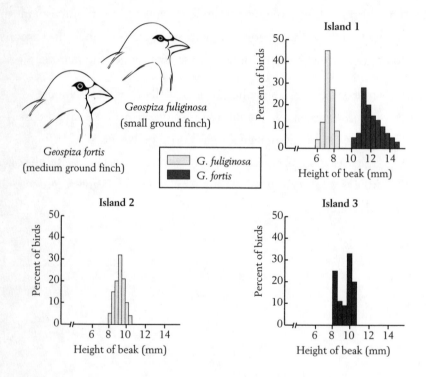

47. Where were G. *fuliginosa* with the greatest beak heights found?

   A.   Island 1
   B.   Island 2
   C.   Island 3
   D.   Islands 1 and 2
   E.   Islands 1 and 3

48. Which of these can MOST LIKELY be inferred from the results?

    A. The populations on Island 1 evolved to occupy different niches.
    B. The populations on Island 1 compete for the same food source.
    C. The populations on Islands 2 and 3 compete for the same food source.
    D. The populations on Islands 2 and 3 evolved to occupy different niches.
    E. The populations on Island 1 are the ancestors of those on Islands 2 and 3.

49. The phenotypes of the populations on Island 1 were MOST LIKELY the result of

    A. disruptive selection
    B. directional selection
    C. stabilizing selection
    D. artificial selection
    E. neutral selection

Questions 50–52 refer to the following.

A geneticist traced a rare disorder through three generations of a family. The geneticist's findings are shown in the pedigree below.

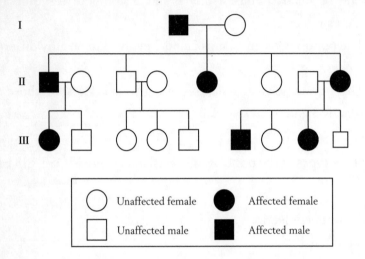

50. How many affected females in generation II passed the disorder to their offspring?

A. 0
B. 1
C. 2
D. 3
E. 4

51. Based on the pedigree, the allele for this disorder is MOST LIKELY

    A. autosomal dominant
    B. autosomal recessive
    C. Y-linked dominant
    D. X-linked dominant
    E. X-linked recessive

52. Which of these is an example of valid reasoning, based on the phe-notypes of individuals in the pedigree?

    A. Individuals I-1 and II-6 indicate that the allele is not X-linked dominant.
    B. Individuals I-1 and II-1 indicate that the allele may be X-linked dominant.
    C. Individuals II-1 and III-1 indicate that the allele may be Y-linked dominant.
    D. Individuals I-2 and II-5 indicate that the allele is not autosomal dominant.
    E. Individuals I-1 and II-1 indicate that the allele is not autosomal recessive.

Questions 53–55 refer to the following.

Ecologists studied the effects of sea stars (*Pisaster ochraceus*) on the distribution of mussels on rocky shores. *Mytilus californianus* mussels normally inhabit the intertidal zone, while sea stars inhabit the deeper low-tide zone. Results are shown in the graph below.

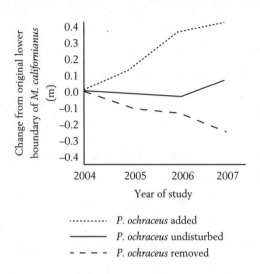

.... *P. ochraceus* added

———— *P. ochraceus* undisturbed

— — — — *P. ochraceus* removed

53. What was the effect of removing *P. ochraceus* on the *M. californianus* population?

A. The *M. californianus* population declined.

B. The *M. californianus* population increased.

C. The *M. californianus* population moved into lower waters.

D. The *M. californianus* population moved into higher waters.

E. The *M. californianus* population was unaffected.

54. What can be inferred from the data about the ecological relation-ship between *P. ochraceus* and *M. californianus*?

    A. *P. ochraceus* constitutes a limiting factor on *M. californianus* populations.

    B. *P. ochraceus* and *M. californianus* occupy the same niche.

    C. *P. ochraceus* and *M. californianus* have a predator–prey relationship.

    D. *P. ochraceus* compete with *M. californianus* for resources.

    E. *P. ochraceus* are better adapted to the environment than *M. californianus*.

55. Based on the study, what is the effect of *P. ochraceus* on the ecosystem?

    A. It is an invasive species.

    B. It decreases species diversity.

    C. It outcompetes other species.

    D. It affects the ranges of other species.

    E. It cannot occupy the same niche as other species.

Questions 56–57 refer to the following.

Experimenters labeled the raw materials used in photosynthesis with radioactive isotopes. They then tested the products of photosynthesis for radioactivity. Their results are shown in the table.

LABELED REACTANT	RADIOACTIVITY OF PRODUCTS		
	O_2	GLUCOSE	H_2O
$H_2{}^{18}O$	+	–	–
$C^{18}O_2$	–	+	+
$^{14}CO_2$	–	+	–

56. Which conclusion can be drawn from the results?

   A. Water molecules remain unchanged in photosynthesis.
   B. Carbon dioxide is the only source of the water produced by plants.
   C. Water is the only source of the oxygen gas produced by plants.
   D. Carbon dioxide is the source of the oxygen gas produced by plants.
   E. Atoms from water are incorporated into glucose in photosynthesis.

57. Based on the findings, which source of matter contributes most of the dry mass of a plant?

    A. Water

    B. Carbon dioxide

    C. Oxygen gas

    D. Glucose

    E. Sunlight

Questions 58–60 refer to the following.

An auxotrophic strain cannot synthesize one or more of the amino acids it requires. These amino acids must be added to the medium on which the strains are grown. A genetic engineer inserted a circular piece of DNA called a plasmid into a strain of *E. coli* that was incapable of synthesizing tryptophan. The plasmid contained a gene enabling tryptophan synthesis (*trp⁺*) and a gene conferring resistance to the antibiotic streptomycin (*strʳ*).

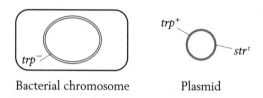

Bacterial chromosome   Plasmid

58. Which nutrient media should the bacteria be plated on to select for cells that successfully integrated the DNA?

   A. Plates with no added tryptophan or streptomycin
   B. Plates with added tryptophan and streptomycin
   C. Plates with no added tryptophan but with streptomycin
   D. Plates with added tryptophan but no streptomycin
   E. Plates with added tryptophan and a different antibiotic

59. When the original auxotrophic strain is plated on minimal medium with no added amino acids, a few colonies sometimes form. These are MOST LIKELY due to

   A. the uptake of DNA from the environment
   B. new alleles resulting from recombination of DNA
   C. mutations that already occurred before plating
   D. mutations caused by stress due to lack of nutrients
   E. mutations resulting from DNA damage during plating

60. The incorporation of the plasmid into the bacterial cell is MOST similar to which of these natural processes?

   A. Binary fission
   B. Homologous recombination
   C. Transformation
   D. Transcription
   E. Translation

**IF YOU ARE TAKING THE BIOLOGY-E TEST,
CONTINUE WITH QUESTIONS 61–80.
IF YOU ARE TAKING THE BIOLOGY-M TEST, GO TO
QUESTION 81 NOW.**

SAT Biology E/M Subject Test
BIOLOGY-E TEST

Directions: Each of the questions or incomplete statements below is followed by five suggested answers or completions. Some questions pertain to a set that refers to a laboratory or experimental situation. For each question, select the one choice that is the best answer to the question.

61. The diagram represents the biomass of different trophic levels in a terrestrial ecosystem. Which level represents producers?

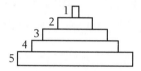

   A. 1
   B. 2
   C. 3
   D. 4
   E. 5

62. Which organisms contributed to the significant change in atmospheric oxygen levels early in the evolution of life?

   A. Plants
   B. Algal protists
   C. Bacteria
   D. Heterotrophs
   E. Anaerobes

63. In which of the following biomes is water, but not energy, a limiting factor?

    A. Temperate grassland
    B. Temperate deciduous forest
    C. Temperate rain forest
    D. Coniferous forest
    E. Tundra

64. Which of these characterize a society that has undergone a demographic transition?

    A. Low birthrates and low death rates
    B. Low birthrates and high death rates
    C. High birthrates and low death rates
    D. High birthrates and high death rates
    E. High birthrates and high emigration

65. What is the most likely role of zooplankton in aquatic ecosystems?

    A. Producers
    B. Primary consumers
    C. Nitrogen fixers
    D. Tertiary consumers
    E. Decomposers

66. A species of spider produces many eggs over its lifetime but provides very little parental care. Only a few offspring survive to adulthood. Which line in the graph below represents the survivorship curve for this species?

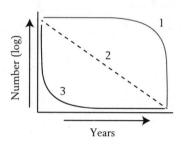

A. Curve 1

B. Curve 2

C. Curve 3

D. Curves 1 and 2

E. Curves 1 and 3

67. Which of these consists of organisms belonging to a single species?

A. Population

B. Community

C. Ecosystem

D. Trophic level

E. Guild

68. How does primary succession differ from secondary succession?

A. Primary succession occurs on soil.

B. Primary succession begins with lichens.

C. Primary succession begins with plant species.

D. Secondary succession involves animal species.

E. Secondary succession involves the weathering of rock.

69. What is the correct order of the events leading to the formation of a dead zone in a body of water?

   I.   Oxygen depletion
   II. Algal bloom
   III. Excess decomposition
   IV. Nutrient runoff

   A. II, I, III, IV
   B. II, IV, III, I
   C. III, II, IV, I
   D. IV, I, II, III
   E. IV, II, III, I

70. In Batesian mimicry, one species resembles another, poisonous, species. Which condition(s) increases the effectiveness of Batesian mimicry?

   I.   Poisonous species is more common than mimic.
   II. Poisonous species is present in same area as mimic.
   III. Poisonous species competes for resources with mimic.
   IV. Poisonous species is distinctly or brightly colored.

   A. I and II
   B. I, II, and III
   C. I, II, and IV
   D. II, III, and IV
   E. I, II, III, and IV

71. The graph below shows the relationship between species A and biodiversity in an ecosystem.

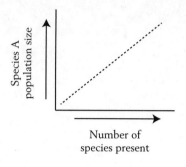

Based on the graph, species A is most likely a/an

A. predator
B. producer
C. invasive species
D. keystone species
E. decomposer

72. The diagram shows a food web in a lake ecosystem. The lake was polluted with PCBs, which do not dissolve easily in water. Which species of organism will contain the greatest concentration of this pollutant in its tissues?

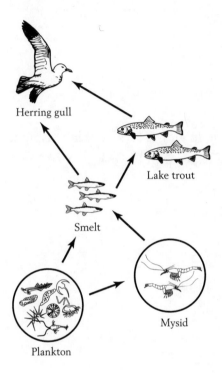

Herring gull

Lake trout

Smelt

Mysid

Plankton

A. Herring gull
B. Lake trout
C. Smelt
D. Mysid
E. Plankton

73. The coefficient of relatedness refers to the probability that two related organisms both inherited a particular allele from a parent or ancestor. What is the coefficient of relatedness between full siblings?

    A. 0.10
    B. 0.25
    C. 0.50
    D. 0.75
    E. 1.00

74. Which of the following is NOT a relationship in which one species benefits at the expense of the other?

    A. Competition
    B. Herbivory
    C. Predation
    D. Parasitism
    E. Commensalism

75. The efficiency of energy transfer from one trophic level to the next is estimated at 10 percent. Assuming that the amount of energy in an ecosystem's producers is equal to 100 units, what is the amount of energy that reaches the secondary consumers?

   A. 1 unit
   B. 25 units
   C. 50 units
   D. 70 units
   E. 80 units

Questions 76–77 refer to the following.

An ecologist measures the level of dissolved oxygen (D.O.) in a collected sample of pond water. She pours equal volumes of the water into a clear jar and a jar covered in opaque paper, and then places the jars under a light source. She measures the D.O. level in both jars after 24 hours.

76. How will the D.O. level MOST LIKELY change after 24 hours?

    A.   It will increase in the covered jar, but decrease in the uncovered jar.

    B.   It will increase in the covered jar, but remain the same in the uncovered jar.

    C.   It will decrease in the covered jar, but increase in the uncovered jar.

    D.   It will increase in both jars.

    E.   It will decrease in both jars.

77. How could the ecologist calculate the rate of photosynthesis in the pond water?

A. By subtracting the level in the covered jar from the level in the original sample and adding that number to the level in the uncovered jar

B. By adding the level in the covered jar to the level in the original sample and subtracting that number from the level in the uncovered jar

C. By subtracting the level in the uncovered jar from the level in the original sample and adding that number to the level in the covered jar

D. By adding the level in the uncovered jar to the level in the original sample and subtracting that number from the level in the covered jar

E. By subtracting the level in the covered jar to the level in the uncovered jar and subtracting that number from the level in the original sample

<u>Questions 78–80</u> refer to the following.

Ecologists studied the effects of herbivory on plant defensive structures. The thorny shrub *Hromathophylla spinosa* is a food source for
grazers. The ecologists surrounded some areas containing this plant
with a fence and left other areas open to grazers. The results are shown
in the graph below.

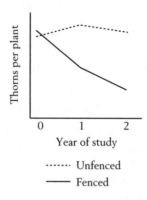

78. In which condition did plants have the greatest number of thorns
    per plant?

    A. Unfenced, year 0
    B. Unfenced, year 1
    C. Unfenced, year 2
    D. Fenced, year 1
    E. Fenced, year 2

79. Which conclusion is BEST supported by the data?

    A. *H. spinosa* grows thorns in response to grazing.

    B. *H. spinosa* thorns are involved in reproduction.

    C. Grazing selects for plants with a greater number of thorns.

    D. Grazing decreases the number of thorns on *H. spinosa* plants.

    E. Plants with more thorns have greater fitness than plants with fewer thorns.

80. The scientists also found that *H. spinosa* plants with fewer thorns produced more fruits and seeds. How could conservationists BEST increase the number of *H. spinosa* plants in the area studied?

    A. By encouraging grazing

    B. By removing the thorns from the plants

    C. By protecting some of the areas from grazing

    D. By selectively breeding plants that produce fewer thorns

    E. By introducing related species that produce fewer thorns

**IF YOU ARE TAKING THE BIOLOGY-M TEST,
CONTINUE WITH QUESTIONS 81–100.**

SAT Biology E/M Subject Test
BIOLOGY-M TEST

Directions: Each of the questions or incomplete statements below is followed by five suggested answers or completions. Some questions pertain to a set that refers to a laboratory or experimental situation. For each question, select the one choice that is the best answer to the question.

81. Which choice correctly identifies a component of the molecule shown below?

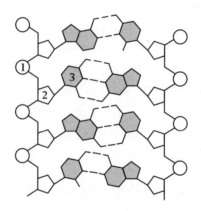

  A. 1 is a sugar.

  B. 2 is a nitrogenous base.

  C. 3 is a phosphate group.

  D. 3 is a sugar.

  E. 1 is a phosphate group.

82. Which of these processes utilizes tRNA?

    I.   Transcription
    II. Translation
    III. DNA replication

    A. I only
    B. II only
    C. I and II
    D. II and III
    E. I, II, and III

83. Which of these must a mammalian embryo receive from its father
    in order to be viable?

    I.   Autosomes
    II. X chromosome
    III. Y chromosome
    IV. Organelles

    A. I only
    B. I and II
    C. I and III
    D. I, II, and III
    E. I, II, III, and IV

84. A normal protein-coding DNA sequence and a mutated sequence are shown below.

Normal: 5'–GCCGATCGCGATCC–3'
Mutated: 5'–GCCGATCGCTATCC–3'

What is the MOST LIKELY result of the mutation?

A. The protein has an incorrect amino acid.
B. A longer-than-normal protein is made.
C. The DNA is not transcribed.
D. The protein is not translated.
E. More of the protein is produced.

85. Which of these are produced by anaerobic respiration in yeast?

I. Carbon dioxide
II. Oxygen
III. Water
IV. Alcohol

A. I only
B. I and II
C. II and III
D. I and III
E. I and IV

86. What is the function of crassulacean acid metabolism (CAM) in plants?

    A. CAM allows plants to produce more glucose from a given amount of raw material.
    B. CAM allows plants to carry out photosynthesis without the use of water.
    C. CAM allows plants to take in carbon dioxide at night instead of during the day.
    D. CAM allows plants to keep their stomata open at all times.
    E. CAM allows plants to conserve energy in cold climates.

87. How does excessive heat negatively affect enzyme function?

    A. It alters the three-dimensional shape of the enzyme.
    B. It alters the amino acid sequence of the enzyme.
    C. It alters the composition of the active site of the enzyme.
    D. It alters the shape of the substrate molecule.
    E. It alters the chemical identity of the substrate.

88. A fruit fly has the genotype *Nn*CC. Which combinations of alleles can it pass on to its offspring?

    I.   *Nn*

    II.   *N*C

    III. *N*c

    IV. *n*C

    V.   CC

    A.   I and V

    B.   I, II, and III

    C.   II and IV

    D.   II, III, and IV

    E.   I, II, III, IV, and V

89. Which of these takes place in the mitochondria?

    I.   Glycolysis

    II.   Citric acid cycle

    III. Oxidative phosphorylation

    A.   II only

    B.   I and II

    C.   I and III

    D.   II and III

    E.   I, II, and III

90. The diagram shows the cloning of an animal.

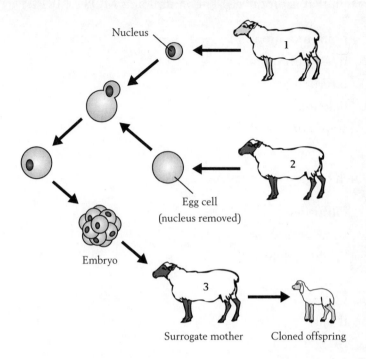

The mitochondrial DNA of the cloned animal will MOST closely match the

A. nuclear DNA of animal 1
B. nuclear DNA of animal 2
C. mitochondrial DNA of animal 1
D. mitochondrial DNA of animal 2
E. mitochondrial DNA of animal 3

91. A mutation in DNA results in no change to the sequence of the protein that is produced. The mutation is MOST LIKELY a

   A.   point mutation
   B.   frameshift mutation
   C.   insertion
   D.   deletion
   E.   stop mutation

92. Which of these requires ATP?

   I.   Diffusion
   II.   Active transport
   III. Facilitated diffusion

   A.   I only
   B.   II only
   C.   III only
   D.   I and III
   E.   II and III

93. The site of transcription in the eukaryotic cell is the

    A.   nucleus

    B.   ribosome

    C.   endoplasmic reticulum

    D.   Golgi body

    E.   cytoplasm

94. The graph shows the amounts of reactant, product, and enzyme over the course of a biochemical reaction taking place in a test tube. Which line is correctly identified?

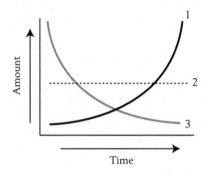

    A.   Line 1 is the enzyme.

    B.   Line 2 is the substrate.

    C.   Line 3 is the product.

    D.   Line 2 is the enzyme.

    E.   Line 1 is the substrate.

Questions 95–97 refer to the following.

A researcher compared the binding of human hemoglobin and myoglobin to oxygen at different oxygen pressures. The results are shown in the graph.

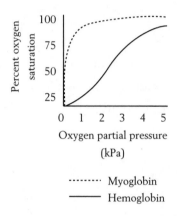

95. At what pressure is the difference in oxygen saturation between hemoglobin and myoglobin the greatest?

A. 1 kPa
B. 2 kPa
C. 3 kPa
D. 4 kPa
E. 5 kPa

96. Myoglobin is expressed in muscle cells. Which BEST explains the difference in oxygen binding between hemoglobin and myoglobin?

    A.   Hemoglobin must retain oxygen in the veins.

    B.   Hemoglobin must remove oxygen from oxygen-poor air.

    C.   Myoglobin must be able to transport oxygen to the brain.

    D.   Myoglobin must be able to remove oxygen from hemoglobin.

    E.   Hemoglobin must bind oxygen even in the presence of myoglobin.

97. A mutation results in hemoglobin with increased saturation at lower pressures. What is the MOST LIKELY result of this mutation?

    A.   Not enough oxygen is absorbed in the lungs.

    B.   Not enough oxygen reaches the muscles.

    C.   More oxygen is transferred to myoglobin.

    D.   Too much oxygen reaches the brain.

    E.   Less oxygen is held by hemoglobin.

Questions 98–99 refer to the following.

Scientists cut a linear piece of DNA with restriction enzymes. They then amplified the DNA and performed gel electrophoresis. The resulting agarose gel is shown.

ENZYME	SITE
EcoR I	5′–GAATTC–3′
BamH I	5′–GGATCC–3′
Hind III	5′–AAGCTT–3′

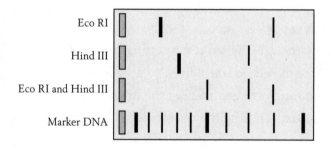

98. When both enzymes were added to the DNA, in how many places was the DNA cut?

    A. 0
    B. 1
    C. 2
    D. 3
    E. 4

99. How many times did the sequence 5'–AAGCTT–3' occur in the DNA?

    A. 0
    B. 1
    C. 2
    D. 3
    E. 4

100. The enzyme BamH I recognizes a palindromic sequence and leaves one strand longer than the other. A piece of DNA is cleaved by BamH I. What does the end of the DNA look like?

    A. ...GATCC–3'
        ...C–5'
    B. ...C–3'
        ...GATCC–5'
    C. ...G–3'
        ...C–5'
    D. ...G–3'
        ...CCTAG–5'
    E. ...CTAGG–3'
        ...GATCC–5'

END OF DIAGNOSTIC TEST

Diagnostic Test Answers and Explanations

Answer Key

1. B	25. C
2. D	26. D
3. D	27. A
4. A	28. D
5. E	29. E
6. D	30. D
7. B	31. B
8. C	32. B
9. D	33. E
10. C	34. C
11. B	35. A
12. C	36. D
13. E	37. D
14. B	38. A
15. C	39. A
16. B	40. E
17. D	41. C
18. B	42. B
19. D	43. C
20. C	44. B
21. A	45. E
22. A	46. D
23. B	47. B
24. A	48. A

49. B	55. D
50. B	56. C
51. A	57. B
52. A	58. C
53. C	59. C
54. A	60. C

Answer Explanations

1. **B.** Photosynthesis uses electromagnetic energy in the form of sunlight to produce glucose molecules. Glucose is broken down in other biochemical processes to release the potential energy stored in its bonds.

2. **D.** Nitrogen fixation converts gaseous nitrogen in the atmosphere (N_2) to nitrogen compounds. The atoms in a molecule of nitrogen gas are held together by a triple bond.

3. **D.** Nitrogen fixation converts nitrogen gas to ammonia.

4. **A.** The carrying capacity of an ecosystem for a species is the maximum population of that species that can be sustained by the resources in the environment.

5. **E.** An r-selected population exists at low population density. Individuals that can produce a large number of offspring quickly are favored in this type of environment, because most offspring will grow to adulthood.

6. **D.** The pancreas is responsible for the regulation of blood glucose levels. Glucose is stored in the liver in the form of glycogen. In response to low blood glucose, the pancreas releases glucagon, which causes glycogen in the liver to enter the bloodstream as glucose.

7. **B.** The parathyroid glands produce parathyroid hormone, which elevates the level of calcium ion dissolved in the blood. It does so, in part, by moving calcium from bone into the bloodstream.

8. **C.** Some lymphocytes are produced in the bone marrow but move to the thymus, where they mature. These become T-cells.

9. **D.** The endoplasmic reticulum contains enzymes that synthesize lipids and hormones. Cells specialized for hormone production have a larger ER.

10. **C.** Ribosomes, which are not bound by membranes, are present in prokaryotes. Ribosomes carry out the translation of mRNA transcripts to produce polypeptides.

11. **B.** Mitochondria are the site of cellular respiration, which harnesses the energy in glucose to produce ATP.

12. **C.** Disruptive selection results when homozygotes have a fitness advantage over heterozygotes. Matings between homozygotes with different alleles produce less-fit offspring. The curve representing this type of selection is bimodal, with peaks to the left and right of the mean for the original population.

13. **E.** Stabilizing selection results in a decrease in average distance from the mean of individuals in a population. The curve representing this type of selection appears thinner and taller than that of the original population.

14. **B.** Directional selection results in a shift in the phenotypic mean of a trait. After selection, the population is, on average, smaller or larger in the particular trait being measured. However, the variation among individuals is the same.

15. **C.** Chordates, which include vertebrates and lancelets, have pharyngeal gill slits at some point in development.

16. **B.** Bryozoa includes sponges, which have tissues but lack differentiation. Sponge tissues are very similar and lack specialized functions.

17. **D.** Members of cnidaria, which include jellyfish and anemones, have radial symmetry.

18. **B.** Motor neurons are part of the somatic nervous system, which is responsible for voluntary muscle movement.

19. **D.** Activation of the parasympathetic nervous system slows the heart

rate, constricts the pupils, and stimulates pancreatic activity. This system promotes relaxation.

20. **C.** The nervous system consists of the central nervous system (brain and spinal cord) and the peripheral nervous system.

21. **A.** An organism's ability to pass its phenotype on to offspring is referred to as its fitness. Some individuals have an advantage in fitness over others, if their phenotype confers some advantage in the current environment.

22. **A.** The four-chambered hearts of birds and mammals are analogous traits because, according to the phylogenetic tree, they did not descend from a common ancestor with this feature.

23. **B.** The endosperm provides nutrients to the plant embryo. Flour is derived from wheat endosperm.

24. **A.** Crossing over, the exchange of DNA segments between pairs of homologous chromosomes, occurs in prophase I of meiosis. In the first round of meiotic cell division, two haploid cells are formed.

25. **C.** Mesophyll, the tissue that forms the interior of the leaf and carries out photosynthesis, is derived from ground tissue. The other two types of plant tissue are vascular and dermal.

26. **D.** In a reflex arc, a sensory neuron sends a signal to the spinal cord, which in turn activates motor neurons originating there. This leads to the reflex movement. Processing of a signal by the brain is not necessary for a reflex to occur.

27. **A.** Gene linkage occurs when two genes are located in close proximity on a chromosome, resulting in a reduced rate of recombination between them. Certain haplotypes therefore tend to occur more frequently, resulting in traits occurring together more often than would otherwise be expected.

28. **D.** Dimorphism refers to the differences between males and females of a species. Birthrate, death rate, emigration, and immigration determine population size.

29. **E.** Both parents are homozygous. Their genotypes can be represented

as *AA* and *BB*. Because their child can only inherit one *A* and one *B* allele, the only possible blood type is *AB*. The alleles for type A and type B blood are codominant.

30. **D.** In a dihybrid cross, the parents are both heterozygous for two different traits. The phenotypic ratios resulting from a dihybrid cross are 9:3:3:1. Only 1 in 16 offspring is expected to be homozygous recessive for both traits.

31. **B.** The principle of competitive exclusion states that two populations in the same ecosystem cannot occupy the same niche. One species will outcompete the other, or character displacement will result such that each species occupies a slightly different niche.

32. **B.** Glucose is completely broken down and released as carbon dioxide in the Krebs or citric acid cycle.

33. **E.** Meiotic recombination, which accompanies sexual reproduction, is carried out by protists, fungi, plants, and animals. Monera (prokaryotes) do not undergo meiosis.

34. **C.** The Calvin cycle of photosynthesis, also known as the dark reactions, converts carbon dioxide gas into other carbon compounds and, eventually, glucose. The Calvin cycle uses ATP produced in the light reactions of photosynthesis.

35. **A.** During the S phase, which occurs between the G1 and G2 phases, a cell's DNA is replicated. However, the replicated DNA still exists as a single chromosome made up of identical sister chromatids bound at the centromere. It is only in mitosis (or meiosis) that the centromeres split and sister chromatids separate.

36. **D.** Tracheids and vessel element cells make up the vascular transport systems of plants. The vascular plant phyla include angiosperms (flowering plants), gymnosperms (conifers), and horsetails, ferns, and club mosses (lycophytes and pterophytes). Bryophytes are nonvascular plants and lack these cell types.

37. **D.** Angiosperms and gymnosperms are seed plants and so do not produce spores. Bryophytes, lycophytes, and pterophytes are spore-producing plants.

38. **A.** A countercurrent exchange system is characterized by fluids flowing in opposite directions. The concentration of dissolved compound is consistently higher in one fluid than in the other, at all points along the system, allowing it to be exchanged across the concentration gradient.

39. **A.** Salivary amylase, produced by the salivary glands of the mouth, digests carbohydrates. Chemical digestion of food therefore begins in the mouth.

40. **E.** Pepsin and trypsin enzymes, produced in the stomach and small intestine, digest protein. These enzymes cleave the bonds between amino acids.

41. **C.** Brain tissue and the epidermis of the skin are both derived from the embryonic ectoderm layer, which is the outermost layer of cells. Bone is derived from mesoderm, the middle layer.

42. **B.** The cells of fungi have cells wall consisting of chitin. Chitin is also found in the exoskeleton of insects. Plant cell walls are composed of cellulose, while the cell walls of some bacteria consist of peptidoglycan.

43. **C.** Birds, reptiles, and some mammals lay eggs that are impermeable to water. The amniotic egg allows these animals to reproduce far from bodies of water. Amphibians lack an amniotic egg and must lay their eggs in water.

44. **B.** Blood circulates from the right side of the heart (1), to the lungs (3), to the left side of the heart (2), to the body (4), and back to the heart (1). The left side of the heart is thicker and stronger than the right because it must pump blood to the entire body.

45. **E.** The systemic circulation consists of the left side of the heart (2) and the veins, capillaries, and arteries that supply the tissues of the body (4).

46. **D.** In response to an increase in blood glucose above this range, the pancreas releases insulin, signaling the liver to convert glucose to glycogen.

47. **B.** *G. fuliginosa* with a beak height of 11.5 mm is found on Island 2. On Island 1, this species has a smaller beak.

48. **A.** The data show character displacement as a result of selection for different food sources. Beak size changed as the two species on Island 1 evolved to occupy different niches, thereby reducing competition.

49. **B.** Directional selection changes the mean of a continuous trait. Beak size shifted downward for *G. fuliginosa* and upward for *G. fortis*.

50. **B.** Only one of the females in generation II, individual II-8, had children. She passed the disorder on to two of these children.

51. **A.** Because it is a rare disorder, it is unlikely that the affected individuals' spouses (I-2, II-2, and II-7) are all carriers. This would be required for the trait to be recessive. In contrast, the pattern of inheritance is consistent with an autosomal dominant mode of inheritance.

52. **A.** Because females inherit one X chromosome from their father, an X-linked dominant trait would be passed on from fathers to all daughters. Individual I-1 did not pass the trait on to daughter II-6, indicating that the disorder is not X-linked dominant.

53. **C.** Removal of the sea star allowed the mussels to expand their lower boundary even lower along the shoreline.

54. **A.** The sea star *P. ochraceus* limits the population of *M. californianus*. Addition of the sea star caused the mussel to move to a higher tideline, while removal of the sea star allowed the mussel to expand to lower depths.

55. **D.** Removal or addition of the sea star affected the range of the mussel species. *P. ochraceus* limits the ranges of other species in the ecosystem.

56. **C.** Radioactive oxygen gas was produced only when the water was radiolabeled. Water is therefore the source of this gas. The source of the hydrogen atoms in water cannot be determined from the experiment, so it cannot be concluded that carbon dioxide is the only source of water.

57. **B.** The dry mass of a plant consists in large part of molecules derived from glucose. Glucose is assembled from the carbon and oxygen atoms in carbon dioxide. Therefore, this gas is the source of most of the dry mass of a plant.

58. **C.** In order to select for cells capable of producing tryptophan, the bacteria are plated on minimal medium, which does not contain tryptophan. To select for cells containing the plasmid, the medium should contain the antibiotic streptomycin. The gene conferring resistance is on the plasmid.

59. **C.** Selection occurs on traits that already exist in a population.

60. **C.** Bacterial transformation involves the intake of DNA from the environment into the cell.

SAT Biology-E Test Answers and Explanations

Answer Key

61. E	71. D
62. C	72. A
63. A	73. C
64. A	74. E
65. B	75. A
66. C	76. C
67. A	77. A
68. B	78. B
69. E	79. A
70. C	80. C

Answer Explanations

61. **E.** Producers (plants) make up the greatest proportion of biomass in a terrestrial ecosystem.

62. **C.** Photosynthetic cyanobacteria are responsible for significantly increasing the level of oxygen gas in the atmosphere, allowing aerobic forms of life to evolve.

63. **A.** In temperate grassland, precipitation varies greatly by season, and droughts are common.

64. **A.** A society that has undergone a demographic transition is characterized by low birthrates and low death rates. The life span is high, and family planning methods are available.

65. **B.** Zooplankton are minuscule organisms that feed on phytoplankton, which are producers. Zooplankton are primary, and sometimes secondary, consumers.

66. **C.** Curve 3 represents a survivorship curve in which many individuals die early in life. It is common among species with large broods and low parental investment.

67. **A.** A population consists of organisms of the same species, occupying the same area. Each ecosystem, community, trophic level, and guild includes multiple species.

68. **B.** Primary succession occurs in areas with no soil and usually begins with lichens, which are capable of extracting nutrients from and weathering rock.

69. **E.** When nutrient-rich runoff enters a body of water, an algal bloom may result. The algae eventually deplete the dissolved nutrients and decomposition increases. This results in the depletion of oxygen, which may form a dead zone.

70. **C.** Predators or herbivores will learn to avoid distinctly or brightly colored species that are noxious. A mimic benefits when the poisonous species is more common (so that predators will encounter it more often than the harmless mimic) and present in the same area.

71. **D.** Removal of a keystone species results in a decrease in species biodiversity. The presence of a keystone species is positively correlated with biodiversity.

72. **A.** Biological magnification results in increased concentrations of water-insoluble pollutions in the tissues of organisms at higher trophic levels. In this ecosystem, the herring gull occupies the highest trophic level.

73. **C.** For any particular allele inherited by one sibling from a parent, there is a 50% change that a second sibling will inherit the same allele. The coefficient of relatedness between siblings is therefore 0.50.

74. **E.** Commensalism refers to a symbiotic relationship in which one species benefits while the other is unaffected.

75. **A.** Multiplying the energy in the primary producers by 0.10 for each transfer yields 100 units $\times$ 0.10 $\times$ 0.10 = 1 unit.

76. **C.** In the covered jar, only respiration is taking place, reducing the D.O. level. Photosynthesis adds oxygen to the water in the uncovered jar.

77. **A.** Subtracting the D.O. level in this jar from that of the original sample results in a measure of the amount of oxygen reduced by respiration. This number is then added to the D.O. in the uncovered jar after 24 hours to add back the oxygen "lost" to respiration.

78. **B.** Of the answer choices given, the plants in the unfenced condition in Year 1 of the study had the greatest number of thorns per plant.

79. **A.** The data indicate that preventing grazing reduced the number of thorns in *H. spinosa*. Therefore, the production of thorns is likely to be a direct response to grazing.

80. **C.** Because *H. spinosa* produces fewer thorns when it is not subject to grazing, it will also produce more seeds. Protecting some of the areas from grazing will encourage seed production and the growth of new plants.

SAT Biology-M Test Answers and Explanations

Answer Key

81. E	91. A
82. B	92. B
83. A	93. A
84. A	94. D
85. D	95. A
86. C	96. D
87. A	97. B
88. C	98. C
89. D	99. B
90. D	100. D

Answer Explanations

81. **E.** In this diagram, 1 represents the phosphate group, 2 represents the deoxyribose sugar, and 3 represents the nitrogenous base. The sugar and phosphate group make up the sides of the ladder, while the hydrogen-bonded nitrogen bases make up the rungs.

82. **B.** Only translation utilizes tRNA, which is the molecule that carries amino acids and binds to the mRNA codons on the ribosome.

83. **A.** Sperm cells normally contribute autosomes and either an X or a Y chromosome to the embryo. However, because the embryo receives an X chromosome from the egg, neither an X nor Y chromosome from sperm is required for viability.

84. **A.** A single-nucleotide point mutation is shown (G to T). Since this does not shift the reading frame, the most likely result is an amino acid substitution.

85. **D.** Fermentation, a form of anaerobic respiration carried out by yeast, produces carbon dioxide and alcohol.

86. **C.** CAM plants convert carbon dioxide to organic molecules before utilizing them for photosynthesis. This allows plants to take in carbon dioxide through their stomata at night and close their stomata during the day. CAM is an adaptation to arid climates.

87. **A.** Excessive heat can denature an enzyme by altering its tertiary, or three-dimensional, structure. This alters the conformation of the active site, preventing it from binding the substrate.

88. **C.** The fruit fly can pass only one allele of each gene to its offspring. The possible allele combinations are NC and nC, since the parent has no c allele to pass on.

89. **D.** Both the citric acid cycle and oxidative phosphorylation take place in the mitochondria. Only glycolysis takes place in the cytoplasm.

90. **D.** Mitochondrial DNA is not contained in the nucleus. The mitochondria of the cloned lamb were derived from mitochondria in the donor egg cell. Its mitochondrial DNA will match that of animal 2.

91. **A.** Only a point mutation, the change of a single nucleotide base to a different base, can result in a silent mutation. This can occur if the change results in a codon specifying the same amino acid as the original sequence.

92. **B.** Only active transport requires the expenditure of energy in the form of ATP. Diffusion and facilitated diffusion (through a protein channel) do not require energy.

93. **A.** Transcription, the copying of a DNA sequence to make an mRNA transcript, takes place in the nucleus.

94. **D.** The enzyme is not altered when it catalyzes a chemical reaction. As a result, the amount of enzyme remains the same while the substrate (3) is converted to product (1).

95. **A.** The greatest difference in saturation between hemoglobin and myoglobin occurs at 1 kPa.

96. **D.** Myoglobin requires a higher affinity for oxygen because it must

remove oxygen from hemoglobin. Hemoglobin carries oxygen to the cells of the body and must release the oxygen at its destination.

97. **B**. If hemoglobin were better able to bind oxygen at lower pressures, it would not as readily release the oxygen to myoglobin in the muscle cells. Therefore, less oxygen would reach the cells.

98. **C**. Adding both enzymes to the DNA resulted in three segments, as seen in the Eco RI and Hind III lane. This means that the linear DNA was cut in three places.

99. **B**. The table shows that 5′–AAGCTT–3′ is the recognition site for Hind III. Because the EcoR I enzyme cleaved the linear DNA into two pieces, the DNA must have contained one recognition site for this enzyme.

100. **D**. The end of the DNA cleaved by BamH I is complementary to the recognition site sequence shown in the table. One strand must also be longer than the other. The sequence CCTAG–5′ is complementary to GATCC–3′.

Using the Diagnostic Test

Calculating Your Score

Calculating your raw score for the SAT Biology E/M Subject Test isn't difficult. Follow the steps below to approximate your raw score.

1. Count the items you answered correctly in each section. Write those numbers here.

   Questions 1–60: _____   E Test: _____   M Test: _____

2. Count the items you answered incorrectly in each section. Write those numbers here, and then perform the calculation:

   Questions 1–60: _____ × 0.250 = _____
   E Test: _____ × 0.250 = _____
   M Test: _____ × 0.250 = _____

3. For each section, subtract the results of #2 from the results of #1.

   Questions 1–60: _____ – _____ = _____
   E Test: _____ – _____ = _____
   M Test: _____ – _____ = _____

4. Calculate your total scores by including the results from the Biology-E and Biology-M Tests. Add the results of #3 for questions 1–60 to each of the subsections.

Questions 1–60 + E Test: _____ + _____ = _____

Questions 1–60 + M Test: _____ + _____ = _____

5. Take the results of #4 and round up or down as necessary to obtain a whole number.

E Test: _____

M Test: _____

These are your raw scores. (Keep in mind that during the actual SAT subject test, your score will be calculated based on *either* the E Test or the M Test, whichever you choose on test day.) The College Board goes one step further and translates your raw score into a scaled score. It isn't necessary to take that extra step to determine how well you'll perform. If you obtained a high raw score (maximum: 80), that would translate to a high scaled score (800). Congratulations! You're definitely ready to ace this test. If, on the other hand, you obtained a low raw score (say, 20 or under), that would translate to a low scaled score, roughly about 450. Remember, you want to hit *at least* the average national score (for 2011, this was 604 for Biology-E and 635 for Biology-M). Although the exact number you must achieve will vary from year to year, you should try to get a minimum raw score of around 50 to hit the average.

Improving Your Score

How do you feel about your performance? Remember, the diagnostic test in this book is meant to help you identify your weak areas and show you where you may need to improve in terms of either the content you are studying or your actual test-taking habits. Don't underestimate the importance of good test-taking habits; for standardized examinations such as this one, your approach is every bit as important as the knowledge you bring to the table.

Assess your performance *honestly*. Go back through the test and review the questions you answered correctly, those you answered incorrectly, and those you skipped. Can you identify patterns or trends in your incorrect or missed answers? Was your score much higher for one subsection than for the other? Did you make dumb mistakes by failing to read all of the answer options or by misreading the questions? Did you miss many core concepts? Also review the vocabulary terms you highlighted. Are these similar in nature or related to particular concepts or ideas? If you have time, follow up on this material. Close the gaps in your knowledge so they aren't a problem when you get to your actual test.

Finally, how did you do with time? Did you run out of time? Were you rushing to finish within the allotted time period? Did you spend too much time on each individual question? Or did you fail to spend *enough* time? Remember, successful test-taking is as much about managing your time as it about understanding the content.

A Final Word about the Diagnostic Test

Finally, don't feel too bad if you didn't do well on this diagnostic test the first time through. After all, the entire point of this book is to give you the opportunity to identify areas for improvement and to give you the materials for practice. Use this book to test and retest, until you feel thoroughly comfortable with both the setup and the content of the examination.

Before moving on, head back to **The Main Course: Comprehensive Strategies and Review** (page 19) and review the test-taking strategies discussed there. Now that you've had an opportunity to take the practice test, some of the test-taking strategies will make a whole lot more sense to you. As you move forward, you'll be able to see more specifically how you can apply these strategies to your advantage.

Review Chapter 1: The Cell

Basic Unit of Life

According to cell theory, the cell is the basic unit of life. All living organisms are either single-celled or multicellular; multicellular organisms have many cells that are specialized to carry out different functions. Cells come in two basic types: *prokaryotic* and *eukaryotic*.

Prokaryotic Cells

Prokaryotic cells are the smallest and simplest cells. They include a plasma membrane and the jelly-like cytosol. Unlike eukaryotes, prokaryotes do not contain membrane-bound organelles. They do, however, have ribosomes, the tiny particles that assemble proteins from the genetic information in the cell's chromosome. A prokaryote's simple, circular chromosome is contained in the cytoplasm, allowing the prokaryote to divide by the simple process of binary fission. Most prokaryotes have a rigid cell wall surrounding the plasma membrane.

Eukaryotic Cells

A eukaryotic cell is larger and more complex than a prokaryotic cell. Its cytoplasm contains membrane-bound organelles, and its genetic material is contained in a nucleus. A eukaryotic cell has the following structures:

- *Cytoskeleton*. This scaffold, made up of tubulin and actin proteins, gives structure and support to the cell. The centrosome is an area that organizes microtubules, and a pair of centrioles may be observed in some cell types (for example, animal cells).

- *Nucleus*. The nucleus contains the cell's genetic material, which consists of long, linear deoxyribonucleic acid (DNA) strands. The strands are wrapped around histone proteins, which coil to form chromosomes. Chromosomes contain the genetic instructions for assembling proteins.

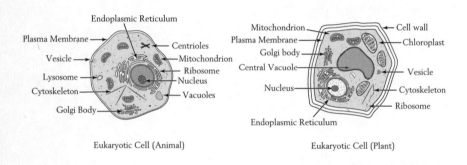

Eukaryotic Cell (Animal)   Eukaryotic Cell (Plant)

- *Endoplasmic reticulum and Golgi body*. Internal membranes enclose the nucleus and make up the endoplasmic reticulum (ER) and Golgi body, or apparatus. The ER consists of a network of membranes surrounding the nucleus. Rough ER is studded with tiny ribosomes, structures made up of ribonucleic acid (RNA) and protein. The ER is where proteins, cell membranes, and other biological molecules, such as hormones and lipids, are synthesized. Proteins are then enclosed in vesicles, which are small sacs that bud off a membrane, forming a sphere. A vesicle transports the material contained inside it, and can merge with another membrane elsewhere in the cell to deposit its cargo. In the case of proteins, the vesicles transport them to the Golgi body.

- *Ribosomes.* Ribosomes are tiny, non-membrane-bound structures made up of protein and RNA. They carry out protein synthesis. In eukaryotes, ribosomes are bound to the ER and are also found floating in the cytoplasm. (Note that prokaryotes also contain ribosomes.)

- *Lysosomes and vacuoles.* Lysosomes are similar to vesicles and contain enzymes that digest, or break down, large molecules. Vacuoles are vesicles of varying sizes that store food or water in the cytoplasm. For example, plant cells often contain a large, central vacuole that stores water and other materials.

- *Mitochondria.* Cells contain many of these organelles, which convert the energy stored in food to small molecules called adenosine triphosphate (ATP). Mitochondria have an external membrane and a highly folded internal membrane, which is important in cellular respiration.

- *Chloroplasts.* These organelles carry out photosynthesis in the cells of eukaryotic producers, such as plants and algae. Their chlorophyll gives producers their characteristic green color. Other plasts may contain starches or pigments.

- *Cell wall.* Some eukaryotic cells are surrounded and supported by cell walls. The presence and make-up of the cell wall is a key characteristic in the classification of organisms.

Mitosis and Cytokinesis

With their large chromosome numbers, eukaryotic cells must undergo mitosis before the cells can divide. Mitosis is the replication of the eukaryotic nucleus and results in two nuclei containing identical genetic information. Eukaryotes species have a characteristic diploid number of paired homologous chromosomes. In sexual reproduction, one homolog from each pair is inherited from each parent.

Before mitosis even begins, the cell has replicated its DNA, with each chromosome forming two identical sister chromatids. However, the number of chromosomes has not doubled because the sister chromatids are joined at the centromeres; they will separate in mitosis. Mitosis proceeds in stages that can be remembered by the mnemonic PMAT: Please Make Another Two.

- *Prophase.* Before mitosis, the chromosomes are in an uncondensed state. In prophase, they condense, and the nuclear membrane breaks down. Spindle fibers emerge from the centrioles, which move to opposite poles of the cell.

- *Metaphase.* The spindle fibers attach to the centromeres of each chromosome, aligning them along the central metaphase plate. Each sister chromatid is attached to a spindle fiber from one centriole.

- *Anaphase.* The centromeres holding sister chromatids together now detach. Sister chromatids separate and are pulled to opposite poles of the cell by the shortening spindle fibers.

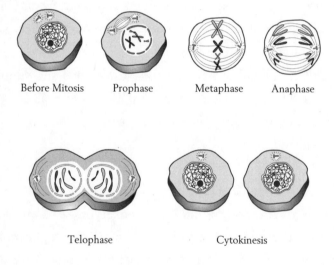

Before Mitosis   Prophase   Metaphase   Anaphase

Telophase   Cytokinesis

- *Telophase.* Now that the sister chromatids have separated, the cell contains two full sets of identical chromosomes. In telophase, a nuclear membrane re-forms around each set, creating a cell with two nuclei. Mitosis is now complete.

- *Cytokinesis.* The division of a cell into two daughter cells can proceed once mitosis is complete. Often, it even begins during telophase. In cells that lack a cell wall, a cleavage furrow forms around the center, constricting the cell and pinching it to form two new cells. In cells with cell walls, a cell plate forms between the two nuclei. This will make up part of the cell wall of the two daughter cells.

The Cell Cycle

Mitosis and cytokinesis make up a very small fraction of the cell cycle, called the *M (mitotic) phase.* The majority of a cell's lifetime is spent in interphase, throughout which the cell grows. Interphase consists of three stages:

- *G1.* A newly formed eukaryotic cell starts out in the G1 ("first gap") phase, during which it grows and accumulates the raw materials needed to replicate its DNA and organelles.
- *S.* In S phase, the synthesis phase, the cell replicates its organelles in preparation for cell division. S phase is also when the chromosomes double their genetic material, forming sister chromatids. (Keep in mind that the chromosome number does not double; sister chromatid pairs are still joined and so are considered single chromosomes.)
- *G2.* In G2 ("second gap") phase, the cell continues to grow in preparation for mitosis and cytokinesis (M phase). The two gap phases are so called because the cell is neither replicating DNA nor dividing.

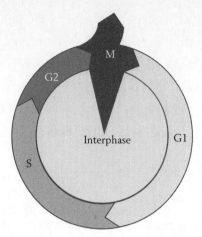

G1: The cell grows and prepares to replicate its DNA

S: The cell replicates its DNA, creating sister chromatids

G2: The cell grows and prepares for cell division

M: Mitosis and Cytokinesis

Checkpoints throughout the cell cycle ensure that DNA is copied correctly and that each new cell receives a complete set of chromosomes. In a multicellular organism, the cell cycle is tightly controlled to ensure that cells do not continue to divide indefinitely. Cancer tumors form due to a disruption of the cell cycle in which cells inherit abnormal numbers of chromosomes (called *aneuploidy*) and/or continue to divide even when external conditions are crowded.

Review Questions

1. Which of these cell structures contains one or more membranes?

   I.   Ribosome
   II. Plasma membrane
   III. Endoplasmic reticulum
   IV. Golgi body

   A. II only
   B. IV only
   C. I and II
   D. I, II, and III
   E. II, III, and IV

2. Cyanobacteria are photosynthetic prokaryotes. Which organelles do cyanobacteria cells contain?

   I.   Chloroplasts
   II. Nucleus
   III. Ribosomes

   A. I only
   B. II only
   C. III only
   D. I and II only
   E. I and III only

3. • A cell normally contains 54 chromosomes. During which phases of mitosis does the cell contain 108 chromosomes?

I. Anaphase
II. Metaphase
III. Prophase
IV. Telophase

A. I and IV
B. II and III
C. II and IV
D. I, II, and III
E. I, II, and IV

4. A cell contains multiple nuclei with identical genetic information. This cell most likely formed by going through

A. multiple rounds of mitosis, but no cytokinesis
B. multiple rounds of the M phase, but no rounds of the S phase
C. multiple rounds of cytokinesis, but no rounds of mitosis
D. multiple rounds of the cell cycle, but no rounds of mitosis
E. multiple rounds of the S phase, but no other phases of the cell cycle

5. What is the correct sequence of these events in the cell cycle?

I.   Nuclear membrane dissolves.

II.   Cell size increases.

III. Two daughter cells form.

IV.   DNA replicates.

A. I, IV, II, III
B. I, IV, III, II
C. II, I, IV, III
D. II, IV, I, III
E. IV, II, III, I

Answer Explanations

1. **E.** The ER, plasma membrane, and Golgi body of a eukaryotic cell consist of membrane composed of a phospholipid bilayer. In contrast, the ribosome is not a membrane-bound organelle.

2. **C.** Cyanobacteria are prokaryotes, and so do not contain membrane-bound organelles such as chloroplasts or a nucleus. All prokaryotes, however, do contain ribosomes.

3. **A.** The sister chromatids making up each of the 54 chromosomes separate in anaphase and move to opposite poles of the cell in telophase. In these two phases, the cell contains 108 distinct chromosomes.

4. **A.** A single cell with multiple nuclei must have undergone multiple rounds of mitosis, which is the replication of the nucleus. It did not, however, undergo cytokinesis, which is the division of a eukaryotic cell to form two daughter cells.

5. **D.** In the G1 and G2 phases of the cell cycle, a newly formed cell grows. It replicates its DNA in the S phase. In mitosis, the nuclear membrane dissolves as the nucleus is replicated. After mitosis, cytokinesis forms two identical daughter cells.

Review Chapter 2: Water, Cell Membranes, and Transport

Water

Because much of life consists of, takes place in, and depends upon water, understanding the special properties of this small molecule is essential. Water is a good solvent for ionic and polar covalent compounds.

Ionic and *covalent* are two basic types of chemical bonds. Ionic bonds form when atoms gain or lose electrons. When dissolved in water, these compounds dissociate to form *ions*, which are atoms or molecules that carry a charge. For example, the sodium ion, Na^+, has lost an electron and carries a positive charge of 1. The calcium ion, Ca^{2+}, carries a positive charge of 2. Chlorine, Cl^-, has an extra electron and carries a negative charge of 1. In contrast, covalent bonds form when two atoms share electrons. Covalent compounds, such as glucose, do not dissociate or carry a charge in water.

In some molecules (such as water), the atoms do not share the electrons equally. Some atoms are more attracted to the bonding electrons, which tend to be found closer to those atoms than to others. This results in the atom having a partial negative or partial positive charge. This is called a *polar covalent bond*, and these molecules are known as polar molecules. Water is a polar molecule: the oxygen atom has a partial negative charge, and each hydrogen atom has a partial positive charge.

Attraction between partial-positive
and partial-negative poles

The polar nature of the water molecule is responsible for water's unique properties. Water molecules participate in hydrogen bonding interactions, both with each other and with other substances. The partially negative oxygen atoms attract the partially positive hydrogen atoms of other water molecules. As a result, water has high *cohesion*. This leads to water's high surface tension, demonstrated when insects are able to walk on water without sinking.

Water also has high *adhesion*, or the ability to attract other surfaces and substances. This is important for water's capillary action. Also, water can dissolve both ionic compounds and many covalent compounds, making it the universal solvent. Lipids, whose molecules are not polar at all, do not interact with water molecules and therefore do not dissolve easily in water. Lipids are termed *hydrophobic*, or water avoiding.

The Plasma Membrane

The plasma membrane is a phospholipid bilayer; it is made up of two layers of phospholipid molecules. A phospholipid has a *hydrophilic* (water-seeking) "head" and a hydrophobic "tail." When these molecules are layered with the hydrophobic tails sandwiched between the hydrophilic heads, the membrane is stable in an aqueous (water) environment.

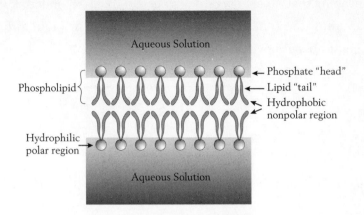

The cell membrane is semipermeable or selectively permeable. Some substances may cross freely; others cannot. Small, hydrophobic molecules easily pass through the phospholipid bilayer. Ions or polar molecules cannot cross this layer easily; even water diffuses through the phospholipid bilayer very slowly.

However, ions and polar molecules do have assistance to help them pass through the cell membrane. The fluid mosaic model depicts proteins floating in the "sea" of phospholipids. These proteins transport molecules across the membrane and are essential for allowing ions, polar molecules, and larger molecules to enter and exit the cell.

Movement of Substances across Cell Membranes

The cell membrane is primarily responsible for allowing substances to enter and exit the cell. Methods of cell transport are divided into two broad categories, depending whether the cell needs to expend energy: *passive* transport and *active* transport.

Passive transport depends on a concentration gradient existing across the membrane. A concentration gradient occurs when a substance exists in different concentrations in adjacent locations, even if no membrane is involved. Over time, ions, molecules, or atoms move "down" the concentration gradient, from an area of greater concentration to an area of lesser concentration. This movement, called *diffusion*, occurs "for free," meaning that no energy or work needed to be expended. Diffusion continues until the concentration is equal throughout (equilibrium), at which point no *net* movement occurs.

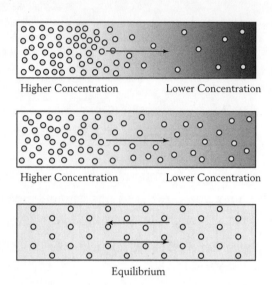

Suppose a cell membrane sits in the middle of a concentration gradient. If the concentration is lower inside the cell, the substance will diffuse into the cell. If the concentration is higher inside the cell, the substance will diffuse out of the cell.

However, because the cell membrane is semipermeable, not all substances may move down a gradient, across the membrane. In some cases, cell membrane proteins act as transport channels that allow these substances to cross. No energy is required; the channel protein simply provides an entry point in this process, called *facilitated diffusion*. Facilitated diffusion is therefore a form of passive transport.

Suppose there is no concentration gradient surrounding a cell membrane. In that case, a cell must expend energy to move substances across the membrane in active transport. Active transport is carried out by cell membrane proteins that pump ions or other molecules against their concentration gradients. For example, cells require a higher concentration of sodium (Na^+) ions outside the cell membrane and a higher concentration of potassium (K^+) ions inside. The cell must continually pump these ions against ("up") their concentration gradients.

Osmosis: The Diffusion of Water

While a dissolved substance, or *solute*, moves "down" a concentration gradient, water moves in the opposite direction of the solute. Osmosis is the diffusion of water across a selectively permeable membrane. All cells must maintain proper water balance, and the surrounding liquid affects osmosis into or out of the cell. This, in turn, depends on the concentration of solutes that **cannot** cross the membrane.

The tonicity of the fluid surrounding a cell affects its water balance. A cell in an *isotonic* solution, or one that has equal tonicity to the cell's cytoplasm, experiences no net change in water balance. In a *hypertonic* (higher-concentration) solution, on the other hand, water will move out of the cell, causing it to shrink. In cells with cell walls, the plasma membrane pulls away from the wall in a process called *plasmolysis*.

In a *hypotonic* (lower-concentration) solution, water will move into the cell. The excess water causes a cell without walls to lyse, or burst. In contrast, a cell with walls becomes turgid (rigid) in hypotonic surroundings, because the wall can withstand the turgor pressure of the water. This causes plants to become firm when watered.

Transport of Larger Materials

Large particles or quantities of liquid are moved across the cell membrane by processes involving vesicle formation: *endocytosis* and *exocytosis*. In endocytosis, the cell membrane surrounds a particle outside of the cell and pinches off to form a vesicle. The vesicle transports the acquired material through the cytoplasm. Two forms of endocytosis are phagocytosis, in which the cell takes in a large particle, and pinocytosis, in which the cell takes in surrounding fluid instead of particles. Exocytosis is the reverse process: a vesicle inside the cell fuses with the cell membrane, ejecting its contents outside of the cell. Because they require energy, these processes are forms of active transport.

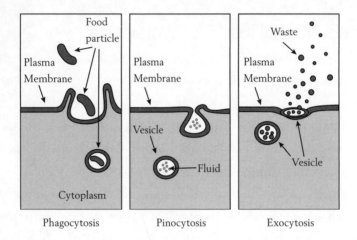

| Phagocytosis | Pinocytosis | Exocytosis |

Review Questions

1. Which of these BEST describes the part of the molecule shown?

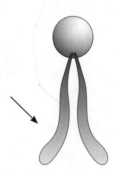

    A. It is hydrophilic.

    B. It forms the outer layer of the plasma membrane.

    C. It is composed of phosphate atoms.

    D. It contains nonpolar covalent bonds.

    E. It is capable of hydrogen bonding.

2. A plant cell is placed in a hypotonic solution. As a result, the cell will

    A. lyse
    B. swell but remain intact
    C. shrivel
    D. remain unchanged
    E. take up solutes

3. A solute cannot move into a cell by crossing the phospholipid bilayer of the membrane. It can, however, enter through a membrane protein. The fact that solute molecules are entering the cell MOST LIKELY indicates that

    A. energy is being expended by the cell
    B. the solute is moving against its concentration gradient
    C. the solute molecules are hydrophilic
    D. the cell is in a hypotonic solution
    E. solute concentration is higher inside than outside the cell

4. How can a water molecule BEST be described?

    I.   It is nonpolar.
    II.   It has an equal electron distribution.
    III. It is able to form hydrogen bonds.

    A. I only
    B. II only
    C. III only
    D. I and II
    E. I and III

Answer Explanations

1. **D.** The lipid tails of a phospholipid molecule are indicated. This region of the phospholipid is hydrophobic (water avoiding), lacks phosphate

atoms, contains nonpolar covalent bonds, and does not participate in hydrogen bonding. It forms the inner layer of the plasma membrane.

2. **B.** A plant cell placed in a hypotonic solution will take up water and swell. However, it will not burst because the rigid cell wall can withstand the turgor pressure of the water. This process keeps plants upright.

3. **C.** The fact that solute molecules are entering a cell via a membrane protein does not necessarily mean that the cell is expending energy (active transport), that the solute is moving against its concentration gradient (which requires energy), or that the solute concentration is greater inside the cell than outside (implying that the solute is moving against its concentration gradient). If the cell were in a hypotonic solution, solutes would tend to move out of the cell while water moved into it. Facilitated diffusion uses membrane protein to allow polar, hydrophilic molecules or ions into the cell. These solutes cannot pass through the nonpolar, hydrophobic inner layer of the cell membrane.

4. **C.** Water is polar, meaning that it has an unequal distribution of electrons. This helps it to form hydrogen bonds.

Review Chapter 3:
DNA, RNA, and Proteins

Two of the most important types of molecules in the cell are *proteins* and *nucleic acids*. Proteins are large, diverse molecules with many roles in cell structure and function. Proteins allow molecules to cross the cell membrane, make up the cytoskeleton, associate with and organize DNA, and compose substances surrounding cells and tissues, such as collagen. Protein enzymes help carry out biochemical reactions. Proteins depend on nucleic acids, DNA and RNA. DNA makes up the chromosomes and contains the cell's genetic information—the instructions for making proteins. RNA plays other crucial roles in protein synthesis.

Proteins and Amino Acids

Proteins are polymers or macromolecules (large molecules) made up of repeating monomers (subunits) called *amino acids*. Just 20 different amino acids make up all the proteins of nearly every living thing. Each amino acid shares the same basic molecular structure. However, they differ in the side group, the one or more atoms attached to the central carbon atom that confer different chemical properties (for example, hydrophilic vs. hydrophobic) to each type of amino acid.

Amino acids are joined end to end in linear chains. Once synthesized, these chains twist and fold to take on their functional, three-dimensional shapes. Four levels of protein structure are considered. The primary structure of a protein refers to the sequence of amino acids making up the chain. The secondary structure refers to shapes or motifs (such as an alpha helix) that may occur in parts of the chain. The tertiary structure refers to the three-dimensional shape of the folded polypeptide chain. Finally, the quaternary structure describes how the polypeptide associates with other polypeptides (for example, if it forms a protein with multiple parts).

Nucleic Acids and Nucleotides

Nucleic acids, DNA and RNA, are polymers made up of nucleotide monomers. The molecular structure of DNA is shown in the figure below. DNA stands for *deoxyribonucleic acid*; each monomer consists of (1) a five-carbon sugar, deoxyribose; (2) a phosphate group, and (3) a nitrogen base (A, C, G, or T). If you consider a double DNA strand as a ladder, the sugar and phosphate groups make up the "sides," while the paired nitrogenous bases make up the "rungs."

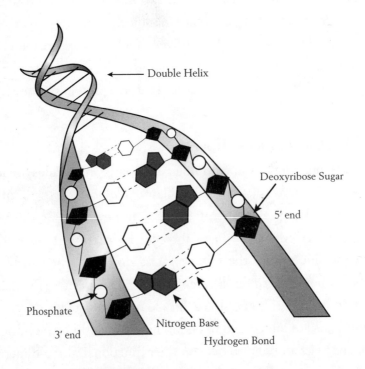

The two strands are held together by hydrogen bonding interactions between complementary bases: adenine bonds with thymine, and guanine bonds with cytosine. The double-stranded DNA twists to form a double helix.

Each DNA strand in a double strand has a direction. One strand is oriented in the 3'-to-5' direction; the other strand is oriented in a 5'-to-3' direction. This means that the strands are antiparallel. (NOTE: The numbers 3 and 5 refer to carbons in the sugar.) Eukaryotic chromosomes are made up of extremely long double strands of DNA wound around proteins called *histones*.

Replication of DNA

When a chromosome replicates its DNA, the DNA double strands "unzip" as the hydrogen bonds between them are broken. Then, free nucleotides pair with the nucleotides of the separated strands, which act as templates. The nucleotides are joined by the enzyme DNA polymerase, creating a new, complementary strand for each original DNA strand. Each new DNA double strand consists of one old (template) strand and one newly formed strand. For this reason, DNA replication is called *semiconservative*.

RNA

RNA (for *ri*bo*n*ucleic *a*cid), like, DNA, is made up of nucleotide monomers linked by their sugar and phosphate subunits. Unlike DNA, the five-carbon sugar in RNA is ribose. In addition, the nucleotide uracil replaces thymine, and RNA does not form a double-stranded helix.

Three important forms of RNA are mRNA, tRNA, and rRNA. Ribosomal RNA (rRNA), along with protein, makes up the ribosome. The others (mRNA and tRNA) are also involved in protein synthesis, as described in the following sections. The relationship between the information in DNA and mRNA, and between mRNA and polypeptide sequence, is known as the central dogma of molecular genetics.

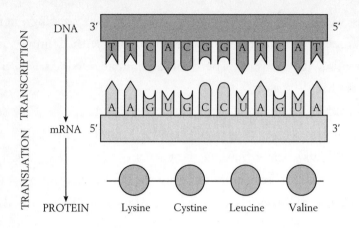

Transcription of mRNA

Genetic information specifies the proteins that a cell may produce. The sequence of nucleotides making up a gene corresponds to the sequence of amino acids in the polypeptide chain that will eventually be assembled. This information is contained in the chromosomes, which reside in the nucleus. Protein assembly, however, takes place in the ribosomes of the ER and cytoplasm. Therefore, the information in DNA must be copied and transported out of the nucleus; this is the function of messenger RNA, or mRNA.

In the location of the gene, the DNA uncoils, and its two strands "unzip," exposing the nitrogen bases. As RNA nucleotides base-pair with the exposed DNA nucleotides, a complementary, antiparallel RNA chain forms. The free nucleotides are joined together by the RNA polymerase enzyme. Once the gene has been transcribed (or copied to RNA), the newly formed mRNA is released and processed in the nucleus. It then exits through a nuclear pore and travels to a free or ER-bound ribosome in the cytoplasm.

Translation of mRNA to Protein

Translation of the genetic information in mRNA to a polypeptide strand is carried out by the ribosome. A nucleotide sequence is read in triplets called *codons*. Each codon corresponds to an amino acid; this is the nearly universal genetic code of life. Because there are four nucleotides making up the codons, there are 64 (4 × 4 × 4) codons. However, there are only 20 amino acids. Most amino acids are specified by more than one codon. There is one codon, a stop codon, that does not specify any amino acid but acts as a signal for translation to stop. The codon signal for translation to start codes for the amino acid methionine. The mRNA strand attaches to a ribosome, and translation initiates at the start codon.

Transfer RNA (tRNA) interprets the genetic sequence into an amino acid sequence. The cell contains different forms of tRNA, each of which has a specific anticodon and carries a specific amino acid. A tRNA molecule is a looped structure with an anticodon at one end and a site that attaches to an amino acid at the opposite end.

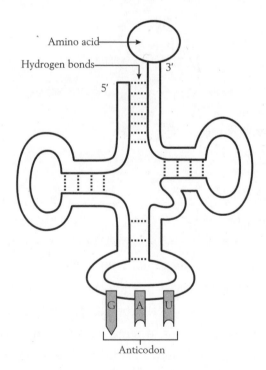

As the mRNA binds to the ribosome, one codon is exposed at a time. The tRNA with the complementary anticodon binds to the mRNA codon in the "hot seat." Once bound, the amino acid it carries is transferred to the ribosome, and the tRNA molecule is released. Then, the mRNA transcript shifts along the ribosome so that the next codon is in the "hot seat." A complementary tRNA binds, its amino acid is joined to the previous amino acid, the tRNA is released, and the mRNA shifts again. As this process is repeated, the polypeptide chain elongates. Eventually, the stop codon is reached and translation is completed. The polypeptide chain is released and allowed to take on its three-dimensional protein conformation.

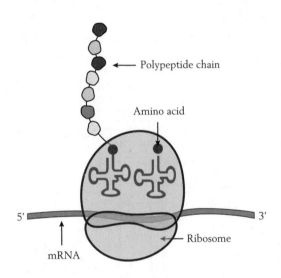

Gene Expression

The transcription of a gene, or *gene expression*, is regulated by DNA sequences (called *promoters* and *enhancers*) located upstream and downstream of the gene. Proteins called *transcription factors* bind to these DNA sequences and either activate or repress the activity of RNA polymerase. Different sets of transcription factors are present in different cells of multicellular organisms, driving the differences in gene expression among the millions of genetically identical cells that make up a plant or animal body. Gene expression differences lead to the differentiation and specialization of cells in multicellular organisms.

Review Questions

1. The genetic code table shows the amino acids that correspond to mRNA codons. Each codon is read from 3' (first nucleotide) to 5' (third nucleotide). A DNA template strand is shown. Which amino acid sequence will be assembled from the mRNA associated with this strand?

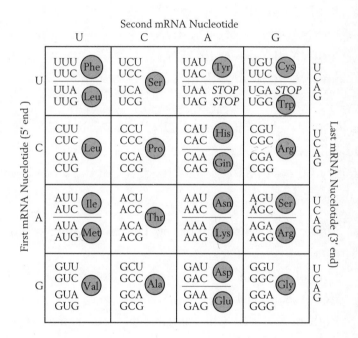

DNA template strand: 5'–GCG ACA TAC ACT–3'

   A.   Ala—Cys—Met
   B.   Arg—Cys—Met
   C.   Ala—Thr—Tyr—Thr
   D.   Ala—Thr—Tyr—Trp
   E.   Arg—Thr—Tyr—Thr

2. Which answer choice matches the functions listed below to the correct RNA types?

    I.   Interprets a codon as an amino acid
    II. Binds to a gene transcript
    III. Contains information for assembling a protein

    A. I. mRNA; II. rRNA; III. tRNA
    B. I. mRNA; II. tRNA; III. rRNA
    C. I. rRNA; II. mRNA; III. tRNA
    D. I. tRNA; II. mRNA; III. rRNA
    E. I. tRNA; II. rRNA; III. mRNA

3. An original cell replicates its DNA. The cell undergoes mitosis and cell division, and one of the daughter cells replicates its DNA. Which of these BEST describes the DNA of the second-generation daughter cells?

    A. One of the cells will contain DNA consisting of one strand from the original cell.
    B. One of the cells will contain DNA consisting of two strands from the original cell.
    C. Both of the cells will contain DNA consisting of one strand from the original cell.
    D. Both of the cells will contain DNA consisting of two strands from the original cell.
    E. Neither of the cells will contain DNA consisting of strands from the original cell.

4. The partial sequence of a single DNA strand is shown. What will be the sequence of the complementary strand produced during DNA replication?

   3′–ATGCTGAACT–5′

   A. 5′–ATGCTGAACT–3′
   B. 5′–CGTAGTCCAG–3′
   C. 5′–GACCTGATGC–3′
   D. 5′–GCATCAGGTC–3′
   E. 5′–TACGACTTGA–3′

5. Which of these labels matches the structure of the partial RNA strand shown?

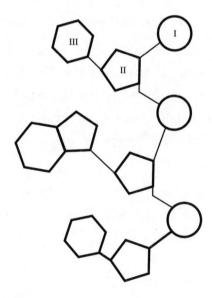

   A. I. phosphate; II. ribose; III. nitrogen base
   B. I. phosphate; II. nitrogen base; III. ribose
   C. I. nitrogen base; II. phosphate; III. ribose
   D. I. ribose; II. nitrogen base; III. phosphate
   E. I. ribose; II. phosphate; III. nitrogen base

Answer Explanations

1. **B.** The DNA template is used to produce a complementary RNA strand with the sequence 3′–CGC UGU AUG UGA–5′. The first three codons specify the amino acids alanine, cystine, and methionine, respectively. The last codon is a stop codon, which tells the ribosome to end translation.

2. **E.** Transfer RNA (tRNA) molecules carry amino acids and bind to specific mRNA codons. Ribosomal RNA (rRNA) makes up the ribosome and binds to the mRNA transcript. Messenger RNA (mRNA) carries genetic information from the nucleus to the cytoplasm.

3. **A.** DNA replication is semiconservative. During the first round of replication, each original single strand pairs with a new complementary strand. The first-generation daughter cells each have DNA consisting of one original and one new strand. During replication, the single original strand will pair with a new strand. The other double strand will consist of nonoriginal DNA.

4. **E.** The complementary base-pairing rule for DNA is that adenine (A) pairs with thymine (T), and cytosine (C) pairs with guanine (G). DNA strands run antiparallel, so the complementary strand will be in the 5′-to-3′ direction. The complementary sequence is, therefore, 5′–TACGACTTGA–3′.

5. **A.** The five-carbon ribose sugar (II) and the phosphate group (I) make up the backbone of the RNA strand. The nitrogen bases (III) are attached to the ribose sugars.

Review Chapter 4: Energy, Respiration, and Photosynthesis

Energy in the Form of ATP

Biochemical reactions may be *endothermic* (energy requiring) or *exothermic* (energy releasing). An endothermic reaction can be paired with an exothermic reaction: one releases energy that the other uses. Endothermic reactions in the cell require a source of energy in the form of a molecule that readily undergoes an exothermic reaction. This energy source must be small, soluble, and readily available. It is ATP, or *a*denosine *tri*phosphate; specifically, the energy comes from the exothermic reaction that occurs when ATP is converted to ADP (*a*denosine *di*phosphate).

A molecule of ATP consists of an adenosine subunit attached to a chain of three phosphate groups. When the bond between the second and third phosphate groups is broken, ADP and an inorganic phosphate molecule are produced, as shown in the equation below. This reaction is exothermic: it releases energy. It can be paired with other biochemical reactions that require energy, allowing these reactions to proceed.

$$ATP \rightarrow ADP + P_{inorganic} \text{ (exothermic, or energy producing)}$$

The equation above describes the breakdown of ATP for energy. When ATP is produced, the opposite reaction takes place, joining phosphate to ADP. This reaction requires energy from another source.

$$ADP + P_{inorganic} \rightarrow ATP \text{ (endothermic, or energy requiring)}$$

Respiration and ATP Production

Where do cells obtain the energy to make ATP? Cells break down organic molecules, most often glucose, and use the energy released to produce ATP from ADP and phosphate. This breakdown of glucose is called *cellular respiration*. The net chemical equation for this process follows:

$$C_6H_{12}O_6 + 6O_2 \rightarrow 6CO_2 + 6H_2O + Energy$$

In *aerobic* (oxygen-requiring) respiration, 36–38 molecules of ATP are produced for every glucose molecule. Heat energy is also produced. Respiration proceeds in three stages: glycolysis, the Krebs (or citric acid) cycle, and oxidative phosphorylation. Most ATP is not produced until the final stage. The earlier stages extract energy from glucose in the form of high-energy electrons carried by the molecules NAD^+ and FADH. These electrons provide energy to create a hydrogen ion (H^+) gradient in the third stage, oxidative phosphorylation; in turn, this gradient provides energy to synthesize ATP.

- *Glycolysis.* This is the first step of respiration and takes place in the cytoplasm. Glycolysis is the breakdown of the six-carbon sugar glucose into two three-carbon molecules of pyruvate, which enter the second stage of respiration. (The root *glyco* means "sugar"; *lysis* means "splitting.") A net of two ATP molecules is produced in glycolysis. In addition, two molecules of NAD^+ accept electrons and are reduced to NADH plus H^+; these will be used in oxidative phosphorylation.

- *Citric acid cycle.* The *Krebs* or *citric acid cycle* takes place in the mitochondria, where pyruvate is actively transported from the cytoplasm. The citric acid cycle is a series of enzyme-catalyzed reactions that further break down pyruvate. This provides additional energy and electrons to reduce NAD^+ to NADH and FAD to $FADH_2$, and produce two more molecules of ATP. Carbon dioxide is produced in this stage of respiration as the original glucose carbons are separated and released.

- *Oxidative phosphorylation.* The final stage of respiration consists of two processes: the electron transport chain and ATP synthesis by chemiosmosis. Most ATP is produced in this stage, and the NADH and $FADH_2$ molecules produced in the previous two stages come into play here. Oxidative phosphorylation takes place along the intricately folded inner membrane of the mitochondria.

- *Electron transport chain.* This consists of proteins and "helper" molecules embedded in the inner mitochondrial membrane. NADH and $FADH_2$ molecules carry high-energy electrons, and donate these to the first member of the chain. (They revert to NAD^+ and FAD.) The first member of the electron transport chain gains energy, which it uses to pump hydrogen ions (H^+) across the mitochondrial membrane. It passes the electrons along to the next member of the chain, which in turns gains energy and pumps more hydrogen ions across the membrane, and so on. At the end of the electron transport chain, the electrons have much less energy and are accepted by oxygen (O_2), which combines with hydrogen to form water (H_2O). No ATP has been produced, but the stage is set for the next step.

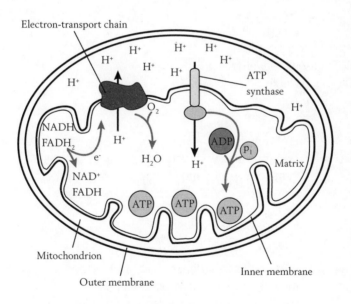

- *Chemiosmosis.* Electron transport pumped hydrogen ions against their gradient, creating a concentration gradient where there was none. Now, diffusion of ions down the gradient works, and ATP is synthesized. ATP synthase is an enzyme in the inner mitochondrial membrane similar to the type of membrane protein that carries out active transport. However, it works in reverse here: hydrogen ions move down their concentration gradient, powering ATP synthase so that it combines ADP and phosphate into ATP. Chemiosmosis produces 32 to 34 molecules of ATP per molecule of glucose.

The table below summarizes the stages of aerobic respiration. Overall, 36–38 molecules of ATP are produced per molecule of glucose.

STAGE	DESCRIPTION	LOCATION	USES	PRODUCES
Glycolysis	Glucose is broken down to two 3-carbon pyruvate molecules	Cytoplasm	Glucose	2 ATP, 2 NADH, 2 H⁺
Citric acid cycle	3-carbon molecules are broken down, energy is used to produce high-energy electron-carrying molecules	Mitochondria	Pyruvate	2 ATP, 8 NADH, 8 H⁺, 2 FADH$_2$, 6 CO$_2$
Electron transport chain	High-energy electrons are passed along chain, providing energy to pump hydrogen ions against gradient	Inner mitochondrial membrane	Oxygen (O$_2$) acts as final electron accepter	Water (H$_2$O)
Chemiosmosis	Hydrogen ions move down gradient, powering ATP synthesis from ADP and phosphate	Inner mitochondrial membrane	Hydrogen ion (H⁺) gradient provides energy	32–34 ATP

Anaerobic Respiration

Anaerobic respiration occurs without oxygen as the final electron acceptor. It is much less efficient, producing only about two ATP molecules per glucose molecule, via glycolysis. The three-carbon pyruvate molecules do not enter the citric acid cycle; instead, they convert NADH back to NAD^+, becoming ethanol (alcohol) or lactic acid in the process. Alcohol fermentation also releases carbon dioxide (CO_2); this is what causes bread dough made with yeast to rise.

Photosynthesis and Glucose Production

Respiration derives energy for ATP from glucose, but where does this energy come from? It comes from the sun. Photosynthesis harvests the energy in sunlight and converts it to chemical energy in the form of glucose. The net equation is shown (compare to the net equation for respiration on page 130).

$$6CO_2 + 6H_2O + Energy \rightarrow C_6H_{12}O_6 + 6O_2$$

In eukaryotes (plants and algae), photosynthesis takes place in the chloroplasts, organelles with double membranes that contain stacks of membrane-bound units called thylakoids in a fluid called stroma.

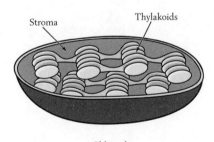

Stroma   Thylakoids

Chloroplast

Photosynthesis takes place in two stages: the light reactions and the Calvin cycle, or dark reactions. The light reactions use light energy to produce ATP and NADPH molecules (from ADP and $NADP^+$ precursors), and the Calvin cycle uses ATP and NADPH to synthesize glucose molecules.

Light Reactions

The light reactions of photosynthesis take place inside the thylakoids of the chloroplast. Chlorophyll pigments in the thylakoid membranes, along with proteins, make up photosystems I and II. Incoming light strikes photosystem II (PS II), exciting one of the electrons in a chlorophyll molecule to a higher energy state. The unstable, excited electron is passed along an electron transport chain.

Photosynthesis produces ATP via a similar method to respiration, creating a hydrogen ion gradient using the energy harvested by an electron transport chain in the membrane. Membrane proteins move ions into the inner spaces of the thylakoids. The ions move out of the thylakoid by passing through the ATP synthase membrane protein, giving this enzyme the energy to synthesize ATP.

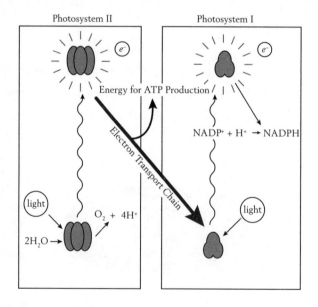

The chlorophyll molecule in PS II needs to replace its missing electron. A water molecule is split, producing free electrons, hydrogen (H^+) ions, and molecular oxygen (O_2). The electrons are accepted by chlorophyll, the hydrogen ions are stored inside the thylakoid to create the concentration gradient, and the oxygen is released.

Meanwhile, light energy also enters photosystem I (PS I), exciting an electron, which is passed along another electron transport chain. These high-energy electrons are donated to $NADP^+$ to produce NADPH. The missing electron in PS I is replaced with the energy-depleted electron from PS II.

Calvin Cycle

The reactions of the Calvin cycle take place in the stroma of the chloroplast. The first step is the fixation of carbon dioxide by combining it with a five-carbon compound in the stroma. The energy of ATP and the electrons of NADPH are used in a series of steps to convert the resulting compounds to a three-carbon glucose precursor. Additional ATP is used to replenish the original five-carbon compound. Three carbon dioxide (CO_2), nine ATP, and six NADPH molecules are required to produce one three-carbon glucose precursor molecule. This precursor is used to produce glucose and other carbohydrates in the cell.

The table below summarizes the stages and components of photosynthesis.

COMPONENT	DESCRIPTION	LOCATION	USES	PRODUCES
PS II	Light excites and energizes electrons in chlorophyll	Thylakoid	Water (H_2O)	Oxygen (O_2), Hydrogen ions (H^+)
Electron transport chain	High-energy electrons are passed along chain, providing energy to pump hydrogen ions into inner space of thylakoid	Thylakoid	Energy in excited electrons	Concentration gradient

COMPONENT	DESCRIPTION	LOCATION	USES	PRODUCES
PS I	Light excites and energizes electrons in chlorophyll, which are used to produce NADPH	Thylakoid	Excited electrons	NADPH and H^+
Calvin Cycle	Series of reactions fix carbon dioxide and produce 3-carbon glucose precursor	Stroma	3 CO_2, 9 ATP, 6 NADPH	3-carbon molecule

Review Questions

1. How does the ATP synthase enzyme function in the cell?

   A. It uses energy to move ions against their concentration gradient by removing a phosphate group from ATP.

   B. It uses the power of ions moving against their concentration gradient to add a phosphate group to ADP.

   C. It uses the power of ions moving down their concentration gradient to add a phosphate group to ADP.

   D. It uses the power of ions moving against their concentration gradient to remove a phosphate group from ATP.

   E. It uses the power of ions moving down their concentration gradient to remove a phosphate group from ATP.

2. Which choice matches each description below to the correct stage of aerobic respiration?

    I.   Produces most of the ATP
    II. Produces carbon dioxide (CO_2)
    III. Uses oxygen (O_2)

    A. I = chemiosmosis; II = electron transport chain; III = citric acid cycle
    B. I = chemiosmosis; II = citric acid cycle; III = electron transport chain
    C. I = citric acid cycle; II = chemiosmosis; III = electron transport chain
    D. I = electron transport chain; II = chemiosmosis; III = citric acid cycle
    E. I = electron transport chain; II = citric acid cycle; III = chemiosmosis

3. Which of these produces a three-carbon sugar from carbon dioxide?

    A. Photosystem I
    B. Photosystem II
    C. Electron transport chain
    D. Calvin cycle
    E. Citric acid cycle

4. Which of these releases carbon dioxide?

    I.   Lactic acid fermentation

    II.   Alcohol fermentation

    III. Aerobic respiration

    IV. Photosynthesis

    A. I and II

    B. I and III

    C. II and III

    D. II and IV

    E. III and IV

5. All of the following take place in the thylakoid of the chloroplast EXCEPT

    A. $NADP^+$ is reduced to create NADPH

    B. hydrogen ions are pumped against their concentration gradient

    C. ATP is produced by the ATP synthase enzyme

    D. excited electrons transfer energy to an electron transport chain

    E. carbon dioxide molecules are converted to a three-carbon sugar

Answer Explanations

1. **C.** The ATP synthase enzyme, present in membranes, uses the power of hydrogen ions moving down their concentration gradient to add a phosphate group to ADP, producing ATP.

2. **B.** The citric acid cycle breaks down glucose, producing carbon dioxide (II). The electron transport chain uses oxygen as a final electron acceptor (III). Most of the ATP in respiration (I) is produced by chemiosmosis, the movement of hydrogen ions down their concentration gradient to power ATP synthase.

3. **D.** The Calvin cycle fixes carbon dioxide, converting it, via a series of reactions, to a three-carbon sugar.

4.   **C.** Aerobic respiration releases carbon dioxide as it breaks down glucose via the citric acid cycle. Alcohol fermentation also releases carbon dioxide, which is a by-product of the production of alcohol. In contrast, lactic acid fermentation does not release carbon dioxide but converts the carbon molecules to lactate. Photosynthesis uses carbon dioxide, rather than releasing it.

5.   **E.** Carbon dioxide is converted to a three-carbon sugar as part of the Calvin cycle, or dark reactions, which take place in the fluid stroma of the chloroplast. The remaining answer choices take place in the light reactions of photosynthesis, which take place in the thylakoids of the chloroplast.

Review Chapter 5: Enzymes and Reactions

Energy in Biochemical Reactions

In order to maintain homeostasis, a single cell must carry out millions of reactions every second. Most of these reactions would occur at a glacially slow pace if not for the action of enzymes. To understand how enzymes work, it is necessary to understand how energy changes in reactions. Most biochemical reactions, whether they are endothermic or exothermic, do not occur spontaneously at the temperatures found in living organisms. Reactions require a certain amount of energy, called *activation energy*, in order to proceed. Heat energy can often spark a reaction. However, because living things must maintain their temperature within a narrow range, heat is not available.

The solution is to lower the activation energy so that the reaction can proceed at normal body temperatures. This is the function of an enzyme. Enzymes are chemical catalysts; they increase the rate of a reaction but are not used up or changed as part of the reaction. The chemical equations below show two ways of representing enzyme action.

$$\text{Reactant}^1 + \text{Reactant}^2 \rightarrow \text{Product}$$
$$\text{Reactant}^1 + \text{Reactant}^2 + \text{Enzyme} \rightarrow \text{Product} + \text{Enzyme}$$

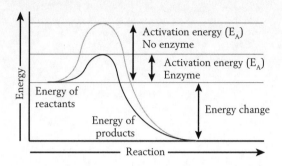

Enzyme Structure

An enzyme is a protein with a functional, three-dimensional shape. Part of the protein's surface forms an active site, which binds to the substrate, a compound that an enzyme causes to react. Each enzyme in the cell catalyzes the reaction of a single substrate or just a few substrates; in other words, enzymes are highly substrate specific. When the enzyme binds the substrate, it lowers the activation energy for the reaction, allowing it to proceed.

Lock-and-Key and Induced-Fit Models

Two models describe how the substrate binds the enzyme's active site. The *lock-and-key model* compares the active site to a lock and the substrate to a molecular key that fits snugly within it. The *induced-fit model* posits that hydrogen binding of the substrate to the active site temporarily changes the three-dimensional structure of the enzyme. The induced-fit model better explains how a single enzyme can have more than one substrate.

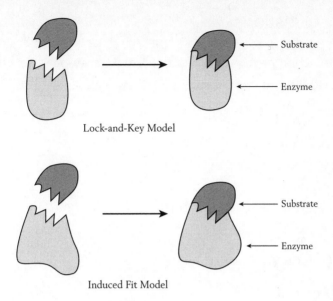

Lock-and-Key Model

Induced Fit Model

Conditions Affecting Enzyme Activity

Enzymes are optimized to function in specific conditions. For example, most human enzymes function best at a temperature of 37°C—body temperature. Similarly, most enzymes work best at a specific pH. Human enzymes tend to function best between pH levels of 6 and 8.

Changes in temperature or pH affect the tertiary structure of the enzyme, disrupting the active site and impairing its ability to bind with the substrate. An enzyme may become denatured by excessive temperature, pH levels that are too high or low, or other changes in the surrounding fluid. A denatured enzyme may or may not regain its shape and function when returned to optimal conditions.

Inhibitors are molecules that can affect enzyme activity. An inhibitor may bind to the active site, blocking the substrate, or it may bind to another part of the enzyme, reducing its ability to catalyze the reaction.

Review Questions

1. As a reaction proceeds, reactants form a transition state, which then forms the products. An enzyme affects the energy of the

    A. products only
    B. reactants only
    C. transition state only
    D. products and reactants
    E. transition state and products

2. Which term most nearly means *substrate?*

    A. Reactant
    B. Product
    C. Activation energy
    D. Active site
    E. Inhibitor

3. Which of these describes a characteristic of the induced-fit model but not the lock-and-key model?

    A. The substrate binds to the active site.
    B. The enzyme lowers the activation energy of the reaction.
    C. The enzyme is changed by the substrate.
    D. The substrate is chemically changed by the enzyme.
    E. The enzyme is altered by the reaction.

4. Which of these is likely to reduce enzyme activity?

    I.   Increasing pH level
    II.   Decreasing temperature
    III. Placing enzyme in a nonpolar liquid

    A. I only
    B. II only
    C. III only
    D. I and II
    E. I, II, and III

Answer Explanations

1. **C.** An enzyme speeds up the rate of a reaction by lowering the activation energy, making the transition state less stable. It does not affect the energy of the products or the reactants.

2. **A.** The reactant of the catalyzed reaction is the substrate, which binds to the active site of the enzyme.

3. **C.** The induced-fit model states that the shape of the enzyme is altered by binding with the substrate. This is not a feature of the lock-and-key model. Neither model posits that the enzyme is changed by the reaction.

4. **E.** Altering temperature and pH beyond the optimal range for the enzyme is likely to reduce enzyme activity. In addition, because proteins function in an aqueous (water) solution, and water is polar, a protein will fold with its hydrophilic (water-seeking) amino acids closer to the surface and its hydrophobic (water-avoiding) amino acids closer to the center. Moving the enzyme to a nonpolar solution will alter its tertiary structure, as hydrophobic amino acids move to the surface instead.

Review Chapter 6:
Genetic Inheritance

Mendel's Laws of Inheritance

The basic laws governing how single-gene traits are inherited were discovered by Gregor Mendel, who crossed pure-bred lines of pea plants. A *pure-bred* or *true-breeding* line is one in which all plants exhibit the same traits. Mendel's laws include the law of dominance, the law of segregation, and the law of independent assortment.

- *Law of dominance.* Mendel crossed a pure-bred plant with white flowers to another with purple flowers. The offspring inherited genetic information for both white and purple flowers. However, they produced all purple flowers and no white flowers. This type of cross established the law of dominance, which states that genes come in versions called *alleles* and that dominant alleles mask the *phenotypes*, or observable expression, of recessive alleles.

- *Law of segregation.* Mendel then crossed F1 plants (offspring) with each other. The resulting F2 generation consisted of both purple-flowered plants and white-flowered plants, in a 3:1 ratio. This cross is shown in the Punnett square on the following page. Note that the parents both have heterozygous genotypes (the alleles inherited for one gene). The white-flowered offspring are homozygous recessive, and the purple-flowered offspring are either homozygous dominant or heterozygous.

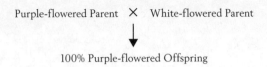

Purple-flowered Parent ✕ White-flowered Parent

↓

100% Purple-flowered Offspring

- *Law of independent assortment.* Mendel's third law was discovered by following the inheritance of two separate traits. The cross below shows a tall, purple-flowered plant crossed with a short, white-flowered plant. The F1 plants are all tall with purple flowers, suggesting that these are the dominant alleles. These plants were then crossed with each other. Are the F2 plants all either tall with purple flowers or short with white flowers? No; some of these plants have new combinations of traits (for example, short with purple flowers).

Parents: *TTPP* ✕ *ttpp*

↓

F1:   *TtPp* ✕ *TtPp*

↓

	TP	Tp	tP	tp
TP	Tall, Purple *TTPP*	Tall, Purple *TTPp*	Tall, Purple *TtPP*	Tall, Purple *TtPp*
Tp	Tall, Purple *TTPp*	Tall, White *TTpp*	Tall, Purple *TtPp*	Tall, White *Ttpp*
tP	Tall, Purple *TtPP*	Tall, Purple *TtPp*	Short, Purple *ttPP*	Short, Purple *ttPp*
tp	Tall, Purple *TtPp*	Tall, White *Ttpp*	Short, Purple *ttPp*	Short, White *ttpp*

F2:

Mendel concluded that the chance of inheriting an allele for one gene (white vs. purple flowers) was independent or unrelated to the inheritance of the allele for another gene (tall vs. short).

Notice that the phenotypic ratio is 9:3:3:1. This means that the probability of inheriting both recessive alleles for both traits is 1 in 16. The probability of two events happening together can be found by multiplying the probabilities of each event happening separately. Because the parent plants are heterozygous for each gene, any offspring has a 1-in-2 (0.5 or 50%) chance of inheriting a recessive allele for a gene from one parent. The formulas below show how to find the probability of inheritance of more than one recessive allele.

- Inheriting two recessive alleles for one gene: $0.5 \times 0.5 = 0.25$
- Inheriting two recessive alleles for a second gene: $0.5 \times 0.5 = 0.25$
- Inheriting two recessive alleles for BOTH genes: $0.25 \times 0.25 = 0.0625 = 1/16$

Non-Mendelian Inheritance

While Mendel's laws predict the inheritance of traits controlled by single genes with dominant and recessive alleles, they do not explain the full range of inheritance found in nature.

- *Codominance* occurs when both inherited phenotypes are expressed in the offspring. The human ABO blood type system is an example of codominance with three alleles: A, B, and O. Children of type A and type B parents can express both A and B antigens.

- *Incomplete dominance* occurs when the offspring's phenotype is a blending of those of the parents. For example, crossing red and white snapdragons produces pink offspring. Pink is a new phenotype, not observed in either parent.

- *Sex-linked traits* occur much more often in one gender (usually male) than the other. The gene for a sex-linked trait is located on either the X or the Y chromosome. In most mammals, males have an X and a Y chromosome, while females have two X chromosomes. Because a boy inherits his Y chromosome from his father, he *must* inherit his single X chromosome from his mother. The Y chromosome is very small and does not have the full set of genes present on the X chromosomes. Therefore, a recessive allele on the X chromosome will be expressed in males. Consider the inheritance of hemophilia, a blood-clotting disorder inherited as an X-linked recessive trait.

	X^H	Y
X^h	$X^H X^h$	$X^h Y$
X^H	$X^H X^H$	$X^H Y$

The mother is a carrier, or heterozygous, with one allele for hemophilia and one allele for normal clotting. Any of her children have a 1-in-2 (0.5 or 50%) chance of inheriting the hemophilia allele. The father has a normal allele on his X chromosome. Any sons of this couple must inherit their father's Y chromosome and must inherit an X from their mother. This means they have a 1-in-2 chance of inheriting the hemophilia allele and expressing the disorder. (In contrast, any daughters must inherit one X chromosome from their father; they will have his normal allele to mask their mother's hemophilia allele, should they inherit it.)

- *Gene linkage* is a pattern that violates Mendel's law of independent assortment, which states that the chance of inheriting the allele for one gene is independent of any other allele that may be inherited. For many genes, this is true because they are located far apart or on different chromosomes. However, alleles for two genes that are located close to each other on a chromosome may often "travel together." For example, individuals with a condition called nail–patella syndrome have a greater chance of also having the B blood type allele (which results in blood types of B or AB). These genes occur next to each other, and so certain alleles are inherited together more often than not.

- *Epistasis* occurs when one gene affects the expression of a second gene. An example is albinism (lack of fur pigment) in mice. The dominant allele for this gene produces pigment; homozygous recessive mice produce no pigment. A second gene determines the color pigment that will be produced: black or brown. However, a mouse that is homozygous recessive for albinism will have white fur, no matter what genotype it inherits for the second gene.

Polygenic Inheritance, Quantitative Traits, and Pleiotropy

Most traits are not simple either–or traits, such as purple or white flowers. Quantitative traits vary along a continuous scale, for example, skin color, foot size, or height. This is because they are determined by the actions of many genes working together—*polygenic inheritance*—as well as environmental factors. *Pleiotropy* refers to the fact that most genes affect multiple traits.

Review Questions

1. In fruit flies, brick-red eye color is dominant to a bright orange color called cinnabar. A fruit fly with heterozygous eye color genotype is crossed with homozygous recessive fruit fly. What is the probability of inheritance for the cinnabar phenotype and the heterozygous genotype?

    A. Cinnabar phenotype = 1.0; Heterozygous genotype = 0
    B. Cinnabar phenotype = 0; Heterozygous genotype = 1.0
    C. Cinnabar phenotype = 0.5; Heterozygous genotype = 0.5
    D. Cinnabar phenotype = 0.25; Heterozygous genotype = 0.5
    E. Cinnabar phenotype = 0.5; Heterozygous genotype = 0.75

2. A woman expresses an X-linked recessive disorder. Which of these conclusions can DEFINITELY be made about the woman's parents?

    I.   Her mother passed on an allele for the disorder.
    II. Her father expresses the same disorder.
    III. Her mother does not express the disorder.

    A. I only
    B. II only
    C. I and II only
    D. II and III only
    E. I, II, and II

3.   Which of these is an example of polygenic inheritance?

    A.   Epistasis
    B.   Dominance
    C.   Segregation
    D.   Pleiotropy
    E.   Independent assortment

Answer Explanations

1. **C.** The Punnett square for the cross is shown below. Each offspring has a 50% chance of inheriting a heterozygous phenotype and an equal chance of inheriting a homozygous recessive genotype (which results in the cinnabar phenotype).

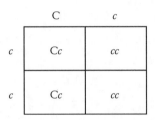

2. **A.** The woman inherited two X chromosomes, one from her father and one from her mother. Because the disorder is recessive, both of her X chromosomes must hold the allele for the disorder. Because one X chromosome must have come from the father (who has only one X), he must also express the disorder. Because the second X chromosome must have come from the mother, she definitely passed on the allele. Whether the mother also expresses the disorder depends on the allele on her other X chromosome.

3. **A.** Polygenic inheritance describes traits that are influenced by multiple genes. Epistasis is an interaction between two genes, both affecting a phenotype. In contrast, pleiotropy occurs when a single gene influences multiple traits.

Review Chapter 7:
Meiosis and Mutations

Inheritance results from chromosomes separating and recombining to form new individuals through sexual reproduction. Chromosomes come in homologous pairs; each homolog has the same genes, in the same locations. However, the alleles of each gene may be the same or different. One homolog from each pair is inherited from the mother, and one homolog from the father. In order to end up with exactly one homolog from each pair in gametes (sperm and egg cells), chromosomes must be carefully separated. This is the job of meiosis, which is key in gametogenesis, or the formation of haploid sperm and eggs cells from diploid cells.

Meiosis

Like mitosis, *meiosis* reproduces the nucleus for cell division. Unlike mitosis, meiosis halves the number of chromosomes in each nucleus by separating homologous pairs. The phases of meiosis mirror those of mitosis, but in meiosis they occur twice, in stage 1 and stage 2. Before mitosis even begins, the cell has replicated its DNA, with each chromosome forming two identical sister chromatids. Sister chromatids will separate in stage 2 of meiosis. Homologs separate in stage 1.

- *Prophase I.* In prophase I, the chromosomes condense, and the nuclear membrane breaks down. Spindle fibers emerge from the centrioles, which move to opposite poles of the cell. Homologous chromosomes pair up alongside each other. This is when *crossing over* occurs, and chromatids from each homolog exchange DNA strands. The four sister chromatids are held together by these exchanges until they separate in anaphase I.

- *Metaphase I.* Spindle fibers attach to the centromeres, aligning the chromosome pairs along the central metaphase plate. Each homolog in a pair is attached to a spindle fiber from one centriole.

- *Anaphase I.* Homologous chromosomes separate, and each homolog is pulled toward one pole by shortening spindle fibers. Each chromosome still consists of attached sister chromatids; however, the chromatids are no longer identical, due to crossing over.

- *Telophase I and cytokinesis.* One homolog from each pair of chromosomes is now at each pole. The cell contains two haploid (halved) sets of chromosomes. In telophase, the cell divides to form two haploid daughter cells with replicated chromosomes.

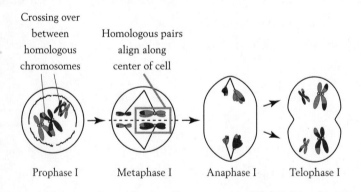

Crossing over between homologous chromosomes	Homologous pairs align along center of cell		
Prophase I	Metaphase I	Anaphase I	Telophase I

- *Prophase II.* The chromatids, which replicated before meiosis I, are ready to separate. Centrioles have replicated again, and they move to opposite poles of the cell.

- *Metaphase II.* Spindle fibers attach to the centromeres, aligning the sister chromatids along the central metaphase plate. Each chromatid is attached to a spindle fiber from one centriole.

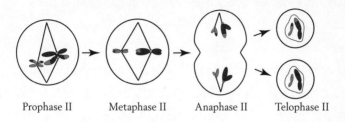

Prophase II   Metaphase II   Anaphase II   Telophase II

- *Anaphase II.* Sister chromatids separate, and each is pulled toward one pole by shortening spindle fibers.
- *Telophase II and cytokinesis.* The cell still contains two haploid (halved) sets of chromosomes, one at each pole, but each chromosome consists of only a single chromatid. In telophase, a nuclear membrane re-forms around each set. The cell separates to form two haploid daughter cells.

A few differences exist between gametogenesis in males and females. In males, four sperm cells are produced from one precursor cell, as expected. In females, however, only one egg cell is produced for every cell that enters meiosis. This is because each cell division produces one viable daughter cell and one small polar body, which is discarded. This allows the egg cell to retain most of the cytoplasmic contents of the original cell.

Mutations

A *mutation* is a change in the genetic material. The cell has mechanisms to prevent errors in DNA replication, meiosis, and mitosis, but occasional errors do occur. A mutation may also be caused by a mutagen, an agent that affects and changes DNA. Mutagens may be physical (for example, X-rays, UV light) or chemical (for example, by-products of cigarette smoke). Mutations can be either large scale, on the level of chromosomes, or small scale, on the level of individual DNA base pairs.

Chromosomal Mutations

- *Aneuploidy* refers to an abnormal number of one or more chromosomes. Meiosis separates homologous chromosome pairs so that each gamete has exactly one chromosome of each type. Nondisjunction is an error in this meiotic process, resulting in a gamete with more or fewer chromosomes of one type. For example, Down syndrome results from a gamete with two homologs of chromosome 21. The fertilized egg then has a total of three copies of this chromosome; it is trisomic.

- *Polyploidy* refers to having more than two complete sets of chromosomes. Many plant species are triploid (three sets) or tetraploid (four sets); this may result when parent plants of different species produce hybrid offspring.

- *Rearrangements* alter the structures of individual chromosomes. A chromosomal *deletion* is the loss of a large chromosome segment. A *duplication* occurs when a segment is repeated. An *inversion* reverses or flips a part of a chromosome. Finally, a *translocation* occurs when a piece of one chromosome detaches and attaches to a different chromosome. Some translocations are reciprocal, meaning that pieces are exchanged between two chromosomes.

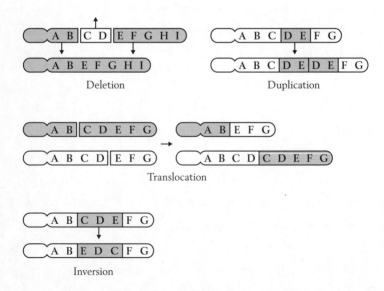

Deletion

Duplication

Translocation

Inversion

DNA-Level Mutations

This type of mutation is a change in the nucleotide sequence of DNA.

- *Substitutions.* The simplest type of mutation is a change from one nitrogen base to another. Substitutions can have different effects on the protein that is made by the gene. A *missense* mutation causes one amino acid to be substituted for another. A *nonsense* mutation changes a codon for an amino acid to a stop codon. Finally, a *silent* mutation causes no change in the protein product, because the codon specifies the same amino acid.

- *Insertions and deletions.* An insertion is the addition of one or more nucleotides into the DNA strand. Similarly, a deletion is the removal of nucleotides. Insertions and deletions may result in a *frameshift*, or a change in the way nucleotides in the rest of the gene are read as codons. Recall that codons are groups of three nucleotides; a frameshift regroups the nucleotides into different codons. If a group of three nucleotides (or a multiple of three) is inserted or deleted, the total number of amino acids may change, but the rest will be produced normally.

Review Questions

1. At which stage of meiosis do cells from a sperm cell precursor contain a haploid set of chromosomes, each consisting of two sister chromatids?

   A. Anaphase I
   B. Metaphase I
   C. Prophase II
   D. Anaphase II
   E. Telophase II

2.   In meiosis, crossing over takes longer than any other process. Which stage of meiosis is most likely the longest?

  A.   Prophase I
  B.   Metaphase I
  C.   Anaphase I
  D.   Prophase II
  E.   Metaphase II

3.   At which stage in meiosis are sister chromatids of each chromosome identical?

  I.   Beginning of prophase I
  II.   Beginning of metaphase I
  III. End of telophase I

  A.   I only
  B.   II only
  C.   III only
  D.   I and II
  E.   II and III

4. The diagram shown compares a normal chromosome with one that has undergone a rearrangement. The rearrangement is BEST described as a/an

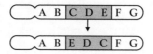

A. deletion
B. duplication
C. nondisjunction
D. inversion
E. translocation

5. Which of these mutations in a gene will MOST LIKELY result in a shortened protein with a long sequence of substituted amino acids?

A. Missense substitution of one nucleotide
B. Insertion of two nucleotides
C. Deletion of three nucleotides
D. Silent substitution of four nucleotides
E. Nonsense substitution of five nucleotides

Answer Explanations

1. **B.** The first stage of meiosis divides the diploid set of chromosomes into two haploid sets. Homologous chromosomes separate in anaphase I, and at the beginning (prophase) of stage 2, each cell contains a haploid set. However, the chromosomes are still replicated and still consist of joined sister chromatids. These separate in anaphase II.

2. **A.** Crossing over takes place in prophase I of meiosis. Homologous chromosomes must be joined by exchanged DNA sequences before they can align at the metaphase plate.

3. **A.** Chromosomes start out as identical sister chromatids. These exchange DNA with nonidentical homologous chromatids during crossing over, resulting in homologs made up of nonidentical sister chromatids. Crossing over happens in prophase I; therefore, all subsequent stages feature nonidentical sister chromatids.

4. **D.** The diagram shows that one section of the chromosome has been flipped or inverted. This type of chromosomal mutation is an inversion.

5. **B.** The insertion of two nucleotides will shift the reading frame of all the codons "downstream" of the mutation, resulting in a series of missense codons and eventually a nonsense (stop) codon.

Review Chapter 8:
DNA Technology

Restriction Enzymes and DNA Ligase

Restriction enzymes were a key discovery in DNA technology. These are naturally occurring enzymes produced by certain types of bacteria. They protect bacteria cells from foreign DNA by cutting or cleaving the DNA. However, each enzyme cuts DNA only at specific recognition sites, or short sequences of four to eight base pairs. Scientists use restriction enzymes as highly specific "molecular scissors."

Many restriction enzymes cleave DNA unevenly, leaving one strand longer than the other. This leaves the DNA end free to base-pair with any complementary DNA. "Sticky" DNA ends cut with the same restriction enzyme can temporarily pair with each other. Adding the DNA ligase enzyme can permanently join these DNA strands. Recombinant DNA can be made by joining cut DNA segments from different organisms.

Cloning and Amplifying DNA in Cells

Bacteria carry nonchromosomal DNA in the form of small, circular plasmids, which can be exchanged between bacteria cells. Using restriction enzymes and ligase, scientists can insert DNA into plasmids. Scientists can remove plasmids from bacteria, genetically engineer them, and reinsert them into bacteria. When the bacteria are allowed to divide, they naturally *replicate*, or clone the plasmid many times over. This method is useful for producing large quantities of DNA.

Selective Plating

When a plasmid is added to a bacterial culture, it enters only a small portion of the cells. The cells containing the plasmid must then be selected from the larger pool of cells. Often, the bacteria are plated on a solid nutrient medium containing an antibiotic. If the plasmid contains a gene for antibiotic resistance, only the cells with the plasmid will form *colonies* on the plates. A colony is a visible dot of bacterial cells that grows from a single cell.

Auxotrophic mutants may also be used. These cells lack the gene for making an essential nutrient, which must be supplied for the cells to grow. These cells are plated on a medium that lacks this essential nutrient. If the plasmid contains a gene that "fixes" the auxotrophic mutation, only those cells with the plasmid will form colonies.

Analyzing DNA Using Gel Electrophoresis

After DNA has been cut with restriction enzymes, it can be analyzed using agarose gel electrophoresis. The agarose gel is made of a gelatin-like substance with pores small enough for DNA to move through. The gel is placed in a chamber containing a conductive solution. Electrodes are attached to points at either end of the chamber and connected to a power supply.

The DNA samples are injected into wells or spaces at one end of the gel, and a current is run through the chamber. The current causes the DNA, which carries a charge, to migrate toward the far end. However, different-sized DNA fragments move at different rates: smaller fragments fit into the gel spaces more easily and therefore travel more quickly, while larger fragments move more slowly. A standard mix of DNA in one of the wells serves as a reference for the DNA fragment sizes.

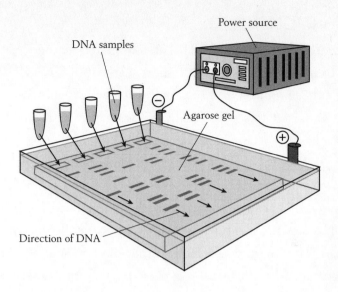

RFLP Analysis

RFLP stands for *r*estriction *f*ragment *l*ength *p*olymorphism. This technique compares DNA by digesting (cutting) it with a restriction enzyme. Recall that these enzymes cleave DNA only at very specific sequences. If the DNA contains the recognition site sequence, it is cut at that point. Different individuals may vary in whether their DNA contains the recognition site at a given location. This variation is called a *polymorphism* ("poly" means *many*, and "morph" means *form*). Digesting DNA samples and analyzing the sizes of the resulting fragments on a gel can help scientists to determine whether the DNA came from different individuals or from relatives. This technique has traditionally been used in forensic science to compare a suspect's blood against blood found at the scene of the crime. It is also used in paternity testing.

In RFLP, two or more DNA samples are digested with the same enzyme. The resulting fragments are separated by gel electrophoresis. The gel shows the number and sizes of the DNA fragments that resulted. A greater number of restriction sequences in the DNA results in more DNA fragments, seen as bands on the gel.

Amplifying DNA Using PCR

Polymerase chain reaction (PCR) is an automated method that allows a scientist to make many copies of a short segment of DNA. Before PCR, studying either impure DNA or small quantities of DNA was quite difficult. PCR solved this problem by allowing the creation of multiple copies of a highly specific DNA sequence.

To carry out PCR, a scientist must know the sequence of DNA upstream and downstream of the sequence of interest. Complementary DNA sequences, called *primers*, are made for each end. They are added to the DNA sample, along with the DNA polymerase enzyme and free nucleotides. The mixture is heated so that the two strands of the DNA sample separate. Then the mixture is cooled so that the primers can bind to complementary sequences on each strand. The DNA polymerase attaches free nucleotides to the 5′ end of each primer, extending the complementary DNA strand along the sequence of interest. After many rounds of heating and cooling, the mixture contains large quantities of the target sequence.

PCR allows a scientist to sequence a segment of DNA, insert the DNA into a plasmid or other vector, or digest the DNA and analyze the results by gel electrophoresis.

Sequencing DNA

To sequence a gene means to determine the order of DNA nucleotides that make up the gene. Improving technology has allowed DNA to be sequenced exponentially faster. However, the basic method for sequencing DNA has remained the same. This method creates complementary DNA strands of many different lengths and then separates the strands by length.

The DNA is mixed with DNA polymerase enzyme (to create the complementary strands), free DNA nucleotides, and abnormal nucleotides with fluorescent labels. DNA polymerase joins the nucleotides that form complementary base pairs with the DNA. However, at some point, a labeled nucleotide will join the strand. When it does, the polymerase enzyme cannot add any more nucleotides, and the strand terminates.

Because the labeled nucleotides can join a chain at any point, termination happens at every point along the DNA strand.

Next, the mix of strands is separated in a long, tubular polyacrylamide gel. As with agarose gel electrophoresis, shorter fragments move faster and pass through the tube first. A machine detects and records the fluorescence of each strand as it passes. Because each type of nucleotide (A, C, G, and T) was labeled with a different color, and each strand moved through the machine according to size, the sequence of the nucleotides in the DNA can be determined.

Sequencing Entire Genomes

The technology that has sped up DNA sequencing has also made it possible to sequence whole genomes of organisms. A genome is the entire set of genetic material contained in an organism's cells. The human genome, as well as that of other organisms, has been sequenced.

Most genome sequencing projects have used the shotgun-sequencing approach. In this method, the DNA is cut into fragments short enough to be sequenced. Because the DNA is cut at random, the sequenced fragments will overlap. Then, the genome sequence can be pieced together by matching the fragment sequences where they overlap.

An alternative approach uses genetic *markers*, which are sequences at known locations in the genome. DNA is cut at these markers to create overlapping fragments whose order is known. The fragments are then cloned (to amplify the DNA) and sequenced.

Genetic Markers from Genome Linkage Maps

Recall that some traits are influenced by genes located close to each other in the genome. By studying the occurrence of traits in many individuals and families, scientists can determine the degree to which certain alleles are linked. This information is used to estimate the distances between genes. Thousands of these genetic markers make up the linkage map of the human genome.

Review Questions

1. Which of these can be used to increase the amount of DNA available for analysis?

    I.   Cloning a plasmid
    II. Gel electrophoresis
    II. PCR

    A.   II only
    B.   I and II
    C.   I and III
    D.   II and III
    E.   I, II, and III

Questions 2–3 refer to the following.

A plasmid containing a normal human beta-globin allele is digested with restriction enzymes. The results are shown in lane 2 of the electrophoresis gel. A second plasmid, contain the beta-globin allele that results in sickle-cell disease, is digested in the same way and placed in lane 3. The standard in lane 1 contains DNA fragments in lengths of 100 base pairs (bp), 200 bp, and so on.

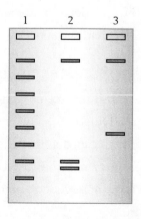

2. Which of these describes the results shown on the gel?

   A. Both lanes 1 and 2 both contain 100-bp fragments.
   B. Only lane 2 contains a 175-bp fragment.
   C. Only lane 3 contains a 375-bp fragment.
   D. Both lanes 2 and 3 contain two equal-sized fragments.
   E. Only lane 3 contains a 300-bp fragment.

3. Based on the results shown, which of these BEST describes the mutation that resulted in the sickle-cell allele?

   A. It created a site that is recognized by the restriction enzyme.
   B. It removed two restriction sites recognized by the enzyme.
   C. It changed a restriction site cut by the restriction enzyme.
   D. It inserted a second restriction site specific for the enzyme.
   E. It inserted a third restriction site specific for the enzyme.

4. A plasmid is added to bacteria cells, which are then spread on plates containing nutrient media. In order to select for cells that took up the plasmid, the

   A. plasmid should contain an auxotrophic mutation, and the medium should contain the missing nutrient
   B. plasmid should contain a gene for producing a nutrient, and the bacterial chromosome should contain an auxotrophic mutation
   C. bacterial chromosome should contain an antibiotic resistance gene, and the medium should contain the antibiotic
   D. plasmid should contain a gene for producing an antibiotic, and the bacterial chromosome should contain a gene for antibiotic resistance
   E. bacterial chromosome should contain an auxotrophic mutation, and the medium should contain the missing nutrient

5.   Which DNA technique depends, in part, on a violation of Mendel's law of independent assortment?

A.   Shotgun genome sequencing
B.   RFLP
C.   PCR
D.   Plasmid cloning and selection
E.   Genome marker mapping

Answer Explanations

1.   **C.** The amount of DNA is amplified by engineering the DNA into a plasmid and cloning the plasmid in cell culture, as well as by performing PCR on the original DNA sample. Gel electrophoresis is a method for analyzing DNA, which often must be amplified first.

2.   **B.** Lane 2 contains three DNA fragments: a very large fragment, a fragment of about 200 bp, and a fragment of about 175 bp. In contrast, lane 3 contains only the large fragment and a fragment of about 375 bp.

3.   **C.** The mutation in the sickle cell allele changed the DNA sequence at one of the recognition sites for the enzyme. This removed a restriction site, causing the 175- and 200-bp fragments seen in lane 2 (the normal allele) to remain joined.

4.   **B.** The goal of selective plating is to allow only those bacteria cells that have taken up the plasmid to grow. This can be accomplished by introducing a plasmid that corrects for an auxotrophic mutation (that is, produces a nutrient) into an auxotrophic mutant strain and then plating the cells on medium that is missing the nutrient.

5.   **E.** Genome marker maps are assembled using gene linkage information. Gene linkage occurs when genes are located next to each other in the genome and do not assort independently.

4. Individuals with favorable phenotypes have a greater chance of passing on their genes to offspring. The degree to which an organism can pass on its genes, as compared to others in the population, is called its *fitness*.

5. Principles 1–4 all lead to changes in the gene pool of a population, as genes leading to favorable phenotypes increase in frequency over generations.

Effects of Natural Selection

Natural selection can have different effects on a population. The examples here consider selection acting on a quantitative (continuous) trait. The vertical line in the center of each graph shows the mean (average) phenotype for the population. The shape of the curve shows the distribution of phenotypes. For each type of selection, examine the graph on the following page.

*   *Directional selection* occurs when individuals on one end of the trait distribution (for example, the largest or smallest, lightest or darkest) have greater fitness. These individuals are better able to pass on their genes, leading to a shift in the population's gene pool and average phenotype. The mean phenotype changes, but the distribution does not.

*   *Stabilizing selection* occurs when individuals that are close to the mean have greater fitness. These individuals are better able to pass on their genes, making the next generation more likely to have a phenotype near the mean. The distribution changes, but the phenotypic mean does not.

*   *Disruptive selection* is the opposite of stabilizing selection: individuals farther from the mean have greater fitness. They pass on more of their genes to the next generation, increasing the number of phenotypes at the tail ends of the distribution. Again, the mean of the trait does not change.

Review Chapter 9:
Evolution and Natural Selection

volution refers to the changes in Earth's species over time. A more technical definition for evolution is "a change in the allele frequency in a population over time." A population is a group of individuals of a species that live in the same area and share a gene pool. Genes come in different versions, or *alleles*, each of which is present in a certain proportion of a population. Evolution changes the proportions of the alleles in the population's gene pool.

Natural Selection

Natural selection is one way that evolution occurs. Natural selection stems from five basic principles.

1. Limited resources keep population sizes in check. Organisms produce more offspring than the environment can support. If resources were unlimited, population sizes would increase exponentially.
2. Individuals in a population vary. Some are able to use available resources more efficiently than others.
3. Some variation within a population is heritable—it can be passed on to offspring through genes.

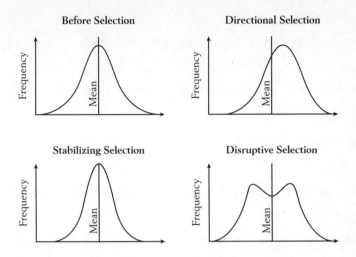

Other Types of Selection and Evolution

Not all evolutionary change is due to natural selection. Sexual selection and genetic drift also change the proportions of alleles in a gene pool.

- *Sexual selection* occurs when individuals with phenotypes that make them more likely to mate have greater fitness. In many species, females select males with "showy" phenotypes. Alleles for these traits then occur more frequently in the next generation of males. The songs and colorful plumage of male birds are a result of sexual selection (whereas females tend to have greater fitness when they are better camouflaged from predators).

- *Genetic drift* is the change in the frequency of a gene variant (allele) in a population due to random sampling. Two examples of genetic drift are population bottleneck and founder effect. In a population bottleneck, a population declines to very few individuals. Simply by chance, some alleles may increase or decrease in frequency, or be eliminated altogether. When the population recovers, its gene pool will reflect that of the bottleneck population. *Founder effect* is somewhat similar; a small number of individuals become isolated from the main population and found a new, separate population. Allele frequencies in the founding group will differ simply by chance, and the new population's gene pool will reflect those differences.

Hardy-Weinberg Theorem

The Hardy-Weinberg theorem predicts that, when there is no selection acting on a population, allele and genotype frequencies will be in *equilibrium*, that is, remain constant over time. Hardy-Weinberg equilibrium is expected when

- a population is large (avoiding effects of genetic drift),
- there is no gene flow in or out of the population,
- no mutations occur in gametes (therefore, no new alleles are introduced),
- all individuals have equal fitness (that is, there is no selection), and
- mating between individuals is random.

The Hardy-Weinberg equation can be used to determine how frequently a genotype occurs in a population, given allele frequencies (or vice versa). For example, in a sample population with alleles A and a, the allele frequencies are as follows. (Notice how, given the frequency of one allele, you can easily determine the frequency of the other.)

Frequency of A = 0.3

Frequency of a = 0.7

Frequency of $A + a$ = 1.0

The frequencies are equal to the probability of an individual's inheriting each allele. From this information, we can find the frequencies of different genotypes. The probability of inheriting one A allele is 0.3. Therefore, the probability of inheriting two A alleles is $0.3 \times 0.3 = 0.09$. This is the proportion of homozygous dominant genotypes in the population. Note that the probability of inheriting one of each allele is *twice* the product of each.

Frequency of AA = 0.09

Frequency of aa = 0.49

Frequency of Aa = $2(0.3 \times 0.7)$ = 0.42

If the letters p and q stand for the frequencies of A and a, respectively, then the Hardy-Weinberg equation states the following:

$$p^2 + 2pq + q^2 = 1$$

That is, the frequencies of each genotype in the population (AA, Aa, and aa) add up to 1. The Hardy-Weinberg theorem can predict whether selection is acting on a population—whether evolution is occurring—by testing whether the observed phenotype frequencies match the expected frequencies.

Speciation

Populations can evolve over time, but how do new species originate? *Speciation* is the formation of new species. Speciation can occur when one isolated population of a species evolves in ways that make the population unable to breed with the original species. Isolation can be geographic or reproductive.

- *Geographic isolation* occurs when a population is physically segregated and unable to mix with other populations. There is no gene flow in or out of the population, allowing it to evolve along its own course.

- *Reproductive isolation* is a result of geographic isolation but can also occur in populations that share the same ecosystem. For example, species that mate at a single point in the year may become separated as early-season maters and late-season maters. Insects that inhabit plants may begin to specialize in different plant types, mating only with those that share their plant preference.

Evidence for Evolution

How do scientists know that these processes have resulted in evolution? Fossil evidence tells us that life on Earth has changed radically over time—species that once dominated Earth are now extinct, and new species have arisen. In addition, several different lines of evidence all support evolution. The shapes and forms of different species suggest that they shared a common ancestor that underwent speciation. So does molecular information (genes and proteins).

- *Homologous structures* share an underlying similarity, though they may differ in function. The front limbs of mammals show homology—the same small set of bones is present in shorter, longer, expanded, and reduced forms depending on whether the animal flies, swims, runs, climbs, or makes tools. (In contrast, *analogous* structures have evolved similar functions independently or from different underlying structures. For example, bird wings and insect wings are analogous.)

- *Vestigial structures* are homologous structures that are no longer useful or that serve a different, less essential function than that for which they originally evolved. For example, the human appendix may play a role in childhood immunity, even though it originally functioned in digestion.

- *Transitional fossils* are evidence that very different types of organisms evolved from a common ancestor. For example, fossils of the earliest whales show that they had rudimentary hind legs, homologous to the hind legs of other mammals. This links whales to mammals that lived on land.

- *Molecular evidence* includes comparisons of DNA and protein sequences among species. For example, the gene coding for part of the ribosome is present in all organisms, but humans and bacteria have many nucleotide differences, while humans and birds have only a few.

- *Silent mutations* and changes in non-protein-coding DNA are especially useful "clocks," because these mutations occur at a constant rate. However, to determine relationships between very distantly related species, it is useful to compare essential, highly conserved genes. The number of differences between two species indicates how distantly they are related.

Review Questions

1. Which of these form the basis of natural selection?

    I.   Random mating
    II.   Limited environmental resources
    III. Stable genotype frequencies over time

    A. I only
    B. II only
    C. III only
    D. I and II
    E. II and III

2. The graph shows the distribution of fur color in a population of rodents. Over time, the environment changes so that it includes only light and dark rocks, with little vegetation. How will natural selection affect the distribution of phenotypes in this population?

    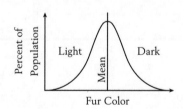

    A. The mean will shift toward the right, and the center of the curve will be higher.
    B. The mean will shift toward the left, and the center of the curve will be higher.
    C. The mean will shift toward the right, and the center of the curve will be lower.
    D. The mean will remain the same, and the center of the curve will be higher.
    E. The mean will remain the same, and the center of the curve will be lower.

3.   A recessive allele accounts for 60% of the alleles of a gene in a popu-
     lation. What proportion of the individuals in this population are
     heterozygous?

     A.   0.16
     B.   0.24
     C.   0.36
     D.   0.48
     E.   0.60

Question 4–5 refer to the phylogenetic tree of fly families shown.

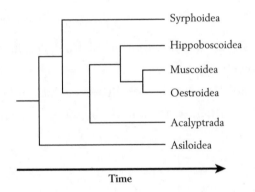

4.   According to the phylogenetic tree, which speciation event occurred
     EARLIEST?

     A.   The event leading to Muscoidea and Oestroidea
     B.   The event leading to Oestroidea and Acalyptratae
     C.   The event leading to Syrphoidea and Hippoboscoidea
     D.   The event leading to Acalyptratae and Hippoboscoidea
     E.   The event leading to Muscoidea and Acalyptratae

5.   Which two families of flies share the GREATEST number of nucle-
     otide base pair sequences?

    A.   Syrphoidea, Hippoboscoidea
    B.   Oestroidea, Hippoboscoidea
    C.   Muscoidea, Acalyptratae
    D.   Acalyptratae, Hippoboscoidea
    E.   Asiloidea, Acalyptratae

Answer Explanations

1.   **B.** A principle of natural selection is that environmental resources are limited and cannot support an infinitely growing population. Therefore, individuals with certain phenotypes are more likely to pass on their alleles (that is, they have greater fitness). Random mating and stable genotype frequencies characterize a population in Hardy-Weinberg equilibrium, in which natural selection is *not* acting.

2.   **E.** Because of the changing environment, rodents at both ends of the curve have greater fitness. Therefore, the frequency curve will become higher at the tips and lower near the current mean. However, the mean will not shift because the average phenotype will still be intermediate in color.

3.   **D.** The frequency of heterozygotes in the population can be deter-mined using the Hardy-Weinberg equation, $p^2 + 2pq + q^2 = 1$. The pro-portion of heterozygotes equals the middle term, $2pq$, where p is the dominant allele frequency and q is the recessive allele frequency. In this example, q is given as 0.6 and p must be 0.4 (because $p + q = 1$). The heterozygote frequency is therefore $2 \times 0.4 \times 0.6 = 0.48$.

4.   **C.** The branches leading to Syrphoidea and Hippoboscoidea diverged from a common ancestor farthest back in time, indicating that this spe-ciation event occurred earliest.

5.   **B.** The branches leading to Oestroidea and Hippoboscoidea diverged from a common ancestor most recently. Therefore, the fewest differ-ences in DNA base pairs will have occurred between these two groups.

Review Chapter 10:
The History and Diversity of Life

The Origin of Life on Earth

Life on Earth has changed radically over time, but so have Earth's physical features. Earth's earliest atmosphere consisted of large amounts of water vapor, nitrogen, nitrogen oxides, ammonia, carbon dioxide, hydrogen, hydrogen sulfide, and methane. Most of these gases are deadly to the life forms that exist today. This early atmosphere was *reducing*, rather than *oxidizing*, and could have led to the formation of simple organic molecules, such as amino acids. This is the Oparin (or Oparin-Haldane) hypothesis.

The Oparin hypothesis was tested in experiments by Miller and Urey, who replicated the conditions of the early Earth in a test tube apparatus. They heated water in a chamber containing hydrogen, ammonia, and methane—all reducing compounds. Sparks from electrodes simulated lightning. The water vapor that formed inside the chamber was condensed and collected. Analysis showed that it contained several amino acids and other organic compounds, supporting the Oparin hypothesis.

Divisions and Kingdoms of Life

Taxonomy is the ordering and assignment of living things into categories. The most recent consensus sorts life into three domains: Archaea,

Eubacteria, and Eukarya (also called Eukaryota). Archaea and Eubacteria consist of prokaryotic organisms, while Eukarya contains the eukaryotes.

DOMAIN	EUBACTERIA	ARCHAEA	EUKARYA			
KINGDOM	Eubacteria	Archaea	Protista	Fungi	Animalia	Plantae

The domain Eukarya is further divided into four kingdoms: Protista, Fungi, Animalia, and Plantae. (When combined with Archaea and Eubacteria, these groups make up the six-kingdom system.) Within each kingdom, organisms are further divided into smaller categories: phylum, class, order, family, genus, and species. Each species has a unique, binomial name made up of its genus name followed by the species name.

Characteristics of Eubacteria and Archaea

Nearly all prokaryotes have a cell wall, helping them to survive hypotonic surroundings. Archaea have cell walls made of polysaccharides. Eubacteria have cell walls made of peptidoglycan. Gram staining divides bacteria into gram positive (simpler walls with more peptidoglycan) and gram negative (complex walls that include other compounds). Gram-negative bacteria are more likely to be pathogenic and develop drug resistance.

Some prokaryotes have flagella, which enable locomotion. This allows taxis, the movement of cells toward or away from an environmental signal. Prokaryotes reproduce asexually via binary fission. Their short generation times allow populations to quickly adapt to changing environments. Prokaryotes include both autotrophs (which use basic inorganic compounds, such as carbon dioxide) and heterotrophs (which must obtain organic compounds from other organisms).

Prokaryotes were the first form of life to evolve on Earth. Cyanobacteria (photosynthetic, autotrophic eubacteria) removed carbon dioxide from the air and pumped large amounts of oxygen gas into the atmosphere. This changed the future course of evolution, since the additional oxygen changed Earth's early reducing atmosphere to an oxidizing atmosphere.

Eubacteria include many familiar species, both helpful and harmful. The *E. coli* and other bacteria that inhabit the large intestine provide needed vitamins. Bacteria are used to produce yogurt and cheese, among other foods. Bacteria such as the *Salmonella* genus are also common causes of disease.

Archaea include species capable of surviving in extreme environments. Thermophiles ("heat lovers") are found in very hot environments, such as hot springs and hydrothermal vents. Halophiles ("salt lovers") thrive in extremely saline waters, such as salt lakes.

Symbiotic Evolution of Eukaryotes

Recall that eukaryotic cells contain membrane-bound organelles. Where did the organelles of eukaryotes originate? Lynn Margulis's endosymbiotic theory partially answered this question: mitochondria and chloroplasts arose from free-living prokaryotes. These organisms were *phagocytized*, or engulfed, by a primitive eukaryote. Instead of being digested, however, they remained in the cytoplasm, helping the host cell to produce ATP (mitochondria) or glucose (chloroplasts).

Several lines of evidence support this theory. Both mitochondria and chloroplasts have two membranes, which would result if vesicle membranes formed around their plasma membranes. Also, free-living prokaryotes that are very similar to these organelles have been found. Finally, both organelles contain their own DNA.

Characteristics of Protists

Protists are a diverse group of mostly single-celled eukaryotes. Though most live in aquatic environments, protists obtain nutrition and move around in a number of different ways. Evolutionary relationships among protists are not well known, and this kingdom is considered a catch-all category for species that cannot be classified as plants, animals, or fungi.

- *Locomotion.* Protists move via cilia or flagella. (Note that the eukaryotic flagellum is very different in form from the bacterial flagellum.) Some protists use amoeboid movement, in which the cytoskeleton forms pseudopods ("false feet") that pull the cell along.

- *Nutrition.* Protists include both heterotrophs and photosynthetic autotrophs, such as algae. Most heterotrophic protists take in and digest food inside the cell. Others, such as slime molds, secrete digestive enzymes and absorb the nutrients.

- *Size.* While most protists are single celled, some form large, multicellular colonies or simple bodies with unspecialized tissues. Algae include both unicellular and large, multicellular organisms.

- *Reproduction.* Like all eukaryotes, protists can divide asexually (via mitosis) or produce spores (via meiosis). Spores result in greater genetic variation and may be produced in response to unfavorable environmental conditions.

Characteristics of Plants

Plants are multicellular, photosynthetic autotrophs with complex, differentiated tissues. (Algae, with their simpler, nondifferentiated tissues, are protists.) Like some protists, a plant cell has chloroplasts, contains a large central vacuole, and is supported by a rigid cell wall. Plant cell walls are composed mainly of cellulose. Plants can reproduce sexually or by various asexual means. New tissues can form from islands of undifferentiated cells in the adult plant, giving plants great flexibility in growth.

Characteristics of Fungi

Fungi are saprophytes, growing on or in their food. They digest food extracellularly, by secreting enzymes and absorbing the resulting nutrients. Fungi may be unicellular or multicellular, and may reproduce asexually (via mitotic cell division) or sexually.

Characteristics of Animals

Animals are multicellular heterotrophs. Animal cells lack cell walls and are instead supported by an extracellular matrix of proteins such as collagen. Like fungi, animals digest their food extracellularly; however, animals usually ingest food into a body sac to digest it.

Animals reproduce sexually; sperm and egg cells join to form a diploid zygote, which cleaves to form an embryo. Animal tissues develop from embryonic germ layers; each layer gives rise to a limited set of tissue types. (Contrast this process with that seen in plants.) Some animals go through a juvenile stage called a *larva*, which differs markedly from the adult form. A larva and adult may inhabit different environments and consume different foods.

Animal Diversity

Animals range from sessile sponges with undifferentiated tissues, to complex, highly intelligent primates. The following describes the major animal phyla. Two distinctions are important in animal taxonomy: protostome vs. deuterostome, and invertebrate vs. vertebrate. During embryonic development, the first opening in the embryo develops to become the mouth in protostomes. In deuterostomes, the mouth develops from an opening that forms later. All protostomes are invertebrates, animals lacking a dorsal (back-side) nerve cord encased in vertebral bones. Invertebrates often have a ventral (stomach-side) nerve cord. Deuterostomes include both vertebrates and invertebrates.

Protostome Phyla

- *Porifera*. Sponges are the simplest animals, lacking true tissues (groups of similar cells that carry out specific functions). Sponges filter food particles from water passing through their bodies. Like all animals, sponges have a gelatin-like extracellular matrix between layers of cells.

- *Cnidarians*. The jellyfishes, hydras, anemones, and corals have radial symmetry and a very simple body plan: a sac that functions as a gastrovascular (digestive) cavity with a single opening surrounded by tentacles. Two body forms in this phylum are the sessile (non-moving) polyp and the floating medusa. Sea anemones, hydras, and corals are polyp forms; jellyfish are medusas. Cnidarians have a simple nervous system, consisting of a nerve net.

- *Platyhelminthes, Nematoda, Annelida*. These are flatworms, roundworms, and segmented worms, respectively. They all have bilateral symmetry.

- *Mollusca*. This phylum includes snails, slugs, clams, oysters, squid, and octopi. Most mollusks live in marine environments, and many secrete a hard shell. The mollusk body plan consists of three parts: a foot used for locomotion, a visceral mass containing the internal organs, and a mantle that surrounds the visceral mass and may produce the shell. Mollusk shells are made mostly of calcium.

- *Arthropoda*. This is the most diverse phylum and includes the insects, spiders, millipedes, centipedes, scorpions, shrimp, crabs, crayfish, and lobsters. Arthropods are characterized by a segmented body plan and jointed appendages. Many arthropods have exoskeletons made of chitin.

Deuterostome Phyla

- *Echinodermata*. This phylum includes sea stars, brittle stars, sea urchins, and sea cucumbers. Echinoderms share a water vascular system, in which canals feed water into tube feet. Hundreds of the suction-cup-like tube feet may cover the body of an echinoderm and perform feeding and locomotion functions. Tube feet also play a role in gas exchange with the environment.

- *Chordata*. Chordates include both invertebrates and vertebrates. Invertebrate chordates include tunicates, lancelets, and hagfishes.

All chordates share four features: a hollow dorsal nerve cord, a notochord, pharyngeal (behind-the mouth) openings, and a strong tail that extends behind the end of the digestive tract. Some of these features are present only in the larval stage or during embryonic development. The notochord is a flexible tube that runs along the nerve cord and provides support. The pharyngeal openings allow water to pass into and out of the mouth. Invertebrate chordates use these openings for filter feeding; in fish, they develop into gill slits and allow gas exchange.

- *Vertebrata.* Vertebrate chordates include humans. Vertebrates feature a backbone in which the dorsal nerve cord is enclosed in vertebrae. The notochord develops into disks that sit between and cushion the vertebrae. Vertebrate classes include cartilaginous fishes (such as sharks) and ray- and lobe-finned fishes, which gave rise to the following classes: amphibians, reptiles (including birds), and mammals. The phylogenetic tree below shows the relationships among these groups.

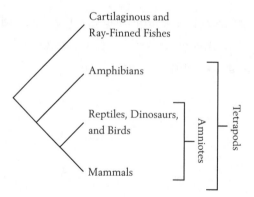

Amphibians, reptiles, birds, and mammals make up the tetrapods, or four-limbed animals. The ancestor of these groups evolved from a species of lobe-finned fish about 360 million years ago. Amphibians are the earliest-branching group, splitting off from the branch that gave rise to amniotes. While the eggs of amphibians and fishes require a moist environment, the amniotic egg is surrounded by a moisture-retaining shell. This adaptation allowed tetrapods to inhabit drier terrestrial environments.

Review Questions

1. In the Oparin-Haldane experiment, the artificial atmosphere they created contained which of the following?

    I.   Hydrogen gas
    II.   Oxygen gas
    III. Reducing gases

    A. I only
    B. II only
    C. I and II
    D. I and III
    E. II and III

2. A unicellular organism contains a Golgi body and ribosomes but lacks a cell wall. It is heterotrophic, ingesting food via phagocytosis. What kingdom does this organism belong to?

    A.   Animalia
    B.   Eubacteria
    C.   Fungi
    D.   Protista
    E.   Archaea

3. Which of these features are found in the phylum that includes centipedes?

    I.   Ventral nerve cord
    II.   Segmented body
    III. Calcium-rich shell
    IV.   Jointed limbs

    A. I and II
    B. I and IV
    C. II and III
    D. I, II, and IV
    E. II, III, and IV

4. Which of these is a tetrapod that is NOT an amniote?

    A. Ostrich
    B. Shark
    C. Rattlesnake
    D. Salamander
    E. Kangaroo

5. How did the results of the Urey-Miller experiment affect the Oparin hypothesis?

    A. The results supported the Oparin hypothesis by showing that organisms contributed to the composition of Earth's present-day atmosphere.

    B. The results contradicted the Oparin hypothesis by showing that Earth's early atmosphere could not produce cells from organic molecules.

    C. The results supported the Oparin hypothesis by showing that replicating membranes could form from simple molecular precursors.

    D. The results contradicted the Oparin hypothesis by showing that Earth's early atmosphere was too hot and volatile to sustain living things.

    E. The results supported the Oparin hypothesis by showing that biological molecules could form in conditions resembling the early Earth.

Answer Explanations

1. **D.** Oparin and Haldane's artificial atmosphere contained hydrogen gas and other reducing gases. It did not contain oxygen gas, which characterizes the current oxidizing atmosphere.

2. **D.** Protists include unicellular, eukaryotic organisms that digest food inside the cell. (Fungi, in contrast, carry out extracellular digestion.)

3. **D.** Centipedes belong to the phylum Arthropoda. Arthropods feature a ventral nerve cord, segmented body plan, jointed appendages, and possibly an exoskeleton of chitin. Mollusks (such as snails) secrete a calcium-rich shell.

4. **D.** Salamanders (along with frogs and snake-like caecilians) are tetrapods that lack watertight, amniotic eggs. Amphibians must lay their eggs in moist environments. Sharks are not tetrapods, and ostriches, rattlesnakes, and kangaroos are all amniotes. (Note that mammals are considered amniotes because they evolved from an ancestor with an amniotic egg.)

5. **E.** Urey and Miller simulated the conditions found early in Earth's history (reducing atmosphere, water vapor, lightning) and showed that organic molecules, such as amino acids, could form spontaneously. Their results support the Oparin hypothesis that life on Earth originated from molecules that formed in such conditions.

Review Chapter 11: Plants

The Diversity of Plants

Plants, from tiny mosses to giant redwoods, are found on almost every continent on Earth. Plants evolved from a species of green algae and have since adapted to terrestrial life. The phylogenetic tree shows the relationships among major groups of land plants.

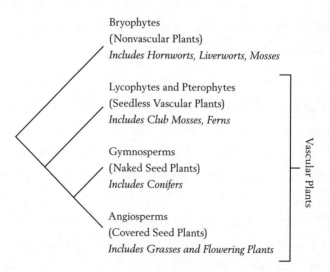

Bryophytes, which include true mosses, liverworts, and hornworts, are *nonvascular* plants. They lack vascular (transport) tissues and therefore remain small. Bryophytes have an important adaptation to land: a tough-walled spore that can travel outside of water without drying out. A *spore* is a haploid cell that undergoes mitosis to produce a multicellular, haploid organism. (Bryophytes have haploid and diploid generations, as described in the next section.)

The remaining groups are the *vascular* plants. The lycophytes and pterophytes (including ferns) still share an important characteristic with bryophytes: they produce spores instead of seeds. However, these plants are able to transport water and dissolved nutrients from their roots to their leaves through a vascular system.

Among vascular plants, gymnosperms and angiosperms produce seeds instead of spores. A *seed* is an embryonic plant that is enclosed, along with food, in a protective covering (called an *integument*). Gymnosperms ("naked seed" plants) have seeds that are partially exposed to the air. Gymnosperms include conifers such as pine, fir, and spruce trees, as well as cycads and gingko trees.

Angiosperms, or flowering plants, produce seeds that are completely encased in an integument. Many angiosperms produce fruits or starchy grains associated with seeds. Angiosperms include deciduous trees, grasses, and all other flowering plants. Almost all agriculturally important plants are angiosperms.

Alternation of Haploid and Diploid Generations

All plants alternate between haploid and diploid generations, or forms. However, plants vary in the generation that forms the mature, or adult, plant. The diploid sporophyte form undergoes meiosis, giving rise to haploid spores. The spores divide mitotically to form a haploid plant body called a *gametophyte*. The gametophyte produces gametes (sperm and egg cells) via mitosis. (Compare to animals, which form gametes directly from the diploid body through meiosis.) Gametes join in fertilization to produce the diploid zygote, which divides mitotically to form the sporophyte generation.

The diagram below summarizes the cycle of plant generations. Note that in mosses, the haploid gametophyte is the dominant generation. The green mosses visible on trees or in soil are all haploid gametophytes.

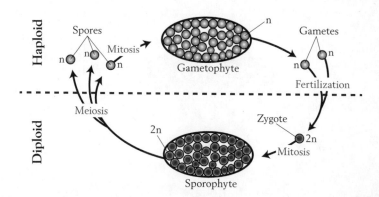

PLANTS	DOMINANT GENERATION	HAPLOID FORM (VIA MEIOSIS)	DIPLOID FORM (VIA FERTILIZATION)
Nonvascular plants (for example, mosses)	Haploid gametophyte	Spores that form the adult plant, which produces sperm and eggs; occurs by mitosis	Zygote, which forms inside the gametophyte; the sporophyte is a small structure dependent on the gametophyte; it produces and releases spores
Seedless vascular plants (for example, ferns)	Diploid sporophyte	Spores that divide mitotically to form small, leaf-like, free-living gametophytes, which produce gametes	Zygote and young and adult plants; adult plants produce haploid spores
Gymnosperms and angiosperms	Diploid sporophyte	Pollen grains and the interiors of ovules	Seeds and young and adult plants

Reproduction in Flowering Plants

Angiosperms are characterized by flowers, seeds, and fruits. (Note that not all angiosperms produce "showy" flowers or fruits.) The structure of a typical flower is shown below.

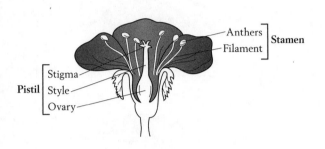

Pollen is produced in the anthers of the stamens. *Pollination*, the transfer of pollen to the stigma, may be carried out by insects, or the pollen may be dispersed by wind. A tube cell in the pollen grain forms a tube from the stigma, through the style, and into the ovary. Pollen also contains two sperm cells. One sperm cell fertilizes the egg cell to form the zygote, which divides mitotically to form the plant embryo contained in the seed. The other sperm cell combines with two nuclei in the ovule, forming a triploid cell. This gives rise to endosperm, the nutrient-rich, starchy tissue that provides food for the embryo within the seed.

Angiosperms: Monocots and Dicots

Most flowering plants fall into one of two main groupings: monocotyledons and dicotyledons. These groups are named for the number of seed leaves (cotyledons) in the embryonic plant. Monocots include palm trees, orchids, and grasses (which include economically important cereal crops, such as corn, wheat, and rice). Monocots do not produce true wood. Dicots include many fruit- and vegetable-producing plants and trees that produce hardwoods (for example, oaks, maples, birches). The criteria for distinguishing monocots and dicots are summarized in the table shown.

COTYLEDONS	PETALS	LEAVES	ROOTS	XYLEM AND PHLOEM
MONOCOTS				
One	Multiples of three	Veins run parallel along the leaf	Fibrous root system with no main root	Distributed throughout stem
DICOTS				
Two	Multiples of four or five	Veins branch out in a net	One main taproot, with smaller roots growing from it	Arranged in a ring

Plant Tissues and Organs

The basic body plan of a plant consists of a root system, which absorbs water and dissolved nutrients from the soil; and a shoot system, which carries out photosynthesis and transports nutrients to the roots. Vascular tissues distribute needed materials throughout the root and shoot systems. Nearly every part of a plant consists of tissue from three types or systems: dermal, vascular, and ground.

- *Dermal.* This is the "skin" of the plant, and includes the root covering, epidermis, and leaf cuticle.
- *Vascular.* This includes xylem and phloem in the plant's roots, stem, and leaves.
- *Ground.* This includes all other tissues that regulate dermal and vascular tissue and carry out photosynthesis.

Leaves

Plant leaves play primary roles in photosynthesis and water regulation. The structure of a plant leaf is shown, with its components described on the following page.

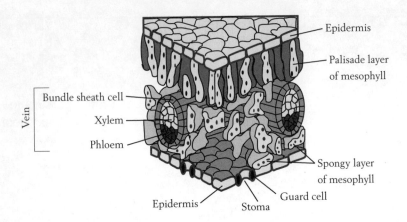

- *Epidermis.* These cells form the upper and lower surfaces of the leaf. They are covered in a protective cuticle and contain openings called *stomata.* The openings allow gas exchange between the air and the leaf cells and may be closed to prevent the loss of water from the leaf.
- *Mesophyll.* This middle layer of the leaf carries out photosynthesis. The mesophyll cells in the upper palisade layer are elongated and tightly packed. The lower, spongy layer is more loosely arranged. Spongy mesophyll cells are key in gas exchange between the mesophyll and the air spaces in the leaf.
- *Vein (vascular bundle).* The leaf vein consists of xylem and phloem cells surrounded by bundled sheaf cells. Materials pass through this outer ring of cells, into and out of the mesophyll.

Vascular Tissues

Vascular tissues transport saps consisting of water, minerals, sugars, and other compounds throughout the plant body. Vascular tissues include xylem and phloem.

- *Xylem.* Xylem conducts water and minerals from a plant's roots to its leaves. Xylem is composed of dead, elongated cells called *tracheids* and *vessel elements.*
- *Phloem.* In contrast, the sugar-transporting phloem consists of living cells. Sap moves along long, narrow sieve cells; in angiosperms,

these are called *sieve-tube members*. These cells are regulated by companion cells that lie alongside them.

Water Transport and Regulation

Water is essential to land plants, which must absorb it from the soil and transport it, sometimes hundreds of feet, to the highest leaves. Two forces affect water transport: root pressure and transpiration. Transpiration is regulated by the opening and closing of stomata.

- *Root pressure.* Water and dissolved minerals from soil enter plants through the roots. A waxy layer within the root, the Casparian strip, prevents water from entering vascular tissue via the spaces between cells. Water must pass through the selective plasma membrane of root endodermis cells. Endodermis cells pump mineral ions (such as potassium, K^+) into the vascular tissue. This increases the amount of water entering the vascular tissue by osmosis. This process creates root pressure, a "push" of water into the plant. Root pressure plays a much smaller role in water transport than transpiration.

- *Transpiration.* Water in the leaf is lost to the environment as vapor that exits through the stomata. This water loss is called *transpiration.* Transpiration causes water from within cells to enter the spaces within the leaf. However, this water must be replaced by water in the xylem. Transpiration pulls water from the veins into plant leaves. Because of water's high cohesion (stickiness between water molecules) and adhesion (stickiness to vascular tissue surfaces), the pull of transpiration acts down the length of the plant. It is primarily responsible for the upward flow of sap through the xylem.

- *Stomata.* These openings in the leaf epidermis control transpiration by regulating the loss of water from the leaves. The pore in each stoma is surrounded by two guard cells, which can expand to open when turgid or wilt to close.

The guard cells pump potassium ions into their vacuoles. This causes water to enter via osmosis, increasing the pressure in the cell and causing turgor. The swollen guard cell opens, allowing gas exchange through the stomata. When water pressure is low, temperature is high, or it is night, potassium ions exit the guard cells, pulling water after them. The wilted guard cells block the stomata opening, preventing water loss from the plant.

Plant Growth

Plants have indeterminate growth thanks to tissues called *meristems*, which consist of cells that can differentiate to form new shoots, roots, and leaves. Apical meristems are located on the tips of shoots and roots and are responsible for *primary* growth, which increases a plant's length. The apical meristem is surrounded by leaf primordia, which form new leaves. During primary growth, meristem cells are left behind at the bases of leaves, forming axillary buds. *Apical dominance* refers to the fact that apical meristems suppress the development of nearby axillary meristems. As the plant grows, the axillary buds may develop and form new leaves or branches.

Lateral meristems are located inside the trunks and roots of woody plants and are responsible for increases in thickness. Vascular cambium and cork cambium are both lateral meristems.

Hormones and Growth

Plant growth is regulated by hormones, chemical signals that are produced in one plant tissue and cause a response in other tissues. The hormone auxin was discovered in studies of phototropic responses in grass seedlings (coleoptiles). A *tropism* is a response toward or away from a stimulus; *phototropism* refers to a plant's bending toward a light source. Plant hormones are summarized below.

- *Auxin* stimulates the growth and differentiation of roots and shoots in fruit and causes tropic responses.
- *Gibberellin* stimulates growth of stems and leaves and stimulates flower and fruit development.

- *Abscisic acid* inhibits growth and germination and causes stomata to close.
- *Ethylene* ripens fruit and may stimulate or inhibit plant growth.
- *Cytokinin* regulates root growth and stimulates the germination of seeds.
- *Brassinosteroid* inhibits root growth as well as leaf abscission.

Review Questions

1. Which of these plant forms are diploid?

   I.   Spore
   II. Sporophyte
   III. Gametophyte

   A. I only
   B. II only
   C. III only
   D. I and II
   E. II and III

2. Which of these correctly matches the plant cells to their tissue systems?

   I.   Guard cell
   II. Palisade mesophyll cell
   III. Sieve-tube member

   A. I = dermal; II = ground; III = vascular
   B. I = dermal; II = vascular; III = ground
   C. I = ground; II = dermal; III = vascular
   D. I = ground; II = vascular; III = dermal
   E. I = vascular; II = ground; III = dermal

3. Which of these is/are responsible for an increase in the thickness of a plant?

    I.   Apical meristem
    II.   Vascular cambium
    III. Cork cambium

    A. I only
    B. II only
    C. III only
    D. I and II
    E. II and III

4. Which of these describes a difference between monocots and dicots?

    A. Monocot embryos form two leaves; dicot embryos form a single leaf.
    B. Monocot flowers may consist of five petals; dicot flowers may consist of six petals.
    C. Monocot leaves have a branching network of veins; dicot leaves have parallel veins.
    D. Monocot roots consist of many small roots growing from a taproot; dicot roots lack a taproot.
    E. Monocot vascular tissue is arranged randomly in the stem; dicot vascular tissue is arranged in a ring.

5.   Which of these increase the movement of sap within the xylem?

    I.   Water moves into guard cells' vacuoles.

    II.   Humidity increases in surrounding air.

    III. Root endodermis prevents ions from entering xylem.

    A.   I only
    B.   II only
    C.   I and III
    D.   II and III
    E.   I, II, and III

Answer Explanations

1.   **B.** Only the sporophyte is diploid. The sporophyte produces haploid spores, which divide mitotically to produce the gametophyte. The gametophyte produces haploid gametes.

2.   **A.** Guard cells, which make up the stomata of the epidermis, are classified as dermal tissue. Palisade mesophyll cells, which carry out photosynthesis, are classified as ground tissue. Sieve-tube members, which make up the phloem, are classified as vascular tissue.

3.   **E.** The vascular cambium and the cork cambium are forms of lateral meristem, which increase the thickness (secondary growth) of woody plants. The apical meristem increases the length of a plant (primary growth) only.

4.   **E.** Monocot vascular tissue is arranged randomly in the stem, while dicot vascular tissue is arranged in a ring. All other answer choices have characteristics reversed.

5.   **A.** Water moving into guard cells increases turgor pressure, causing them to swell. Swollen guard cells open the stomatal pore, allowing water vapor to exit the leaf via transpiration. This, in turn, draws water up from the roots. In contrast, increasing humidity decreases water loss from the leaves. Root endodermis increases root pressure by pumping ions into the xylem.

Review Chapter 12: Animal Organ Systems, Part 1

Animals are complex, multicellular organisms. They must coordinate the actions of many specialized cells and tissues in order to meet the basic cellular needs: obtain nutrients and oxygen; dispose of carbon dioxide and other metabolic wastes; maintain osmotic (water) balance; and keep conditions within a narrow, optimal range for biochemical reactions. These functions are summed up by the term *homeostasis*. This chapter describes how the major mammalian body systems help to maintain homeostasis and carry out other life functions. A comparison with other types of animals is also provided.

The Muscular and Skeletal Systems

The muscular and skeletal systems function in locomotion, as well as in gas exchange and digestion. Mammalian muscle tissues are divided into three types, as follows:

- *Skeletal muscle* is found beneath the skin and attached to bone. Voluntary contractions of skeletal muscles allow movement. Skeletal muscle has striations (stripes) due to the arrangement of muscle fibers.
- *Smooth muscle* lines the bladder, digestive tract, and arteries. It lacks striations and is not under voluntary control.

- *Cardiac muscle* is found in the heart. It shares characteristics of both smooth and skeletal muscle.

Contracting Muscle Fibers

Muscle fibers are long, thin, multinucleated cells packed together to make up muscle tissue. Each muscle fiber contains long strands made up of the proteins actin and myosin. Actin and myosin filaments are arranged in units called *sarcomeres,* as shown below; note how they partially overlap. When a muscle fiber is stimulated, the region of overlap increases, causing the fibers to contract. This is the sliding-filament model of muscle contraction.

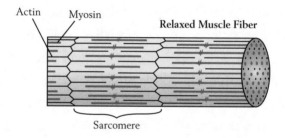

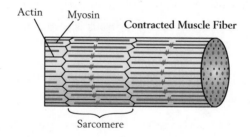

Opposing Muscles Contract

Tendons attach muscles to the bones of the skeleton. Because muscles can only voluntarily contract but cannot extend, they often work in opposing pairs. As one muscle contracts, the opposing muscle is extended, and the limb moves toward the contracting muscle. To move the limb in the opposite direction, the opposing muscle must contract.

Skeletal Joints

Joints between bones allow for a range of motion. The following describes some of the joints in the body. Note that some structures in the body may include a combination of joint types.

- *Ball-and-socket joints* allow for the rotation of limbs. They occur where the upper arm bone attaches to the shoulder and where the upper thigh bone attaches to the hip.
- *Hinge joints* allow swinging motion in one dimension. Hinge joints can be found at the elbows and the knees.
- *Pivot joints* allow rotational motion in one dimension. They can be found at the elbows and neck.
- *Saddle and condyloid joints* allow movement in two planes. They are found in the hands, feet, wrists, and ankles.

Comparison: Hydrostatic Skeleton

Contraction of opposing muscle pairs also occurs in organisms with exoskeletons (for example, arthropods). Animals that lack a skeleton (for example, annelids) may use a hydrostatic skeleton—fluid in a closed sac. Pressure applied to one part of the sac is distributed throughout the fluid, affecting other regions of the sac. For example, an earthworm contracts segments of its body, elongating other segments and thus moving forward.

The Nervous System

The cells of the brain, spinal cord, and body receive signals from the environment, process information, and carry out movements. They make up the nervous system, which includes cells called *neurons*.

Neurons and Action Potentials

A neuron consists of dendrites, which receive signals from other neurons; a cell body that contains the nucleus; and an axon that transmits a signal down its length and through the terminal branches. Cells called *glia* form myelin, which wraps around and insulates the axons of some cells. The long axons of neurons make up nerve fibers, and clusters of neuron cell bodies constitute ganglia.

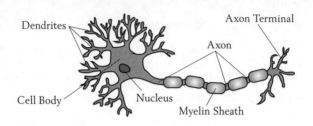

Electrical signals called *action potentials* travel through neurons. An action potential results from a temporary shift in the balance of positively and negatively charged ions inside and outside the cell membrane. Action potentials are initiated when sodium ion (Na^+) channels are opened, allowing sodium into the cytoplasm. The balance is restored when potassium ions (K^+) exit the cytoplasm.

Neurotransmitters

Besides action potentials, the nervous system uses chemical messengers called *neurotransmitters*. When an action potential reaches the terminal axon branches, neurotransmitter molecules are released into a space called a *synapse*. Here, they bind to receptor proteins on the membrane of the adjacent cell's dendrites. Neurotransmitters affect the sodium and potassium channels of the cell and can create a new action potential. Serotonin, acetylcholine, and dopamine are examples of neurotransmitters.

Divisions of the Nervous System

The two major divisions of the nervous system are the central nervous system (CNS), which includes the neurons of the brain and spinal cord; and the peripheral nervous system (PNS), which includes all other neurons and originates in the cranium and between the vertebrae. The PNS is further divided into somatic and autonomic systems. The somatic system links the skeletal muscles to the CNS. The autonomic system regulates involuntary muscles and endocrine glands. It consists of the following divisions:

- *Sympathetic.* This division results in arousal and alertness, stimulating production of the "fight or flight" hormones (epinephrine and norepinephrine), increasing heart rate, and easing breathing.

- *Parasympathetic.* This division promotes "rest and digest" activities. It slows the heart rate, constricts the lungs, and stimulates the digestive organs.

- *Enteric.* This division controls the digestive organs and can be regulated by the other two autonomic divisions.

Comparison: Nerve Nets and Nervous System Complexity

Almost all animals are capable of motion due to the existence of a nervous system, whether simple or complex. The simplest type of nervous system is the nerve net of cnidarians (jellyfish, anemones, and hydras). The next level of complexity features nerve nets that coordinate the movements of multiple body parts. Still more complex nervous systems feature a brain, nerve cord (CNS), and ganglia (neuron clusters) that innervate specific sections of the body.

The Endocrine System

Endocrine organs or glands secrete hormones into the bloodstream. A *hormone* is a substance that has specific effects on certain tissues types. Hormones function by binding to receptor proteins on the plasma membranes of target cells. This binding changes the cell's activity. Some hormones pass directly into the cell's nucleus and affect gene transcription.

The endocrine system includes the following glands and their hormones:

- *Adrenal medulla.* Epinephrine and norepinephrine, responsible for the "fight or flight" response.

- *Pancreas.* Insulin, which lowers blood glucose, and glucagon, which raises blood glucose.

- *Thyroid.* Calcitonin, which lowers blood calcium, and thyroid hormones, which increase metabolism.
- *Parathyroid.* Parathyroid hormone, which increases blood calcium.
- *Gonads (testes and ovaries).* Androgens, which promote male secondary sex characteristics; estrogens, which promote female secondary sex characteristics and growth of the uterine lining; and progesterone, which maintains the uterine lining in pregnancy.
- *Hypothalamus.* Regulates the pituitary via gonadotropin-releasing hormone (GnRH) and other hormones.
- *Pituitary.* The "master gland"; secretes a variety of hormones, including thyroid-stimulating hormone (TSH); growth hormone (GH); antidiuretic hormone, which promotes water retention; and follicle-stimulating hormone (FSH), luteinizing hormone (LH), prolactin, and oxytocin, all of which have roles in reproduction and pregnancy.

Calcium Regulation Feedback Loop

The body uses negative feedback loops to regulate internal conditions and maintain homeostasis. The level of calcium ions (Ca^{2+}) in the blood is maintained within a very narrow range. When levels fall too low or rise too high, the endocrine system responds by secreting hormones that correct the imbalance. When calcium falls too low, the parathyroid glands release parathyroid hormone (PTH). This hormone acts on the kidneys and small intestine to increase their absorption of calcium. PTH also acts on bones, causing them to break down and release calcium into the bloodstream. When calcium levels rise too high, the thyroid is stimulated to release calcitonin. This hormone causes the bones to take up calcium from the bloodstream, and the kidneys to decrease their calcium absorption.

Reproduction and Development

In mammals, both gamete production and secondary sex characteristics are regulated by sex hormones: androgens (such as testosterone), estrogens, and progesterone. Androgens are secreted in larger quantities by testes; ovaries secrete mainly estrogens and progesterone.

Production of Sperm

In males, sperm are produced inside the seminiferous tubules that make up the testes. Sperm cells then travel through the epididymis, where they develop further. From there, they exit the male reproductive tract through the vas deferentia, which pass through the prostate gland and connect to the urethra of the penis. The structure of a sperm cell is shown. Note that the head, which fuses with the egg, does not contain organelles other than a nucleus. Mitochondria packed in the midpiece ("neck") provide energy to the flagellum and allow the sperm to "swim."

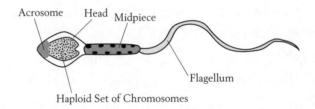

The Female Reproductive Cycle

The female reproductive cycle involves hormones secreted by the hypothalamus and pituitary, which affect the ovaries, which in turn drive changes in the uterine lining. Positive feedback regulates this cycle, which consists of two phases: follicular and luteal. The follicular phase drives the maturation of a follicle, which releases the egg cell into the Fallopian tubes leading to the uterus. The estrogen and progesterone secreted by the follicle cause the uterine lining to build up.

The luteal phase is driven by the corpus luteum, which develops from the follicle. It causes the uterine lining to thicken; if the egg is fertilized, it will implant in the uterine wall, and the corpus luteum will continue to secrete hormones to maintain pregnancy. Usually, the egg is not fertilized, and the corpus luteum degenerates. This causes a drop in estrogen and progesterone, which in turn causes the uterine lining in humans to be shed via menstruation. This cycle takes an average of 28 days.

Development of the Embryo

An animal develops from a single-celled, diploid zygote, which undergoes mitosis and differentiates to form tissues and organs. The zygote first undergoes *cleavage*, mitotic divisions that do not increase the size of the embryo. A cavity begins to form inside the solid ball of cells, resulting in a hollow sphere containing an inner cell mass. This stage is called a *blastocyst* in mammals. The blastocyst implants in the uterine wall, and the outer layer begins to form the placenta. After implantation, the inner cell mass undergoes gastrulation. Cells migrate to form three distinct cell populations called *germ layers*. Each layer will give rise to a specific set of tissues, as follows.

- *Endoderm.* This germ layer gives rise to the lining of the digestive system and other internal organs, as well as the pancreas, liver, thymus, thyroid, and parathyroid glands.

- *Mesoderm.* This germ layer gives rise to the muscular, skeletal, circulatory, lymphatic, excretory, and reproductive systems; the outer muscle layer of the digestive system; and the dermis of the skin.

- *Ectoderm.* This germ layer gives rise to the nervous system, several bones of the cranium, and skin epidermis. The ectoderm forms a hollow neural tube along the dorsal side of the embryo, which will form the CNS.

Comparison: The Amniotic Egg

Mammals—along with turtles, reptiles, and birds—are considered *amniotes* because they evolved from an ancestor that laid an amniotic egg. This type of egg has a leathery or hard shell that prevents the contents from drying out. Embryos produce specialized membranes that aid in gas exchange, nutrition, and protection from injury. These layers are described and shown on the next page.

- *Yolk sac.* Holds a nutrient-rich yolk that "feeds" the embryo through blood vessels.
- *Amnion.* Holds the embryo and amniotic fluid; protects the embryo.
- *Allantois.* Holds metabolic wastes; aids in gas exchange.
- *Chorion.* Exchanges gases (oxygen and carbon dioxide) with the air outside the egg.

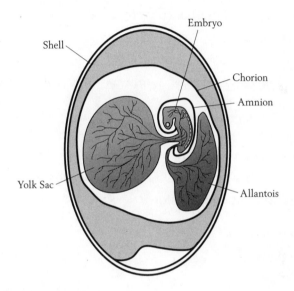

Review Questions

1. Which of these correctly matches each structure to the germ layer from which it arises?

   I. Femur
   II. Brainstem
   III. Lungs

   A. I = endoderm; II = ectoderm; III = mesoderm
   B. I = endoderm; II = mesoderm; III = ectoderm
   C. I = ectoderm; II = endoderm; III = mesoderm
   D. I = mesoderm; II = endoderm; III = ectoderm
   E. I = mesoderm; II = ectoderm; III = endoderm

2. Which precedes an action potential traveling down the axon of a neuron?

    A. Neurotransmitters bind to receptors on the dendrite of the neuron.
    B. Neurotransmitters are released from the axon terminals of the neuron.
    C. The action potential travels through the synapse from a nearby neuron.
    D. Vesicles in the axon terminal release their contents at the synapse.
    E. The cell body releases neurotransmitters down the length of the axon.

3. A nerve leading to the small intestine causes the rate of digestion to increase. This nerve MOST LIKELY belongs to which of the following systems and divisions?

    I.   Autonomic
    II. Sympathetic
    III. Peripheral
    IV. Enteric

    A. I and II only
    B. II and III only
    C. I, II, and III
    D. I, III, and IV
    E. II, III, and IV

4.   Which of these is the MOST LIKELY result of blood calcium levels falling too low?

   A.   The thyroid gland releases calcitonin, which binds to bone cells.
   B.   The parathyroid glands release PTH, which binds to kidney cells.
   C.   The thyroid gland releases thyroid hormone, which binds to small intestine cells.
   D.   The pancreas releases glucagon, which binds to liver cells.
   E.   The pituitary gland releases growth hormone, which binds to bone cells.

5.   Which correctly describes a process or event in the female reproductive cycle?

   A.   The cycle is regulated via a negative feedback loop.
   B.   The corpus luteum releases an egg into a fallopian tube.
   C.   Estrogen and progesterone cause a follicle to mature.
   D.   Pituitary hormones cause the uterine lining to be shed monthly.
   E.   A maturing follicle causes the uterine lining to build up.

Answer Explanations

1.   **E.** The long bones are derived from the mesoderm; the nervous system, from the neural tube of the ectoderm; and the lungs, from the endoderm.

2.   **A.** Action potentials are transmitted from input at the dendrites of a neuron, travel down the axon, and release neurotransmitters into the synapse between adjacent cells. These neurotransmitters bind to receptors on the dendrite of the second neuron, helping to produce a new action potential. Action potentials cannot travel through synapses.

3.   **D.** The nerve is outside the CNS and so belongs to the peripheral nervous system (PNS). Because it is not under voluntary control, it must belong to the autonomic system. Because it promotes "rest and digest" functions, it must belong to the parasympathetic (rather than

sympathetic) nervous system. Finally, because it innervates the intestines, it is likely part of the enteric nervous system.

4.   **B.** Parathyroid hormone (PTH) is secreted in response to low blood calcium levels. This hormone acts on the kidneys to take up more calcium and causes bones to release calcium into the blood.

5.   **E.** Pituitary hormones cause a follicle in the ovary to mature and release an egg. The maturing follicle secretes estrogen and progesterone, causing the uterine lining to build up. After the egg is released, the follicle forms a corpus luteum, which disintegrates if pregnancy does not occur. This loss of the corpus luteum causes estrogen and progesterone levels to drop, which in turn causes the uterine lining to be shed.

Review Chapter 13: Animal Organ Systems, Part 2

C hapter 12 focused on those systems that regulate internal conditions and coordinate actions; this chapter focuses on the exchange of the body's materials with the environment. For example, the digestive system takes in food and digests it to produce nutrients, which can then be distributed to cells. The respiratory system exchanges oxygen and carbon dioxide with the air, and the excretory system eliminates the chemical by-products of metabolism. The circulatory system is essential to all of the other organ systems, as it transports these materials throughout the body.

The Digestive System

Animals ingest food and digest it (break it down) into simple nutrients. Digestion occurs in the tube-like digestive tract. Once food is digested, nutrients are absorbed into the body and transported through the bloodstream. Food may be digested mechanically or chemically (by enzymes). Three classes of nutrients are digested, as follows:

- *Proteins* are broken down into amino acids. Amino acids are used to build proteins in the cells.

- *Carbohydrates* (starches and sugars) are broken down into simple monosaccharides, such as glucose. Glucose is a preferred energy source.

- *Fats* or lipids are broken down into fatty acids and monoglycerides. Fats are also used for energy.

Mouth and Esophagus

The mouth, teeth, and tongue mechanically digest food, breaking it down into a soft mixture. Chemical digestion begins in the mouth, as salivary amylase begins to break down carbohydrates.

Food is swallowed, passing over the epiglottis that closes off the trachea and then into the esophagus. Peristaltic contractions of the esophagus push food to the stomach.

Stomach

The stomach lining secretes highly acidic gastric juice, with a pH between 1 and 3. This breaks down food chemically, and the enzyme pepsin begins to cleave proteins into smaller polypeptides. The stomach stores and churns food for several hours, producing a mixture called *chyme*.

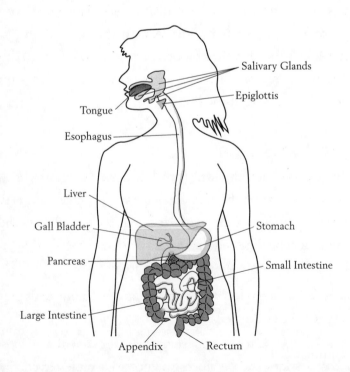

Small Intestine: Digestion in the Duodenum

The chyme is then released into the duodenum (upper portion) of the small intestine. Here, it mixes with secretions from the duodenum, liver, and pancreas and is further digested.

Accessory Organs: Pancreas, Liver, and Gall Bladder

These are accessory organs in digestion; food does not pass through them, but they release substances into the digestive tract. The liver produces bile, which both helps to emulsify fats and raises the pH of the chyme. The emulsification of fats increases their surface area, allowing them to be digested by lipase from the pancreas. The pancreas secretes enzymes that digest carbohydrates, fats, proteins, and nucleic acids.

The gallbladder stores bile produced by the liver and releases it into the duodenum when needed. This allows a larger volume of bile to be released at one time.

Small Intestine: Absorption of Nutrients

After food is digested, it is absorbed in the remaining length of the small intestine. Tiny fingerlike projections, called *villi*, line the inner wall of this organ. The cells of the villi have projections called *microvilli*. Together, the villi and microvilli maximize the surface area available for absorption. Dissolved nutrients enter the cells of the villi and pass into tiny capillaries, where they enter the bloodstream to be distributed throughout the body. The first stop on this journey is to the liver, which regulates the balance of nutrients in the blood.

Large Intestine: Reabsorption of Water

Undigested material passes into the large intestine (colon), which houses a rich bacterial flora. These symbiotic bacteria use the nutrients in unabsorbed or undigested food and in return produce several essential vitamins, such as vitamin K. The remaining undigested matter, along with some bacteria, make up feces. Feces are stored in the rectum until they can be eliminated.

The large intestine is crucial in water regulation, absorbing much of the water released into the digestive tract up to this point. Too little water reabsorption leads to diarrhea; too much reabsorption results in constipation.

Glucose Regulation Feedback Loop

The level of glucose in the blood is regulated so that it remains within a tight range. The ingestion of a large meal leads to the absorption of glucose, raising blood glucose levels. The pancreas responds by secreting the hormone insulin, which stimulates the cells of the liver, brain, muscles, and other body tissues to take up more glucose. This depletes the glucose in the blood.

The liver converts glucose molecules to a polymer called *glycogen*, a storage form of glucose. When blood glucose drops too low, the pancreas secretes glucagon. This hormone causes the liver to convert stored glycogen to glucose and release it into the bloodstream, raising the glucose level. The regulation of blood glucose is an example of a negative feedback loop.

Comparison: Carnivores and Herbivores

The herbivore digestive system must work harder to extract nutrients from food. Herbivores generally have longer, more extensive digestive tracts, which may consist of multiple stomachs. In contrast, carnivores have shorter digestive tracts and can easily digest their protein-rich diets.

The Respiratory System

The respiratory system is responsible for obtaining the oxygen required for cellular respiration, and expelling carbon dioxide. Pulmonary (lung) respiration moves air into and out of the lungs. Gas exchange takes place within the alveoli of the lungs.

Air enters the body through the nasal cavity and pharynx (throat) and passes into the cartilage-lined trachea, which splits into two bronchi that enter the lungs and branch into a series of bronchioles. Cells along this tract are covered in *cilia*, microscopic "hairs" that keep the airways free of debris.

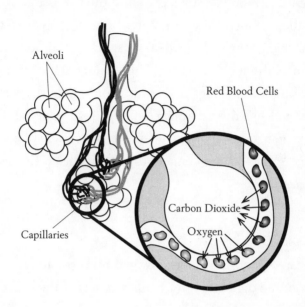

The bronchioles transport air to the sac-like alveoli. Oxygen dissolves into the liquid lining the alveoli and crosses into the network of capillaries just beyond it. Hemoglobin in red blood cells binds to the oxygen molecules and carries them away. Carbon dioxide moves in the opposite direction, from the bloodstream, through the alveoli, and into to the air of the bronchioles.

Breathing: Inhalation and Exhalation

Air is inhaled and exhaled from the lungs by the action of the diaphragm (the muscle below the lungs) and the muscles of the ribcage. During inhalation, the diaphragm contracts and moves downward, and the rib cage expands. This increases the volume of the chest cavity, creating a negative pressure in the chest, which pulls air into the lungs. On exhalation, the diaphragm relaxes and moves upward and the ribs move inward, constricting the chest cavity and pushing air out of the lungs.

Comparison: Gills and Tracheal Systems

Fish use gills instead of lungs to exchange oxygen and carbon dioxide. Gills are composed of many delicate filaments. When water moves over these filaments, carbon dioxide passes into the water and dissolved oxygen enters them. Gills use a countercurrent exchange system, which allows gas exchange through passive transport. Blood flows in the opposite direction as the moving water. This ensures that the concentration of oxygen in the water is higher, at every point, than that of the blood.

Insects do not use these familiar types of respiratory and circulatory systems to exchange gases, but instead rely on a system of air-filled tubes called *tracheae*. These tubes connect to the outside air through openings called *spiracles*.

The Circulatory System

The circulatory system transports oxygen from the lungs and nutrients absorbed from the digestive tract to all the cells of the body. It also carries away wastes produced by the biochemical processes within these cells. The circulatory system consists of the heart, arteries (which carry blood away from the heart), veins (which carry blood toward the heart), and tiny capillaries (which allow substances to pass between the blood and individual cells).

Blood may be oxygenated, as when it returns from the lungs, or deoxygenated, as when it returns from the capillaries that feed the body's tissues. Capillaries from the lungs merge to form the pulmonary veins to the heart, which then pumps the oxygen-rich blood throughout the body.

The heart is divided into four chambers: the left and right atria (top) and the left and right ventricles (bottom). Veins connect to the atria, and blood passes from atrium to ventricle, where it is pumped out of the heart through an artery. The right and left sides of the heart are divided by a septum (wall), and make up two different circuits: pulmonary (right) and systemic (left). The pulmonary circuit collects deoxygenated blood from the two major veins called venae cavae. The heart pumps this blood via the pulmonary arteries to the lungs. The systemic circulation collects newly oxygenated blood from the pulmonary veins and pumps it via the aorta to the tissues of the body.

The aorta branches into ever-smaller arteries, vessels, and capillaries. Oxygen passes through the capillary walls into cells, and waste compounds pass into the capillary blood. They are transported back to the heart as the capillaries merge to form larger vessels and veins, which form the venae cavae leading into the heart. Blood cycles through the body from the lungs, to the left atrium, left ventricle, aorta, body tissues, venae cavae, right atrium, right ventricle, and back to the lungs.

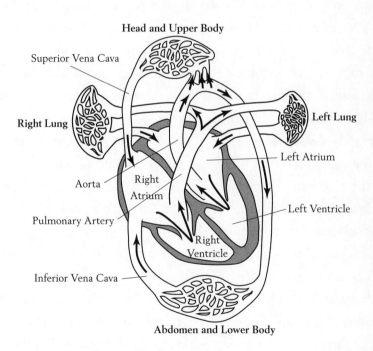

Comparison: Open Circulatory Systems

The simplest invertebrates—sponges and cnidarians—lack a circulatory system. Solutes simply diffuse the short distances through cells. Arthropods and some mollusks have *open* circulatory systems, in which a tubular heart pumps a fluid called *hemolymph* into sinuses, or spaces, that contain the organs.

Contrast this with the *closed* circulatory systems of annelids and other animals (including vertebrates, squids, and octopuses). This type of system involves one or more hearts pumping blood through vessels. Although materials are exchanged between the blood and the cells, the blood does not directly contact the cells. Organisms with faster metabolisms have closed circulatory systems, in which higher pressure facilitates the exchange of materials.

The Excretory System

This system filters waste compounds from the blood and helps to maintain water balance (osmoregulation). Vessels transport blood to the kidneys, where wastes are filtered and water is returned to the circulatory system. Urine, consisting of waste compounds and some water, passes through the two ureters into the bladder, where it is stored until it can be eliminated through the urethra.

The task of the kidneys is to eliminate waste while conserving water. This is accomplished by filtering a larger volume of water and solutes from the blood and then selectively reabsorbing water and other useful substances from the filtrate. While the first step requires little energy, the second relies on both passive and active transport.

The mammalian kidney is packed with functional units called *nephrons*. Each nephron consists of a ball of capillaries called a *glomerulus*, which is enclosed in one end of a long tube. The glomerulus and tube covering it form the Bowman's capsule. Extending from the Bowman's capsule, the tube forms a hairpin at one point along its length, called the loop of Henle. The loop of Henle descends deeper into the center of the kidney and ascends back to the level of the Bowman's capsule. Last, the tube feeds into a urine-collecting duct.

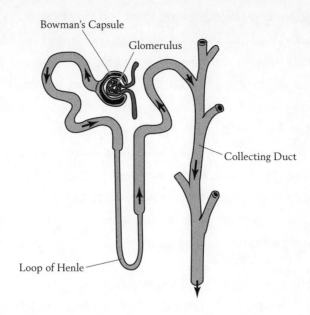

Water and small molecules pass from the glomerulus to the tube via passive transport; cells and proteins are too large to pass into this filtrate. The filtrate contains glucose, salts, vitamins, and minerals that the body needs, as well as water that must be conserved. As the filtrate passes through the rest of the nephron, these substances are collected through both passive and active transport.

The loop of Henle is key in the reabsorption of water and salt. This is accomplished by varying both the permeability of the membrane throughout the loop and the concentration of the fluid outside of the loop. As filtrate moves down the loop, it becomes more concentrated. However, the fluid surrounding the loop also increases in concentration, due to its location within the kidney. Therefore, water can still move out of the loop through passive transport. (Recall that water will move osmotically from an area of low solute concentration to an area of high solute concentration.)

Comparison: Water Conservation

The purpose of urine is to prevent a buildup of nitrogen compounds from digested proteins and nucleic acids in the body. The simplest form of these nitrogen compounds is ammonia (NH_3). However, ammonia is highly toxic and must be dissolved in large volumes of water for excretion. Mammals solve this problem by converting ammonia to a less toxic compound, urea. Urea can be excreted in a smaller volume of water.

Mammals produce urine that is hyperosmotic (more concentrated) relative to the body's fluids, a process that allows them to conserve water. Desert mammals generally have longer loops of Henle, resulting in more concentrated urine. Birds have short loops, but produce uric acid (which is excreted as a paste) instead of urea (which must be dissolved). Freshwater fishes, in contrast, can excrete large volumes of water; they do not convert their ammonia to urea.

The Immune System

Multicellular animal bodies are susceptible to invasion by bacteria and viruses. Viruses enter a cell and use its transcription and translation capabilities to make multiple copies of themselves; the viruses then burst from the cell to invade others. The immune system protects the body by recognizing and destroying foreign cells and viruses. *Innate* immunity is present at birth and protects against a wide range of microbes. *Acquired* (or *adaptive*) immunity develops after exposure to a pathogen, or agent of infection. Acquired immunity is specific, while innate immunity is generic.

Innate Immunity

The skin and mucous membranes provide an external first line of defense against a wide range of microbes. Pathogens that pass these defenses are destroyed by white blood cells called *phagocytes* ("eater cells"), which engulf and digest the invaders. Macrophages are phagocytes that display molecules from the ingested pathogen on their surfaces. Cells called *natural killer cells* destroy body cells that are infected with bacteria or viruses.

The complement system aids in immunity by producing blood proteins that either destroy pathogens or prevent them from reproducing.

For example, virus-infected body cells secrete interferon proteins that induce other cells to prevent the production of viruses.

Inflammation also prevents infection. At sites of injury, mast cells release histamines, which dilate capillaries and allow immune cells and proteins to flood the site. Inflammation also promotes clotting, which forms a barrier to infection.

Acquired Immunity

Lymphocytes play a key role in acquired immunity by recognizing and responding to foreign molecules called *antigens*. The surface of B and T lymphocytes (cells) have antigen receptors, Y-shaped proteins that can bind to foreign molecules. B cells becomes activated by recognizing and binding to an antigen. Helper T cells may bind to an antigen displayed on the surface of a macrophage. Helper T cells stimulate B cells by releasing cytokines.

B cells may also produce antibodies and, instead of displaying these proteins on the cell surface, release them into the bloodstream. In this case, the proteins are called *immunoglobins*. Once exposed to an antigen, some of these cells retain a "memory" that allows the body to mount an immediate immune response the next time it is encountered. This memory is the basis for vaccines, which provide immunity by exposing B and T cells to antigens.

Review Questions

1. Which of these carries deoxygenated blood?

    I.   Pulmonary veins
    II. Anterior vena cava
    III. Pulmonary arteries

    A. I only
    B. II only
    C. III only
    D. I and II
    E. II and III

2. What sequence is followed by the path of blood from the heart?

    A. Vena cava, right atrium, right ventricle, aorta, lungs
    B. Lungs, pulmonary vein, right atrium, right ventricle, aorta
    C. Vena cava, right atrium, right ventricle, lungs, pulmonary vein
    D. Vena cava, left atrium, left ventricle, lungs, pulmonary artery
    E. Left ventricle, lungs, pulmonary vein, pulmonary artery, right atrium

3. Which of these does NOT secrete any digestive enzyme?

    A. Salivary glands
    B. Liver
    C. Pancreas
    D. Small intestine
    E. Stomach

4. Which of these describes an adaptation to an arid environment?

   A. A short loop of Henle, which allows more filtrate to be removed
       from the blood
   B. A short loop of Henle, which allows less water to be removed
       from the filtrate
   C. A long loop of Henle, which allows more filtrate to be removed
       from the blood
   D. A long loop of Henle, which allows more water to be removed
       from the filtrate
   E. A long loop of Henle, which allows less filtrate to be removed
       from the blood

5. Which of these would a researcher test the blood for to determine
    if a person has been infected with a virus in the past?

   A. Antigens
   B. Antibodies
   C. Macrophages
   D. Pathogens
   E. Natural killer cells

Answer Explanations

1. **E.** The anterior and posterior venae cavae return blood to the heart
after it has traveled to the tissues of the body. Because the blood has supplied oxygen to cells, it is deoxygenated. The heart pumps this deoxygenated blood to the lungs through the pulmonary arteries. It picks up
oxygen and returns to the heart via the pulmonary veins.

2. **C.** Deoxygenated blood collects in the vena cava, which feeds into
the right atrium of the heart. Blood from the right atrium enters the
right ventricle, where it is pumped to the lungs via the pulmonary arteries. Oxygen-rich blood returns to the heart via the pulmonary veins.

3. **B**. The liver secretes lipase, which emulsifies fats and allows them to be digested by pancreatic lipase. However, the liver does not produce digestive enzymes.

4. **D**. A long loop of Henle allows more water to be removed from the filtrate before it is excreted as urine. This causes the urine to be even more hyperosmotic and conserves water.

5. **B**. Antigens or immunoglobulins produced by B and T cells are specific and provide a "memory" that helps to fight previously encountered pathogens, or infectious organisms. Antigens, produced by pathogens, would not linger in the blood. Macrophages and natural killer cells are part of the innate immune system and would not be specific to a particular virus.

Review Chapter 14:
Ecology, Part I

Population Ecology

An important unit of species is the population. A *population* refers to the organisms of a species that share an ecosystem. Populations differ in *density* (the number of individuals per unit area) and *dispersion* (how individuals are spread out over the total area). Species may have uniform, clumped, or random dispersion patterns.

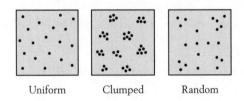

Uniform   Clumped   Random

The size of a population increases when organisms are added to the population, via birth or immigration. It decreases when organisms are removed via death or emigration. The change in a population's size (N) can be determined as:

$$\Delta N = (\text{Birth} + \text{Immigration}) - (\text{Deaths} + \text{Emigration})$$

Every population is limited by finite environmental resources, habitats, water, nutrients, and energy. Limiting factors may be density dependent, which means they affect populations only at certain densities. Alternately, limiting factors may be independent of density. For example, land may be a density-dependent limit on population for territorial species, while a drought that limits a plant population may be a density-independent factor. An ecosystem has resources to support a maximum population size for a particular species. This is called the *carrying capacity* (*K*) for the ecosystem for a given population.

Life History Strategies and Survivorship Curves

Graphs of survivorship curves represent the fates of a *cohort* of individuals (those born at the same time). The number of individuals still alive is plotted over time. Note that the *y*-axis of a survivorship graph is a logarithmic scale, meaning that each unit is 10 times more than the previous unit. Three types of life history curves are shown.

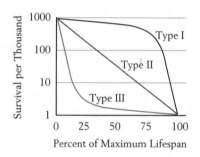

Percent of Maximum Lifespan

- *Type I* characterizes a species with low juvenile death rates and long average life spans.
- *Type II* characterizes a species in which individuals of different ages have roughly equal chances of dying.
- *Type III* characterizes a species with high mortality among offspring but relatively low mortality among adults.

The three curves represent different reproductive and life history strategies. For example, many spiders and fish produce large numbers of offspring but do not invest much in caring for them. These species have type III curves. Primates, elephants, and other large mammals produce few offspring but invest a great deal of care to ensure survival. Type I curves characterize these species.

In addition, species may reproduce once in a lifetime (such as annual plants and some salmon) or several times throughout their lives. Each strategy has trade-offs and is subject to natural selection. For example, if the environment is hostile to offspring, natural selection favors organisms that produce many offspring, because this increases the chance that at least some will survive.

Exponential and Logistic Growth Models

When resources are unlimited, population growth is exponential. Even if the per capita birthrate, or number of offspring per individual, remains constant, the population will follow the J-shaped curve shown in the graph below. As the number of individuals increases, the number of offspring born also increases. In reality, resources are never infinite. However, a population may be much smaller than its environment's carrying capacity. For example, a small group may inhabit a previously uninhabited island, or a disaster may eliminate all but a small number of individuals in a population.

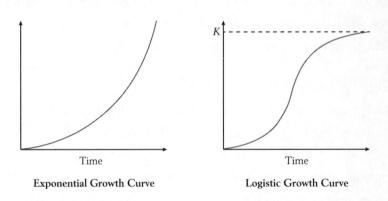

Exponential Growth Curve   Logistic Growth Curve

In contrast, the logistic model of population growth takes resource limitation into account. In the graph above, the population size increases exponentially until it approaches its carrying capacity, K. It then begins to level off, indicating that the number of births equals the number of deaths. Whereas exponential growth describes equal *rates* of increase, no matter the population density, a logistically growing population increases at different rates depending on its density. As the population density increases, its growth rate decreases.

The logistic growth model predicts that natural selection will act differently on a population, depending on its density. When density is low, individuals that can produce greater numbers of offspring have higher fitness. (A population may overshoot K and drop before leveling off.) Life history strategies that maximize reproduction in environments with plentiful resources result from r-selection.

In contrast, when density is high, population size is near K, and resources are limited, individuals that can compete for and efficiently use resources have higher fitness. K-selection favors the production of few offspring along with the investment of parental care and resources to ensure their survival.

The Allee Effect

The logistic growth model predicts that an increase in population size generally leads to a decrease in its rate of growth. However, when population size is extremely low, organisms may be less likely to either survive or find mates and reproduce. In this case, increasing population size actually leads to an *increase* in the rate of growth.

Mark–Recapture Method

Ecologists estimate population sizes using the mark–recapture method. A number of individuals are captured and marked and then released back into the wild. After some time, ecologists recapture the same number of individuals and note any that have been tagged. In a larger population, the chances of capturing the same individual twice is small, so few of the recaptured organisms will have been tagged. If the population is smaller, the probability of recapturing a tagged individual is greater. Comparing the number tagged with the number of those recaptured allows ecologists to estimate the population size.

Methods of marking can vary and often involve placing a numbered metal or plastic band on an animal's body. For example, the legs of birds may be banded, or tags may be attached to ears or gill coverings. Newer technologies, such as digital chips and GPS, allow more sophisticated methods of tracking animals.

Human Population Demographics

Until recently, the global human population has experienced exponential growth. Though it is still increasing, the rate of increase has slowed. Currently, different populations are increasing or decreasing at different rates. The study of human populations is called *demographics*.

Populations of the same size may vary in terms of age structure, or the distribution of individuals among different age groups. Age structures are represented in graphs such as those shown below. Populations that are rapidly growing will have graphs that are wider at the bottom, representing the larger proportion of young people. In populations with very slow or no growth, individuals are more evenly distributed among age ranges.

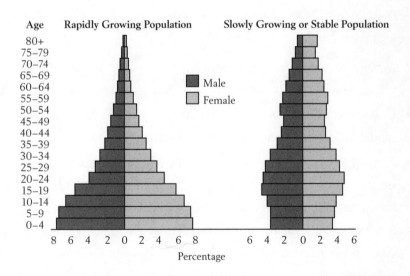

Populations may achieve the same low rate of growth through very different means. In developing countries, both birthrates and death rates are high. In countries that have undergone a demographic transition, birth and death rates are both low.

Ecological Relationships

Populations share the environment with populations of other species, making up a *community*. Community ecology examines the interactions between species. Each species in an ecosystem is characterized by a preferred habitat and a niche. A suitable habitat allows an organism to obtain the resources needed to survive and reproduce. An organism's niche is its method of obtaining resources. For example, a large grassland area with an extensive deer population is a suitable habitat for the gray wolf, which occupies the niche of carnivorous, pack-hunting predator.

Ecologists describe ecological relationships as +/+ (both species benefit), +/0 (only one species benefits), and +/– (one species benefits while harming another). This section describes common ecological relationships.

Symbiotic Relationships

Symbiosis refers to organisms of different species living in close association. One or both species obtain food, protection, or shelter from the association. A symbiotic relationship may benefit or harm the species involved.

- *Mutualism* refers to a relationship in which both species benefit. Often, the species "exchange" food, defense mechanisms, or shelter.

- *Commensalism* refers to a relationship in which one species benefits while the other remains relatively unaffected.

- *Parasitism* refers to a relationship in which one species (the parasite) benefits at the expense of the other (the host). Unlike predators, parasites do not usually kill their hosts. Many parasites have lost the ability to live independently of their hosts. For example, tapeworms cannot ingest and digest foods but must absorb nutrients from their host's digestive tract. Other parasites live on the skin, feathers, or fur of the host, or lay eggs on the host. Organisms that carry parasites or pathogens are called *vectors*.

Predator-Prey Cycles

Predators depend on prey species as food sources. Naturally, the population sizes of predators and their prey are inextricably linked. An increasing prey population can sustain a larger predator population. In turn, the larger number of predators can diminish the number of prey. Predator and prey populations may vary cyclically, as shown in the graph below. Predation and herbivory (feeding on plants) are both +/– relationships.

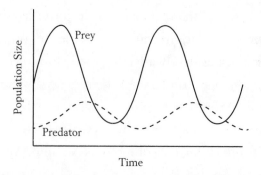

Competition

Competition may be interspecific (between different species) or intraspecific (between members of the same species). Both types of competition drive natural selection.

Interspecific competition results when two species in an ecosystem share overlapping niches and therefore rely on the same limited set of resources. The competitive exclusion principle states that two species cannot share the same niche. Interspecific competition may result in the population of one species rapidly surpassing or even replacing that of the other.

In some cases, one or both species may evolve to occupy different niches. For example, they may evolve to feed on different food sources or to nest in different trees. This divergence in traits due to competitive exclusion is known as *character displacement*.

Keystone and Invasive Species

A keystone species is one that has widespread, detrimental effects on the entire community when its population declines. A keystone species helps to keep the populations of other predators or herbivores in check, thereby increasing the species diversity of the ecosystem. For example, sea otters are a keystone species in the kelp forests of the Pacific Northwest. By feeding on and suppressing the populations of kelp-eating sea urchins, the otters allow kelp density to remain high. This is beneficial for the other species that depend on kelp-forest habitats. In contrast, declining sea otter populations cause sea urchins to multiply and reduce the density of kelps, negatively affecting the kelp-forest community.

Keystone species help to maintain the species diversity of an ecosystem by maintaining the structure of a community. In contrast, ecological relationships may be disrupted by invasive species, which are often nonnative, or introduced from a different ecosystem. An invasive species usually faces little predation and finds abundant resources in its new home. Therefore, its population increases rapidly, often to the detriment of other species.

Animal Behavior

Ecologists are interested in the behavior of animal species, which often determines the niche a species may occupy and represents adaptation to the community and environment. The study of animal behavior is known as *ethology*. Behavior ranges from simple and innate to complex and learned.

- *Fixed action patterns* are sequences of behaviors in response to external stimuli.
- *Imprinting* is an innate response to an environmental stimulus, such as when a duckling follows its mother. Imprinting occurs only during a sensitive period in a young animal's development and happens in response to whatever stimulus the environment provides (which is the reason ducklings can imprint on humans).

- *Habituation* is the *loss* of a response to a repeated, harmless stimulus.
- *Territoriality* and *aggression* toward members of the same species allow an individual animal to monopolize the resources in an area. Often, only one sex of a species will defend a territory, while the opposite sex is allowed to move about freely.
- *Migration* is the coordinated, seasonal movement of a population from one ecosystem to a second ecosystem.
- *Mating rituals* may involve complex movements or displays (for example, the elaborate nests of bower birds). Mate choice and mating are often influenced by pheromones, chemicals that signal and influence other individuals of the same species. Sound (for example, birdsongs) is also used to attract or signal to potential mates.

Review Questions

1. Which of these best describes the population growth shown in the graph?

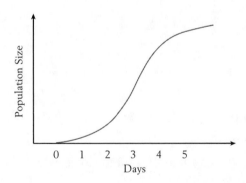

A. On day 1, the resources of the population limit its growth.

B. On day 2, the birthrate per individual is greater than on day 1.

C. On day 3, the population size is equal to K.

D. On day 4, the curve is most similar an exponential growth curve.

E. On day 5, the number of deaths approaches the number of births.

2. Compared to a country that has undergone demographic transition, a country that has NOT undergone this transition has which of the following?

    I.   Higher birthrate
    II. Lower death rate
    III. Higher growth rate

    A. I only
    B. I and II
    C. I and III
    D. II and III
    E. I, II, and III

3. Which of these examples is represented by the Type III curve shown?

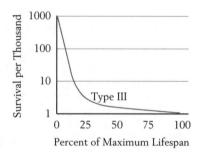

    A. Most redwood seeds are eaten, but a few produce trees that live for decades.
    B. The growth of a bamboo stand slows as space becomes limited.
    C. The probability of a squid being captured and eaten is independent of its age.
    D. The growth of a bacterial colony increases as new individuals are produced.
    E. A few pandas are born in a population, but they survive through adulthood.

4. Which of these relationships results in harm to one of the species involved?

    I.   Commensalism
    II. Predation
    III. Herbivory

    A. I only
    B. III only
    C. I and II
    D. II and III
    E. I, II, and III

5. All of these are likely consequences of removing a keystone species from an ecosystem, EXCEPT a/an

    A. decrease in species diversity
    B. increase in other community populations
    C. increase in the types of ecological interactions
    D. decrease in the carrying capacity for most of the community
    E. increase in the rate of growth of one or more populations

Answer Explanations

1. **E.** Logistic population growth has different rates of increase over time. Growth rate decreases as the population size approaches the carrying capacity (K) of the ecosystem. Early logistic growth resembles exponential growth, in which the per capita rate of increase is constant.

2. **C.** Demographic transition is characterized by lower birthrates, death rates, and population growth.

3. **A.** A type III survivorship curve characterizes species that produce a large number of offspring with only a few of the species surviving into adulthood.

4.   **D**. Predation and herbivory, along with parasitism, result in harm to one of the species involved. Commensalism benefits one species while leaving the other largely unaffected.

5.   **E**. Keystone species maintain the structure of a community. Removing a keystone species is not likely to increase the number of ecological interactions, because the species diversity of the community also decreases.

Review Chapter 15:
Ecology, Part 2

An ecosystem consists of the biological (community) and physical factors of an area, as well as their interactions. The term *ecosystem* is not specific to a small or large scale—for example, both a biome and a puddle can be considered ecosystems. Ecologists are particularly interested in ecosystem processes that lead to the cycling of nutrients and the flow of energy. The nutrients in an ecosystem must originate from some other part of the ecosystem or from another ecosystem on Earth. Nutrients are continuously recycled. In contrast, energy continually flows from the Sun to Earth. From Earth, energy is lost to space.

Trophic Levels

Ecosystem communities are organized into trophic, or feeding, levels. The most important trophic level consists of producers, or photosynthetic autotrophs (plants, algae, and cyanobacteria). These organisms convert inorganic carbon from carbon dioxide and other elements into organic molecules that make up their bodies: carbohydrates, proteins, fats, and nucleic acids. Producers make up the base, or lowest trophic level, of an ecosystem.

The higher trophic levels contain heterotrophs, or consumers, which obtain their nutrients from other organisms. Primary consumers (herbivores) feed on producers. Secondary consumers feed on primary consumers, tertiary consumers feed on secondary consumers, and so on. All consumers ultimately depend on producers to convert matter into a form they can use.

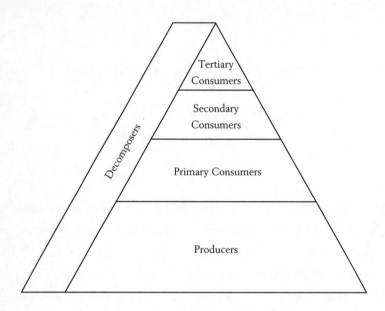

Decomposers are heterotrophs that feed on nonliving organic matter, such as dead plants and animal waste. Decomposers may also be called *detritivores* (detritus eaters) or *saprophytes* (organisms that grow on the material they digest, such as fungi). Decomposers include many prokaryotes, fungi, insects, and earthworms. Their essential function is to break organic matter into simple, inorganic compounds that can be used by producers. Decomposers help to recycle the nutrients in an ecosystem.

Biogeochemical Cycles

Biogeochemical cycles describe how materials move between the living and nonliving components of an ecosystem. Plants convert simple inorganic compounds to organic matter, which then enters higher trophic levels as it is consumed by heterotrophs. Decomposers recycle the organic matter in an ecosystem back into simple inorganic compounds.

These compounds enter the air, soil, and water, where they once again become available to producers. The major contribution of living things to the water cycle is the transpiration of water through plant leaves, which enters the atmosphere. The biogeochemical cycles of two important elements, carbon and nitrogen, are described below.

The Carbon Cycle

Photosynthesis uses carbon dioxide gas in the air to produce organic, carbon-containing molecules, such as glucose. This carbon remains in the form of an organic compound until it is digested by a consumer. The consumer uses the organic carbon as fuel for cellular respiration, converts each carbon atom to a molecule of carbon dioxide, and releases it into the atmosphere. Decomposition also moves the carbon from organic matter to carbon dioxide in the atmosphere.

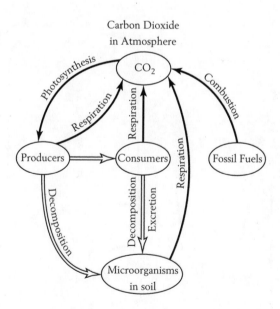

The addition of carbon dioxide from the atmosphere by respiration and decomposition is nearly balanced by its removal via photosynthesis. An additional source of atmospheric carbon is the combustion (burning) of fossil fuels, which are derived from fossilized organic matter.

The Nitrogen Cycle

Although 80% of the atmosphere consists of nitrogen gas (N_2), this inorganic form of nitrogen is biologically available to very few organisms. However, all living things require nitrogen, which is a component of proteins and nucleic acids. Consumers obtain nitrogen in the form of organic compounds in the foods they eat. Plants and algae cannot use atmospheric nitrogen gas directly; they can use the inorganic ions ammonium (NH_4^+) and nitrate (NO_3^-).

Atmospheric nitrogen must be converted to one of these compounds before it can be used by producers and consumers. This is accomplished through nitrogen *fixation*, the chemical conversion of nitrogen gas to forms that are usable by producers. This is the role of nitrogen-fixing soil bacteria. Some nitrogen is also fixed by lightning and much is fixed by the industrial production of fertilizers.

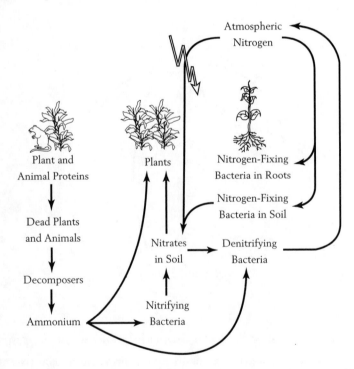

Bacteria may also carry out nitrification (conversion of ammonia to nitrate), denitrification (conversion of nitrate to nitrogen gas), or ammonification (conversion of organic compounds to ammonium). However, more nitrogen is removed from the atmosphere by fixation than is replaced by denitrifying bacteria.

Disruptions of Nutrient Cycles: Eutrophication

Producers depend on large quantities of nitrogen, phosphorus, and other elements from the surrounding soil or water. The scarcity of one or more of these elements limits the growth of plants or phytoplankton, which can only grow as much as the single most limiting nutrient allows.

The unintentional addition of nutrients can disrupt aquatic ecosystems, a process called *eutrophication*. For example, nitrogen and phosphorus compounds added to soils in the form of fertilizers can be carried, via run-off or other processes, into bodies of water. Sewage from waste-treatment plants and livestock farms can also increase nutrients in lakes and rivers.

Because nitrogen and phosphorus are required by phytoplankton, they can cause an increase in phytoplankton growth called a *bloom*. A bloom can turn an oligotrophic lake, in which photosynthesis is low, into a productive eutrophic lake. The increase in photosynthesis may initially raise the level of dissolved oxygen. However, the added oxygen is used during the night by cellular respiration. In addition, as the added nutrients are depleted, the phytoplankton die off and feed decomposers. The increase in decomposition further reduces the level of oxygen in the water. Oxygen depletion can lead to the deaths of fishes and other consumers and may, in some instances, create an enduring "dead zone" of low-oxygen water.

Plant Symbiotic Associations

Some plants, particularly legumes and their relatives, form a mutualistic association with nitrogen-fixing bacteria. The plants have swellings, called *nodules*, along their roots. Each nodule houses the nitrogen-fixing bacteria, *Rhyzobium*, which converts atmospheric nitrogen gas into ammonium. In return, the plant provides the bacteria with energy-rich carbon compounds.

Plants also form associations with root fungi, forming root structures called *mycorrhizae*. The fungus forms strands called *hyphae*, which increase the surface area through which water and minerals can be absorbed and actively take up minerals from the soil. Again, the plant provides the mycorrhyzal fungi with organic carbon compounds for energy.

Energy Flow and Trophic Levels

Unlike matter, which is continually recycled through Earth's systems, energy continuously reaches Earth from the Sun and dissipates as heat. Of the Sun's energy, only a small portion is incorporated into ecosystems. Producers (plants, algae, and photosynthetic bacteria) harness the energy in sunlight and convert this electromagnetic energy to a form that consumers can use—the chemical energy in food.

Of the vast amount of solar energy that reaches Earth, producers harness only a fraction of a percent. Some of this energy is used by the producers themselves. What is left is called *net primary production* (NPP) and represents the maximum amount of energy available to the rest of the ecosystem. NPP can be considered in terms of energy or in terms of biomass, the dry weight of vegetation. NPP is equal to the yearly *increase* in the biomass of producers in an ecosystem.

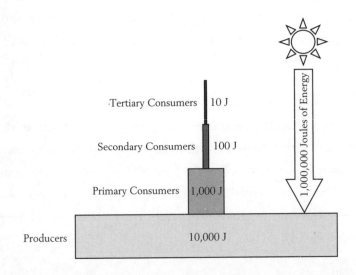

The energy stored in the biomass of producers is transferred to higher trophic levels. A primary consumer, such as the gazelle, uses the energy in grasses for metabolism, locomotion, and other processes involving cellular respiration. A small portion of the energy is used for growth, adding to the biomass of this trophic level. When the gazelle's biomass is consumed by a cheetah, energy again enters a higher trophic level.

Typically, only between 1% and 20% of the energy stored in one trophic level is transferred to the next trophic level; a common estimate is 10%. Of the energy entering an ecosystem via producers, only a small percentage reaches the highest trophic level.

Biomes

Earth's ecosystems are classified into *biomes*, or regions of similar organisms and processes. Biomes are characterized by abiotic factors, such as energy (light and temperature), water, and nutrient availability. Biotic factors, such as vegetation type and abundance, also distinguish biomes. Biomes differ in their NPP, largely due to abiotic differences. Biomes can be aquatic or terrestrial.

Aquatic Biomes

The typical producers in aquatic biomes are algae and photosynthetic bacteria, which make up floating phytoplankton. (Phytoplankton, the base of the aquatic energy pyramid, may have less biomass than zooplankton, the level of primary consumers. However, new plankton are rapidly produced, and biomass is added at the rate it is consumed.)

The NPP of aquatic biomes is limited by the penetration of light. Enough light energy penetrates the upper photic zones of lakes and ocean for photosynthesis to take place. However, little light reaches the lower aphotic zone.

Terrestrial Biomes

Terrestrial biomes are distinguished by climate, which varies with latitude and elevation. Latitudes located closer to the equator receive more solar energy and therefore have higher temperatures and longer growing seasons than higher latitudes. Along with energy, water is another determining abiotic difference among terrestrial biomes. Major biomes are described below.

- *Rain forest.* Characterized by high annual rainfall. Tropical (equatorial) rain forests are warm year-round, while temperate rain forests have mild seasonal variation. Broadleaf trees form a dense canopy.
- *Temperate deciduous forest.* This biome has less precipitation than rain forests, with precipitation falling year-round. Temperature varies with the season, and broadleaf trees lose their leaves each year.
- *Savannah/grassland.* Characterized by seasonal precipitation. Ground is covered by grasses and forbs. Temperature varies seasonally in grassland, with cold winters. Temperature is warm throughout the year in the savannah. The savannah includes sparse trees and fire-adapted plants.
- *Chaparral.* Characterized by mild, wet winters and arid summers. Features small trees, shrubs, grasses, and nonwoody plants. Plants adapt to drought and fire.
- *Desert.* Arid biomes located in belts at 30° latitude north and south of equator, due to global convection currents. Characterized by infrequent rainfall, large daily variations in temperature, and sparse, desert-adapted vegetation, such as succulent plants.
- *Taiga (coniferous forest).* This biome is relatively arid, with long, very cold winters. Landscape is dominated by conifers.
- *Tundra.* This biome occurs at high latitudes and altitudes. Characterized by low-growing plants, such as mosses, grasses, and shrubs, and a permanently frozen soil layer *(permafrost)*.

Plant Adaptations to Hot and Arid Climates

Succulent plants, such as cacti, often have a watertight cuticle and are able to store water. Many succulent plants have modified leaves or carry out photosynthesis in stems instead of leaves. Plants have also evolved metabolic adaptations for preventing water loss.

In response to high rates of evaporation from the leaf, plants close the stomata (leaf openings). Although this prevents water loss, it also prevents required carbon dioxide from entering the leaf. Low carbon dioxide and high oxygen levels lead to an inefficient and unnecessary process called photorespiration. Some plants have evolved adaptations to prevent photorespiration. These adaptations alter photosynthesis and allow plants to conserve water.

Many grasses use C_4 photosynthesis, which fixes carbon in two stages. First, carbon dioxide is incorporated into a four-carbon molecule. This compound is then transported to cells deeper within the leaf, which carry out the Calvin cycle (conversion of carbon dioxide to glucose). By increasing the amount of carbon in the cells where it is needed, C_4 plants avoid photorespiration.

Some succulent plants have evolved crassulacean acid metabolism, or CAM. CAM plants fix carbon at night, when evaporation decreases and stomata can be kept open. The carbon is converted to compounds that are stored in the cells until the daytime, when light energy allows them to be used in photosynthesis.

Review Questions

1. Which processes remove nitrogen from the atmosphere?

    I.   Fertilizer production
    II.   Eutrophication
    III. Nitrogen fixation
    IV.   Denitrification

    A. I and II
    B. I and III
    C. I and IV
    D. II and III
    E. II and IV

2. The net primary production (NPP) of a stable lake ecosystem is roughly equal to the amount of

    A. phytoplankton present in the photic zone
    B. phytoplankton consumed by heterotrophs
    C. dissolved nutrients used by phytoplankton
    D. dissolved oxygen used by phytoplankton
    E. dissolved oxygen used by all consumers

3. Which type of biome is found at the lowest latitudes?

    A. Rain forest
    B. Desert
    C. Chaparral
    D. Tundra
    E. Taiga

4. Which of these are plant adaptations to hot, dry climates?

    I.   CAM
    II.   Mycorrhizae
    III. C_4 photosynthesis

    A. I only
    B. II only
    C. I and II
    D. I and III
    E. I, II, and III

Answer Explanations

1. **B.** Atmospheric nitrogen gas is used to produce fertilizers and is fixed by nitrogen-fixing bacteria. Eutrophication does not remove nitrogen from the atmosphere, and denitrification returns nitrogen gas to the atmosphere.

2. **B**. NPP is not equal to the total biomass of producers, but to the amount of biomass that is added. In a stable lake, the added phytoplankton biomass will equal that consumed by zooplankton.

3. **A**. Tropical rain forests occur in regions close to the equator. In contrast, deserts occur about 30° latitude both north and south of the equator.

4. **D**. CAM and C_4 photosynthesis are adaptations to hot, dry environments. In contrast, mycorrhizae are present in nearly all land plants.

THE BIG PICTURE: HOW TO PREPARE YEAR-ROUND

No matter how far in the future you plan to take the SAT Biology E/M Subject Test, the time to start preparing is *now*. And this part of your book is here to help. Here you will learn how to register for the test, make the most of your preparation time both in the classroom and outside of it, and manage the stress a test of this magnitude may bring. As you get closer to your test date, make sure you are using all of the materials provided in this book. That way, when the day of the test arrives, you'll be ready to earn your top score!

Step 1: Get Registered

The SAT Biology E/M Subject Test is offered several times a year. According to the College Board, the majority of students take the SAT for the first time in the spring of junior year and again during the fall of senior year. Taking the test twice gives you the opportunity to increase your score, as most students do better the second time around. The

College Board also recommends taking the test as soon as possible after completing your course of study in the subject, because the material will be fresher in your mind.

Test locations and registration requirements vary by location, so visit the College Board website (go to www.collegeboard.org and search for SAT II, Biology E/M Subject Test, or follow the links) as soon as possible to learn how to register for the test and where can take it. You also want to check admissions requirements with the colleges and universities you're interested in attending; if you plan to pursue a degree in the sciences, you may be required or recommended to take one test or the other, or to achieve a particular score.

Note that SAT Subject Tests are available to homeschooled students as well as those in traditional high schools. Advance registration is required, and you may need to pay a fee if you do not register far enough in advance. Check the College Board's website for the information that applies in your circumstances.

Here are some important points to keep in mind as you get started.

- **Do you know what you need to know?** We can't emphasize enough how important it is to make sure you have accurate information about this test. Refer to the College Board's official website (www.collegeboard.org) for current information about the test, including eligibility, late testing, special accommodations for students with disabilities, and reduced testing fees for low-income students. This site also allows you to register (and gives alternative registration options, such as how to register by phone or mail) and tells you how your score will be reported to the colleges and universities you're interested in attending. Don't depend on getting this information from anyone else! Since you purchased this book, obviously you're interested in doing well on the examination. So don't risk losing points by not knowing what you need to know. Time spent on early research can pay off for you down the road.

- **It's all about the timing.** The tricky thing about an examination like the SAT Biology E/M Subject Test is that you really don't want to take it more than twice, and you do want to take it somewhere close to your relevant coursework. You should try to take the test once in your junior year and a second time in your senior year. If you're worried about coordinating the testing date around your studies, don't be! The test is actually offered several times a year; as long as you do some advance planning, you should be able to get a test date that works for you.

- **Be proactive.** If you're *not* enrolled in a suitable class at school, take the initiative! Do some reading to refresh yourself on the topic. Borrow some suitable books from the library. Review the study guide carefully and determine exactly what you need to know.

- **You don't have to choose your emphasis when you register, but you should still know in advance what you're doing.** As you know, you will take either the Biology-E Test or the Biology-M Test. You don't have to select the specific test when you register for Biology E/M, but it IS better if you know in advance which test you plan to take. The tests are NOT designed with one more difficult than the other, and most colleges don't actually care which emphasis you choose, as long as you do well on the test. Therefore, select the emphasis that you feel most confident about, and go in knowing what you want to do.

- **Remember, it's worth it!** You might be worried about your anxiety level for this test. You might be thinking that, in the overall scheme of senior year and college prep, this test is less important than others you need to worry about. You may be concerned about not doing well. If your thought process is running in this direction, slow down for a minute! Consider how little you have to lose if you score poorly on the test and how much you have to gain if you do well. Plus, you may do better than you expect if you make the best use of study time and material at your disposal. (Consider especially the resources in this book!) Even if, after all is said and done, you *don't* do well, remember, a low score doesn't have to be devastating—you can take the test again if you wish. Plus, if you're concerned, the Score Choice service allows you to choose the particular scores you want to share with the colleges of your choice.

Step 2: Become an Expert Student

To do well on the test, you must retain a lot of information both in and out of the classroom. You will have to work hard and study. Did you know that studying is a discipline in and of itself that many people just don't know how to do well? It's true. Even the smartest people need to learn *how* to study in order to maximize their ability to learn.

One of the most critical study skills involves notes. More specifically, it involves taking effective notes rather than just writing down everything your teacher says. Don't underestimate how important good note taking is both during class *and* while you're studying alone or with a partner. Good note taking serves several purposes. First (and most obviously), note taking is important for making sure you have recorded the key points being made by your teacher (or your study partner). Since this person is very familiar with the material and the test, he or she knows where you should focus your time, so you should glean as much knowledge as you possibly can. Second, effective note taking is important because the process of working on notes can actually help you retain the material. For example, the deceptively simple act of writing and rewriting reinforces your memory just from doing the activity. Additionally, writing in conjunction with listening or reading helps to reinforce the information, making it more likely that you will remember it.

Here are some tips for taking great notes.

- **Listen actively.** The first key to taking good notes is to practice *active listening*—that is, listening in a structured way to understand and evaluate what's being said. Active listeners are not distracted, thinking about other things, nor are they considering what they will say next (in the classroom, this means opening up your mind rather than thinking about some question you might ask your teacher). Active listening also does not involve writing down every single thing the teacher says. Rather, it means listening in a structured way so that you hear the main ideas, pay attention to cues that impart meaning, and keep your eyes on the speaker (not on your notebook).

- **Listen for main ideas.** Before you even begin the note-taking process, consider the topic under discussion and be ready to organize your notes around that topic. Is it a person, place, or hypothesis? Is it a particular era or concept? Do some prethinking about the topic and work from that angle. Also listen for transitions into new topics as the teacher works his or way through the material.

- **Pay attention to cues.** If you're taking notes in class, certain words and phrases tend to reflect the way the discussion is organized. For example, the teacher usually starts with an introduction, and this introduction generally provides the framework around how the topic will be treated. For example, "Today we will trace the origins of early primate species and think critically about the physical diversity within modern human populations." Listen for transition words such as "next," "the following," and numbered or bulleted lists.

- **Don't just stare at your notebook.** Information is conveyed by speakers in a number of ways, many of them nonverbal. Keep an eye on the instructor's body language and expressions. These are the type of nonverbal cues that will help you to determine what's important and what's not.

- **What do good notes look like?** Good notes are not just a jumbled mass of everything. It's unrealistic and ineffective to try to write down everything there is to say about a topic. Instead, you should learn to focus on key words and main ideas. Here are some tips on how to proceed.

- **Start with a clean sheet.** Indicate today's date and the main/ primary topic. This will jog your memory later on when you study these notes.

- **If the instructor is using slides, don't just copy the slide word for word.** Instead, jot down the title of the slide and the key idea, concept, or overall topic under discussion (this should be apparent from either the title of the slide deck, the title of the slide itself, of the instructor's introduction).

- **Listen actively to your instructor's treatment of the material and his or her points of emphasis**. Try to *really listen* to what is being said. Then, as your teacher makes important points, write them down in bullet-point/summarized fashion. Don't worry too much about organization in the moment. Just do your best to capture the discussion in a way that makes sense to you.

- **If you're confused about something, ask for clarification.** Many students make the mistake of not asking for help when the teacher makes a statement that is confusing or unclear. Sometimes even the best teachers go too fast or fail to transition you through the material plainly. It's much better to ask for help than to write down a bunch of information that makes no sense to you later.

- **This is an important and often-overlooked point: once class is over, *rewrite* or *retype* your notes, using the opportunity to also fold in information from your textbook or other resources.** This is your opportunity to bring real organization, clarity, and understanding to the material. You should rewrite or retype your notes regularly (preferably daily, but if that's not possible, at least weekly). You'll be amazed at how much more sense the material makes if you take the time to look at it critically and rework it in a way that makes sense to you on a regular basis.

- **Take notes from your books and other resources as well as your class notes—see the section on the next page titled "How do you** read to understand?" This test covers *a lot* of material. Paying attention to what gets attention in resources can help you focus.

○ **Review your notes before class every day.** Doing so serves as a reminder of where you are chronologically and also helps you to transition from concept to concept and era to era. Work mindfully to make connections among the material that you're learning. Those connections will serve you well later.

• **How do you read to understand?** Material such as this book and your class textbook can make the difference between a passing and failing grade or between a so-so and an excellent score. However, you need to understand what you're reading so that you can supplement your class notes.

○ **Do a complete read-through.** Start with the objectives of the chapter. Review the questions at the end.

○ **Map out the main ideas.** Once you've read through the material and have an overall understanding, write down the main ideas and leave space to fill in details. Wherever possible, do so in your own words. Avoid copying text exactly from the book. Paraphrasing the material in your own words helps you engage with the material and facilitates your learning.

○ **Reread the material.** Once you have the main ideas mapped out, you should reread the material with an eye toward filling in details under each of the main ideas.

○ **Fill in the details.** Now that you've reread, write details under each main idea—again, do not copy the words exactly from the book, but use your own words so that you retain the information. Use details from the book or other resource AND from your class notes.

○ **Put the book aside and read through your notes.** Do you understand what you've written? Have you accurately represented the main ideas? Did you fill in the appropriate level of detail?

○ **Review, review, review.** Read your notes over and over again. That's how you get the information to stick.

Step 3: Create a Realistic Study Plan

If you're like many students with challenging classes, extracurricular activities, and other priorities, you may have only a limited amount of time to review for this test. This section will help you get the most out of your limited test preparation time and make it really count. You need a plan specifically for you—one that addresses *your* needs and considers the time you have available. No two people will have exactly the same plan or use this book in exactly the same way. To develop a personalized test prep plan, you'll need to identify your weak points and then allocate time to address them efficiently and effectively.

Here are the three basic steps to creating a personalized test prep plan.

1. **Identify your weak points.** Start by taking the diagnostic test in this book. This will show you what you're up against. It will also help you get a feel for the test and identify the subject areas where you need to focus. Based on your performance, you can prioritize the subjects to review, starting with the areas in which you are weakest. If your time is limited or if you feel you're not ready to take a complete practice test, focus your review by skimming the diagnostic test and identifying those areas where you have the most difficulty with understanding.

2. **Develop a review plan and a schedule.** Figure out how much time you can devote each week to test preparation and reserve specific blocks of time for this purpose. Create a written schedule that includes specific time slots and activities or content areas for review. This will help you pace yourself to get through all of the material you want to review. You'll likely find there are content areas or question types you want to focus on more than others. Also make sure your plan includes time to master test-taking strategies and actually take the practice tests.

3. **Marshal your self-discipline.** The hard part about a plan for test prep is making yourself stick to it. Schedule your test prep time actively in your calendar. Don't let it get pushed aside by more

seemingly urgent activities. You've come a long way; don't blow the test by failing to prepare for it. Develop a plan for your needs in the time you have available and then stick with it.

For some people, it helps to have a study partner. A partner may make it easier to hold to the schedule and may also help you to study more effectively. You and your partner can quiz each other, share information, and exchange ideas. However, for other people, having a study partner makes it harder to stay on topic and focus on studying. Try to figure out, based on past experience, how you can best enforce your study plan and most effectively use your time.

Step 4: Use All the Resources at Your Disposal

This book is an excellent way to prepare for this test. It includes not only the diagnostic test but two *full* practice tests. Each test has unique questions, so you get the opportunity to address all different areas of the content in all different ways.

Additionally, another practice test is available to you free of charge at mymaxscore.com.

Check out the website for the College Board (www.collegeboard.org). At this site, you can find actual released tests that are no longer in circulation, along with general information about the test and testing advice.

You'll also find lots of other test resources in your library, at the local bookstore, or online. Look around to see what's available and figure out ways to work that material into your study time if you can.

Good luck! Happy studying!

This book contains two practice tests. Visit mymaxscore.com to download your free third practice test with answers and explanations.

SAT Biology E/M Subject Test Practice Test 1

SAT Biology E/M Subject Test
Time—60 minutes
80 questions

Directions: The set of lettered choices below refers to the numbered questions or statements immediately following it. Select the one lettered choice that best fits each statement. A choice may be used once, more than once, or not at all in the set.

Questions 1–4 refer to the following organs.

    A.   Thyroid
    B.   Pancreas
    C.   Parathyroid
    D.   Adrenal medulla
    E.   Anterior pituitary

1.   This organ secretes growth hormone (GH).

2.   This organ secretes thyroxine.

3. This organ secretes the hormone responsible for the "flight-or-flight" response.

4. This organ secretes a hormone that causes the liver to break down glycogen.

Questions 5–7 refer to the following phases of meiosis.

    A.   Anaphase I
    B.   Prophase I
    C.   Anaphase II
    D.   Prophase II
    E.   Metaphase I

5. Crossing over occurs in this phase.

6. Homologous chromosomes separate in this phase.

7. Sister chromatids separate in this phase.

Questions 8–10 refer to the following diagram of floral structures.

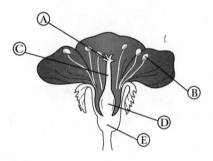

8. The site of fertilization

9. The site of pollen production

10. The site of pollen tube development

Questions 11–14 refer to the following.

   A. Xylem

   B. Phloem

   C. Cambium

   D. Bark

   E. Pith

11. Tissue that conducts sugars downward from the leaves

12. Tissue that conducts water upward from the roots

13. Tissue that gives rise to all vascular tissue

14. Ground tissue with no specialized function

Directions: Each of the questions or incomplete statements below is followed by five suggested answers or completions. Some questions pertain to a set that refers to a laboratory or experimental situation. For each question, select the one choice that is the best answer to the question.

15. Which tissue, formed during the gastrulation phase of embryonic development, later differentiates to form the nervous system?

   A. Archenteron

   B. Blastopore

   C. Ectoderm

   D. Endoderm

   E. Mesoderm

16. What is the role of mRNA in protein synthesis?

   A. To make up the structure of the ribosome
   B. To carry amino acids to the ribosome
   C. To catalyze bonds between nucleotides
   D. To serve as a template for the synthesis of DNA
   E. To carry information determining amino acid sequence

17. Oxygen gas (O_2) is produced by plants and algae. What is the source of oxygen atoms in these molecules?

   A. Water
   B. Glucose
   C. Carbon dioxide
   D. Atmospheric oxygen
   E. Atmospheric nitrogen

18. Which of the following describes a behavior of organisms of the same species?

   A. Periodical cicadas that emerge the same year
   B. Fish that become fertile during different seasons
   C. Ungulates that mate frequently and yield sterile offspring
   D. Rodents that mate frequently and yield no viable offspring
   E. Tropical birds that court their mates with differing dances or songs

19. A mature gymnosperm will possess all of the following EXCEPT

   A. seeds
   B. leaves
   C. flowers
   D. vascular tissue
   E. woody growth

20. Which of the following patterns of inheritance describes interactions between multiple genes?

    A. Epistasis
    B. Sex linkage
    C. Codominance
    D. Simple dominance
    E. Homozygous recessive

21. Which situation describes an incidence of artificial selection acting upon a single population?

    A. Weak prey animals successfully hunted by predators
    B. Excessive rains providing additional water resources
    C. Males choosing the healthiest females to reproduce with
    D. An early warm front resulting in premature plant blooming
    E. Insecticides eliminating all crop pests except resistant individuals

22. The following change is an example of which type of mutation?

    Original DNA sequence: ATGGA–AGC
    New DNA sequence: ATTGACAGC

    I.   Point mutation
    II. Deletion
    III. Frameshift

    A. I only
    B. II only
    C. III only
    D. I and II
    E. I and III

23. With a limited amount of chemical substrate, all of the following factors could directly affect an enzyme's activity EXCEPT

   A. pH level
   B. inhibitors
   C. temperature
   D. enzyme cofactors
   E. enzyme concentration

24. The loop of Henle is a structure within the urinary tract responsible for reabsorbing water. Compared to a terrestrial species, how might this structure appear in a freshwater aquatic species?

   A. Absent
   B. Longer
   C. Shorter
   D. Withered
   E. Thinner

25. The coyote, *Canis latrans*, belongs to each of the taxonomic groups in the answer choices below. Which group's members are most closely related to each other?

   A. Order Carnivora
   B. Class Mammalia
   C. Subfamily Vertebrata
   D. Family Canidae
   E. Phylum Chordata

26. Terrestrial snakes and aquatic eels have a similar elongated morphology. However, they are not closely related evolutionarily. Their resemblance is an example of

   A. analogy
   B. homology
   C. speciation
   D. divergent evolution
   E. artificial selection

27. Edward's syndrome is the result of an additional 18th chromosome present in a fertilized embryo. Which of the following events could lead to the presence of this additional chromosome in a zygote?

   A. Crossing over in meiosis I
   B. Nondisjunction in meiosis II
   C. A deletion during meiosis II
   D. A deletion during meiosis I
   E. Replication error in meiosis II

28. The steps of protein synthesis and modification take place in several different locations throughout the cell. What is the proper order of these locations, from start to finish?

   I.   Ribosome
   II. Nucleus
   III. Golgi apparatus
   IV. Endoplasmic reticulum

   A. I, II, III, IV
   B. II, I, IV, III
   C. III, II, IV, I
   D. II, I, III, IV
   E. IV, III, II, I

29. A somatic cell of the common octopus (*Octopus vulgaris*) has 56 chromosomes. What number of chromosomes will an octopus gamete contain?

    A. 14
    B. 28
    C. 56
    D. 112
    E. 168

30. A genetic mutation results in a DNA sequence that continues to synthesize the same protein, at the same rate as a nonmutated sequence. This mutation would be BEST classified as a

    A. deletion
    B. insertion
    C. missense mutation
    D. nonsense mutation
    E. silent mutation

31. A unicellular prokaryote belongs to which kingdom?

    A. Animalia
    B. Eubacteria
    C. Fungi
    D. Plantae
    E. Protista

32. Which of the following organisms has the highest evolutionary fitness?

    A. A cheetah that catches the most prey
    B. A fox that successfully avoids predators
    C. A tortoise that has lived for over 100 years
    D. A wolf that recovers quickly from a wound
    E. A gorilla that reproduces several times

33. Flowering plants are divided into two subgroups, monocots and dicots. These groups differ significantly in all of the following characteristics EXCEPT

    A. seed structure
    B. floral parts
    C. leaf venation
    D. stomata structure
    E. vascular organization

34. An organism produces many offspring each reproductive season, only a few of which survive.

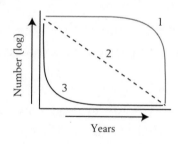

The survivorship curve for this organism can BEST be described as

    A. closely matching curve 1
    B. closely matching curve 2
    C. closely matching curve 3
    D. fitting between curves 1 and 2
    E. fitting between curves 2 and 3

35. An association between two organisms in which one benefits and neither is harmed is called

    A. commensalism
    B. mutualism
    C. parasitism
    D. predation
    E. omnivory

36. Centrifugation is a laboratory technique used to separate materials by their relative masses. More massive substances will sink to the bottom of a test tube while those with less mass will float to the top. A cell culture is centrifuged. Which cellular organelle would be concentrated at the top of the centrifuged mixture?

    A. Nuclei
    B. Endoplasmic reticulum
    C. Mitochondria
    D. Ribosomes
    E. Membrane-bound proteins

37. Which of the following shows the proper order of blood flow through the heart, entering from the vena cava?

    A. Left atrium → left ventricle → right ventricle → right atrium
    B. Left ventricle → left atrium → right atrium → right ventricle
    C. Right atrium → right ventricle → left atrium → left ventricle
    D. Right ventricle → right atrium → left atrium → left ventricle
    E. Right ventricle → right atrium → left ventricle → left atrium

38. What would happen to a blood cell moved from an isotonic solution to a hypertonic solution?

    A. The cell would swell.
    B. The cell would shrivel up.
    C. The cell would immediately lyse.
    D. The cell membrane would be reinforced.
    E. Nothing; the cell would be in equilibrium.

39. Triticale is a hybrid of wheat (*Triticum turgidum*) and rye (*Secale cereale*), bred to demonstrate the most desirable characteristics of both species. The resulting hybrid possesses four chromosome sets from the maternal wheat plant and two sets from the paternal rye plant. What is the ploidy of these hybrids?

    A. Diploid ($2n$)
    B. Triploid ($3n$)
    C. Tetraploid ($4n$)
    D. Hexaploid ($6n$)
    E. Octoploid ($8n$)

40. A group of biologists wishes to isolate an antifreeze gene found in a cold-water species of fish and introduce it into the genome of a different organism. Which of the following techniques must they use?

    A. Cloning
    B. Artificial selection
    C. Selective breeding
    D. Genetic engineering
    E. Sexual recombination

41. If the allele for dark-colored hair is dominant over the allele for light-colored hair, which is LEAST likely?

    A. A light-haired couple produces a baby with dark hair.
    B. A dark-haired couple produces a baby with light hair.
    C. A light-haired woman and a dark-haired man produce a light-haired baby.
    D. A dark-haired woman and a light-haired man produce a light-haired baby.
    E. A dark-haired woman and a light-haired man produce a dark-haired baby.

42. Which of the following are in order of least complex to most complex, in terms of the amount of genetic information they carry?

    I.   Chromosome
    II. Base pair
    III. Codon
    IV. Gene

    A. I → II → III → IV
    B. II → III → I → IV
    C. III → II → I → IV
    D. II → III → IV → I
    E. II → IV → II → I

43. An organism that demonstrates radial symmetry and an exoskeleton would be classified into which phylum?

    A. Arthropoda
    B. Cnidaria
    C. Echinodermata
    D. Mollusca
    E. Porifera

44. Crabs and lobsters are both members of the suborder Pleocyemata. Both possess a tail; however, in the crab, this structure is very small and not used. This structure can be considered an example of all of the following EXCEPT

    A. convergent evolution
    B. vestigial structure
    C. divergent evolution
    D. genetic fitness
    E. homologous structure

45. A human hereditary disorder that is present only in males is most likely

    A. maternally inherited
    B. a Y-linked trait
    C. an autosomal recessive trait
    D. an X-linked recessive trait
    E. an X-linked dominant trait

46. What prevents ions from crossing the plasma membrane via simple diffusion?

    A. Ions are too large.
    B. Ions carry a charge.
    C. Ions are hydrophobic.
    D. Ions do not produce a concentration difference.
    E. Ions cannot interact with membrane-bound proteins.

47. An ecosystem undergoes a sudden drastic change that now favors organisms with an extreme phenotype. This is an example of

    A. genetic drift
    B. founder effect
    C. artificial selection
    D. disruptive selection
    E. directional selection

48. All of the following organs serve a role in excreting metabolic wastes EXCEPT the

    A. skin
    B. large intestine
    C. lungs
    D. liver
    E. kidney

49. In a system where only two genes are responsible for determining skin pigmentation, a woman is heterozygous for one gene and homozygous for the other. The woman herself only exhibits the homozygous trait. This pattern of expression is known as

    A. epistasis
    B. X-linkage
    C. pleiotropy
    D. codominance
    E. simple dominance

50. A test cross with an organism with a homozygous recessive geno-type results in 50% of the offspring exhibiting the recessive trait. What is the genotype of the test-cross parent?

   I.   Homozygous recessive
   II. Homozygous dominant
   III. Heterozygous

   A. I only
   B. II only
   C. III only
   D. I or III
   E. II or III

51. Which biological molecule is associated with iron (Fe) ions?

   A. Histone
   B. Catalase
   C. Chlorophyll
   D. Hemoglobin
   E. RNA polymerase

Questions 52–54 refer to the following.

The graph depicts the population size of a species over time.

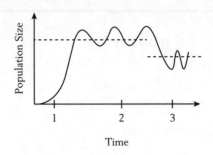

52. What growth pattern is the population demonstrating at time 1?

  A. Gradual
  B. Declining
  C. Continual
  D. Oscillating
  E. Exponential

53. The dashed lines most likely represent

    A. independent climax communities
    B. carrying capacities for different populations
    C. carrying capacities for the same population
    D. similar effects of predation on different populations
    E. similar effects of predation on the same population

54. Which of the following could account for the differences in population size between time 2 and time 3?

    A. Decline in populations of parasitic species
    B. Decline in predator population size
    C. Decline in interspecies competition
    D. Decline in intraspecies competition
    E. Decline in available food resources

Questions 55–57 refer to the following.

Medical researchers tested two different medications for treating type I diabetes. Both Drug 1 and Drug 2 mimic the effects of insulin on muscle, brain, and liver cells. The graph depicts the serum (blood) levels of the drugs in patients through eight hours after injection.

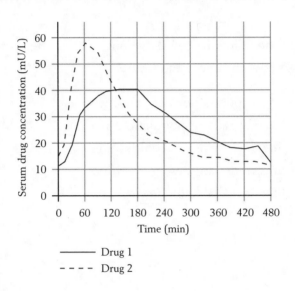

55. Which of the following can be inferred from these data?

A. The effects of Drug 2 are longer lasting.

B. Drug 1 is faster acting than Drug 2.

C. Drug 1 is at its highest concentration upon injection.

D. Drug 1 and Drug 2 have about equal concentrations after four hours.

E. Drug 2 is most highly concentrated within two hours of injection.

56. A patient with type I diabetes eats a large meal and then takes a dose of Drug 2. If the drug is effective, what changes will occur in the patient?

  I.   The amount of glucose in the blood will increase.
  II. The amount of glucose in muscle cells will increase.
  III. The amount of glucose stored in the liver will decrease.

  A. I only
  B. II only
  C. III only
  D. I and II
  E. II and III

57. How will the two drugs most likely differ in their effects on a diabetic patient's blood glucose level?

  A. Drug 2 is more likely to cause blood glucose to drop too low.
  B. Drug 2 is more likely to cause blood glucose to rise too high.
  C. Drug 1 is more likely to cause blood glucose to remain high after a meal.
  D. Drug 1 is more likely to cause the liver to break down glycogen.
  E. Drug 2 is more likely to cause the liver to break down glycogen.

Questions 58–60 refer to the following.

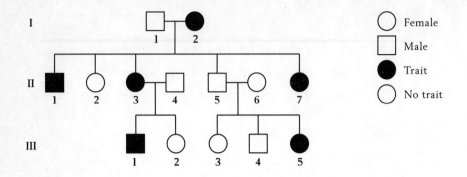

58. According to the pedigree, what is the most likely genotype of individual III-5?

    A.   Carrier

    B.   Unaffected

    C.   Homozygous recessive

    D.   Homozygous dominant

    E.   Heterozygous

59. Which individual is most likely to be a carrier of the trait in question?

    A. II-2
    B. II-4
    C. III-2
    D. III-3
    E. III-4

60. Considering the phenotypes of generations II and II, what is the most likely genotype of the man in generation I?

    A. Autozygous
    B. Hemizygous
    C. Heterozygous
    D. Homozygous recessive
    E. Homozygous dominant

**IF YOU ARE TAKING THE BIOLOGY-E TEST,
CONTINUE WITH QUESTIONS 61–80.
IF YOU ARE TAKING THE BIOLOGY-M TEST, GO TO
QUESTION 81 NOW.**

SAT Biology E/M Subject Test
BIOLOGY-E TEST

Directions: Each of the questions or incomplete statements below is followed by five suggested answers or completions. Some questions pertain to a set that refers to a laboratory or experimental situation. For each question, select the one choice that is the best answer to the question.

61. A biome that contains a layer of permanently frozen soil, called permafrost, would be classified as

    A. taiga
    B. desert
    C. tundra
    D. savannah
    E. temperate deciduous forest

62. All of the following can be considered decomposers EXCEPT

    A. fungi
    B. bacteria
    C. hyenas
    D. earthworms
    E. dung beetles

63. Which pair of organisms is likely to engage in interspecific resource competition?

    A. Hare and rat
    B. Rat and beetle
    C. Hawk and tree
    D. Deer and hare
    E. Hawk and hare

64. In a single ecosystem, two similar species can coexist peacefully as long as they do not share the same

    A. niche
    B. predators
    C. mutations
    D. ecosystem
    E. pheromones

65. *Myriophyllum spicatum*, or water milfoil, native to Eurasia, is an aggressive, invasive aquatic plant in North America. All of the following are reasons this species is successful as an invasive species EXCEPT

    A. milfoil evolved from North American plant species
    B. milfoil has few natural predators in a nonnative environment
    C. milfoil has few natural competitors among North American plant species
    D. milfoil is a hardy plant capable of succeeding in harsher environments
    E. milfoil is resistant to many native diseases that are adapted to native plant species

66. An example of a secondary consumer is

    A. a fish that feeds on algae
    B. a hawk that feeds on a mouse that feeds on an insect
    C. a plant that is parasitic to another plant
    D. a lion that eats a gazelle that feeds on grass
    E. a beetle that feeds on nectar

67. Which of the following is considered a biotic factor capable of influencing a plant species's population growth?

    I.   Intraspecies competition
    II.   Predation
    III. Nutrient availability

    A. I only
    B. II only
    C. III only
    D. I and II
    E. II and III

68. A lake filled with algae that are choking out aquatic plants and fish is likely experiencing which process?

    A. Succession
    B. Eutrophication
    C. Denitrification
    D. Carbon fixation
    E. Acid rain runoff

69. In a tropical food web, 800,000 kJ of energy are produced by auto-trophic species. Approximately how much energy will exist at the level of secondary consumers?

    A. 80 kJ
    B. 800 kJ
    C. 8,000 kJ
    D. 80,000 kJ
    E. 800,000 kJ

70. Nitrogen-fixing bacteria are most likely found in which environment?

    A. Stomach of a reptile
    B. Lower epidermis of leaves
    C. Gills of freshwater fish
    D. Large intestine of humans
    E. Root systems of plants

71. Plants that inhabit warm, dry environments have evolved which of the following adaptations?

    I.   Conversion of carbon dioxide to a four-carbon compound
    II.   Stomata that remain closed throughout the night
    III. Photorespiration

    A. I only
    B. II only
    C. I and II
    D. II and III
    E. I and III

72. A grassy field experiences an increase in growth in an area where phosphorus has been added. However, no such growth occurs in a second area to which nitrogen has been added. Which is a limiting nutrient for this ecosystem?

   A. Nitrogen, because addition of this nutrient did not affect plant growth

   B. Phosphorus, because addition of this nutrient did not affect plant growth

   C. Nitrogen, because addition of this nutrient resulted in increased plant growth

   D. Phosphorus, because addition of this nutrient resulted in increased plant growth

   E. Both nitrogen and phosphorus, because addition of one nutrient increased plant growth

<u>Questions 73–77</u> refer to the following.

Ecologists measured the evapotranspiration and net primary production of different ecosystem types. Their results are shown in the graph.

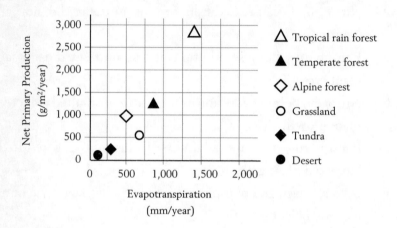

73. How many ecosystem types have a higher rate of evapotranspiration than grassland?

    A. 1
    B. 2
    C. 3
    D. 4
    E. 5

74. How much plant biomass is added to a square meter of temperate forest in one month?

    A. 100 g
    B. 500 g
    C. 1,000 g
    D. 1,200 g
    E. 1,500 g

75. Which factor leads to a higher rate of net primary production?

    A. Biodiversity
    B. Competition
    C. Elevation
    D. Latitude
    E. Precipitation

76. According to the chart, which best describes the relationship between solar energy and net primary production?

    A. Solar energy is unrelated to net primary production.
    B. Solar energy is positively correlated with net primary production.
    C. Solar energy is negatively correlated with net primary production.
    D. Solar energy increases net primary production where water is not limited.
    E. Solar energy increases net primary production by increasing evapotranspiration.

77. The graph shows net primary production. Based on the data, which biome could potentially have a gross primary production rate equivalent to 500 grams per square meter per year?

    A. Tropical rain forest
    B. Temperate forest
    C. Alpine forest
    D. Grassland
    E. Tundra

Questions 78–80 refer to the following.

In a long-running ecological study, the species richness of mosses, shrubs, and trees was calculated for one hectare (10,000 m²) of land every 50 years for 200 years. The data are shown in the table.

YEAR	MOSSES	SHRUBS	TREES
1800	16	2	0
1850	21	7	4
1900	10	5	3
1950	13	12	6
2000	17	28	14

78. What ecological process do the data suggest is occurring?

   A. Evolution
   B. Succession
   C. Destabilization
   D. Primary growth
   E. Artificial selection

79. During which time period do the data suggest this area may have experienced a natural disaster?

    A. 1750–1800
    B. 1800–1850
    C. 1850–1900
    D. 1900–1950
    E. 1950–2000

80. According to the data, has this community reached a climax?

    A. Yes; all densities continue to change.
    B. No; there is continual change in species' densities.
    C. Yes; moss species are constantly present throughout time.
    D. No; moss species are always present in high densities.
    E. Yes; in 1800 there are relatively many more tree species found.

    **IF YOU ARE TAKING THE BIOLOGY-M TEST,
    CONTINUE WITH QUESTIONS 81–100.**

SAT Biology E/M Subject Test
BIOLOGY-M TEST

Directions: Each of the questions or incomplete statements below is followed by five suggested answers or completions. Some questions pertain to a set that refers to a laboratory or experimental situation. For each question, select the one choice that is the best answer to the question.

81. The phenomenon depicted in the diagram is known as

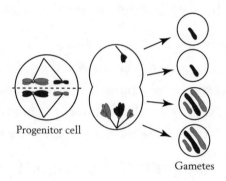

Progenitor cell

Gametes

- A. linkage
- B. independent assortment
- C. crossing over
- D. nondisjunction
- E. mutation

82. The graph shows the changes in free energy before, during, and after a biochemical reaction.

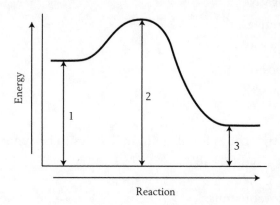

Which describes the effect of a catalytic enzyme on this reaction?

A.   Energy decreases at point 1.
B.   Energy increases at point 1.
C.   Energy decreases at point 2.
D.   Energy increases at point 2.
E.   Energy decreases at point 3.

83. A cell that receives more than the normal number of chromosomes can be called all of the following EXCEPT

A.   aneuploid
B.   gametic
C.   monosomic
D.   polyploid
E.   trisomatic

84. People with an A-positive blood type may safely donate blood to those with which blood type?

    A. A negative
    B. B positive
    C. O negative
    D. AB positive
    E. AB negative

85. An allele that codes for all actin molecules to be synthesized in linear chains would result in

    A. immovable muscles
    B. smooth muscle tissue
    C. normal sarcomere structure
    D. degeneration of muscle tissue
    E. muscle tendons that cannot attach

86. A horse has 64 chromosomes, while a zebra has 46. In rare cases, it is possible to cause these two species to hybridize, creating offspring that are

    A. fertile, with 46 chromosomes
    B. fertile, with 55 chromosomes
    C. sterile, with 46 chromosomes
    D. sterile, with 55 chromosomes
    E. sterile, with 64 chromosomes

87. A genetic mutation that adds a nucleotide to a protein-coding sequence of DNA creates an early stop codon. How will this influence the resulting protein?

    A. The primary structure of the protein will be unaffected.
    B. The secondary structure of the protein will be unchanged.
    C. The protein will not be translated at all.
    D. The protein will be complete but function abnormally.
    E. The protein will be synthesized normally up to the mutation.

88. What are the three structural components of a nucleotide?

    A. A carboxyl, a sugar, and a phosphate
    B. A phosphate, an amino acid, and a carboxyl
    C. An amino acid, a carboxyl, and a phosphate
    D. A sugar, a phosphate, and a nitrogenous base
    E. A nitrogenous base, an amino acid, and a sugar

89. Human immunodeficiency virus (HIV) is a retrovirus that integrates its own DNA into a host cell's genome using

    A. DNA polymerase
    B. helicase
    C. primase
    D. ligase
    E. reverse transcriptase

90. How will the function of a neuron be affected if the potassium channels of the membrane remain open?

    A. It will continue to function normally.
    B. It will function inconsistently.
    C. It will no longer function due to sodium leakage.
    D. It will continue to function but not transmit any impulses.
    E. It will no longer function due to an overly positive charge.

91. Which can affect the primary structure of a protein?

    I.   Genetic mutation
    II. Increase in temperature
    III. Decrease in pH

    A. I only
    B. I and II
    C. I and III
    D. II and III
    E. I, II, and III

92. Which type of bond is broken by the helicase enzyme?

    I.   Covalent bonds
    II. Hydrogen bonds
    III. Ionic bonds

    A. I only
    B. II only
    C. III only
    D. I and II
    E. I, II, and III

93. A sample of DNA is sequenced and is found to consist of 32% guanine. Which conclusion can be drawn about the composition of the DNA sample?

   A. It consists of 18% cytosine and 18% thymine.
   B. It consists of 18% adenine and 18% cytosine.
   C. It consists of 32% cytosine and 18% thymine.
   D. It consists of 32% adenine and 18% cytosine.
   E. It consists of 32% thymine and 18% adenine.

94. During mitosis, a checkpoint ensures that all chromosomal kinetochore proteins, present at the centromere of each sister chromatid, are attached to spindle fibers. Kinetochore proteins that are unattached produce a signal that prevents mitosis from proceeding to the next stage. This checkpoint occurs at the transition from

   A. anaphase to telophase
   B. prophase to metaphase
   C. metaphase to telophase
   D. prophase to anaphase
   E. metaphase to anaphase

<u>Questions 95–97</u> refer to the following.

Scientists constructed a phylogenetic tree of modern lizard genera based on DNA sequences, shown below.

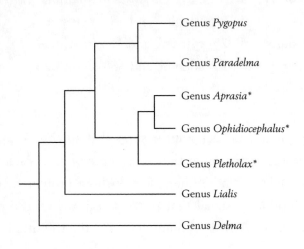

*Diminished external ear

95. Which genus can be identified as the closest relative of the genus *Pletholax*?

    A. *Delma*
    B. *Aprasia*
    C. *Paradelma*
    D. *Lialis*
    E. *Pygopus*

96. Lizards from which two genera most likely have the greatest number of noncoding DNA differences between them?

   A. *Aprasia* and *Ophidiocephalus*
   B. *Pygopus* and *Ophidiocephalus*
   C. *Lialis* and *Aprasia*
   D. *Pygopus* and *Pletholax*
   E. *Lialis* and *Delma*

97. Within this group of lizards, several genera have evolved characteristics similar to those found in snakes. One mutation contributed to a diminished external ear in the genera indicated by an asterisk. What is the most recent point at which this mutation most likely occurred?

   A. After *Aprasia* diverged from *Paradelma*
   B. After *Lialis* diverged from *Pletholax*
   C. When *Aprasia* and *Pletholax* last shared a common ancestor
   D. When *Lialis* and *Pygopus* last shared a common ancestor
   E. After *Aprasia* diverged from *Ophidiocephalus*

Questions 98–100 refer to the following.

A female chimpanzee recently gave birth to an infant while in captivity. Because the paternity of the infant is unclear, scientists tested the DNA from two male chimpanzees, along with the female and infant. The resulting electrophoresis gel is shown.

98. Which labeled DNA fragment is largest?

    A. 1

    B. 2

    C. 3

    D. 4

    E. 5

99. Which fragments must the infant have received from its father?

    A.   1 and 2
    B.   2 and 5
    C.   3 and 4
    D.   3 and 5
    E.   4 and 5

100. Based on the gel electrophoresis result, what can be concluded?

    I.   Male 1 could possibly be the parent.
    II. Male 1 can be ruled out as the parent.
    III. Male 2 could possibly be the parent.
    IV. Male 2 can be ruled out as the parent.

    A. II only
    B. I and III
    C. I and IV
    D. II and III
    E. II and IV

END OF PRACTICE TEST 1

Practice Test 1 Answers and Explanations

Answer Key

1. E	25. D
2. A	26. A
3. D	27. B
4. B	28. B
5. B	29. B
6. A	30. E
7. C	31. B
8. D	32. E
9. B	33. D
10. C	34. C
11. B	35. A
12. B	36. C
13. C	37. C
14. E	38. A
15. C	39. D
16. E	40. D
17. A	41. A
18. A	42. D
19. C	43. C
20. A	44. A
21. E	45. B
22. C	46. B
23. E	47. E
24. C	48. B

49. A	55. E
50. E	56. B
51. D	57. A
52. E	58. C
53. C	59. B
54. E	60. C

Answer Explanations

1. **E.** The anterior pituitary, located beneath the brain, secretes growth hormone.

2. **A.** Thyroxine can only be secreted by the thyroid.

3. **D.** The adrenal medulla is a gland that responds to stress and creates a lasting response on the sympathetic nervous system, which none of the other options have an effect on.

4. **B.** The pancreas secretes glucagon in response to low blood glucose levels. This causes the liver to release glucose into the bloodstream.

5. **B.** Crossing over occurs during prophase I of meiosis. These exchanges hold homologous chromosomes together during metaphase.

6. **A.** In the meiotic cell cycle, meiosis I is the only phase that includes a DNA replication step, or else the process would not result in haploid cells. As in mitosis, prophase is the step within which replication occurs.

7. **C.** As in mitosis, homologous chromosomes are physically pulled apart during anaphase. In meiosis this occurs in the same step, but specifically in meiosis I, because this half of the cycle is the only half that includes replicated DNA.

8. **D.** During pollination, pollen sticks to the stigma (A) and then germinates and grows down the style (C) in order to reach the ovule (D) to achieve fertilization.

9. **B.** Pollen is the product of meiosis by the male floral reproductive structure known as the anther (B).

10. **C.** During pollination, pollen sticks to the stigma (A) and then germinates and grows down the style (C) in order to reach the ovule.

11. **B.** Phloem is the plant vascular tissue responsible for conducting water and dissolved sugars throughout the plant, downward from the leaves. It is always exterior to xylem, from which it is separated by the vascular cambium.

12. **B.** Xylem is the plant vascular tissue responsible for conducting water and dissolved nutrients upward from the roots to other plant tissues. This tissue is always interior to phloem, from which it is separated by the vascular cambium.

13. **C.** Vascular cambium is oriented directly between xylem and phloem. It is a meristematic tissue that gives rise to both types of vascular tissue.

14. **E.** Pith is a source of unspecialized ground tissue that adds structure to a stem at the very center.

15. **C.** During embryonic development, three layers of tissue arise. The outermost layer is ectoderm, which develops into the nervous system, skin, and bones of the skull.

16. **E.** During transcription, an mRNA transcript is copied from a DNA template. This transcript transports genetic information out of the nucleus.

17. **A.** Water is the source of oxygen molecules released by the photosynthetic process, when water molecules are dissociated to free hydrogen ions.

18. **A.** Organisms that reach sexual maturity at the same time are more likely to be the same species. Periodical cicada nymphs emerge from the ground when they are ready to enter the adult stage.

19. **C.** All gymnosperms are vascular plants that produce leaves, though they may be modified into needles. This group also produces wood and "naked" seeds that are not enclosed. This group does not produce flowers, as angiosperms do.

20. **A.** Epistasis is the condition in which the genotype at one locus affects the expression of a gene at another locus. For example, an allele for a gene for black fur may mask the alleles at another locus, no matter which alleles are present at that locus.

21. **E.** Artificial selection is any selective pressure acting on a community or population that is not natural. A nonnatural condition can severely affect population demographics.

22. **C.** A point mutation refers to a DNA mutation where a single base is changed. A frameshift mutation occurs when bases are inserted or deleted, and the entire reading frame changes. The example shows an insertion that results in a frameshift.

23. **E.** Substrates are the limiting factor in a chemical reaction. No matter how much enzyme is available to catalyze a reaction, only so much product can be made unless the substrate is present in excess. Inhibitors, pH level, temperature, and the presence of cofactors could all potentially affect how an enzyme carries out its function and change the reaction rate.

24. **C.** Freshwater aquatic animals require less ability to reabsorb water than do terrestrial or saltwater species, which require a greater capacity for water reabsorption and thus a longer loop of Henle.

25. **D.** The taxonomic hierarchy moves from most general groupings to most specific as follows: kingdom, phylum, class, order, family, genus, and species. The group with the fewest number of species listed in the answer choices is the family *Canidae*.

26. **A.** Analogy is the result of convergent evolution, wherein two distantly related organisms adapt the same strategy or morphology.

27. **B.** Nondisjunction occurs when two homologous chromosomes or chromatids fail to segregate; if this were to occur in meiosis I or II, the resulting zygote could have three copies of a chromosome.

28. **B.** DNA in the cell's nucleus is a template for mRNA, which carries the information to the ribosome for translation. The new translated protein is further modified at the ER and Golgi body, respectively.

29. **B.** A somatic cell is diploid. If the organism's diploid chromosome number is 56, then the haploid gamete will possess half of this number of chromosomes, which is 28.

30. **E.** A silent mutation is not phenotypically visible because the protein product remains unchanged.

31. **B.** Fungi, plants, and animals are all multicellular and possess nuclei within their cells, so this cannot be the answer. Many protists are unicellular, but they are still eukaryotic. Only Archaea and Eubacteria contain unicellular prokaryotic organisms.

32. **E.** Fitness is defined as an organism's ability to successfully reproduce and put its genetic information into future generations. While answers A through D demonstrate successful organisms, only answer E provides any information specifically about reproductive success.

33. **D.** Stomata are pores in leaves formed by guard cells. They are organized the same way across the plant kingdom. In contrast, monocots possess seeds with only one cotyledon (embryonic leaf tissue) while dicot seeds possess two, making Choice A incorrect. Monocots possess flowers with parts in multiples of three, whereas dicot floral parts occur in multiples of four or five, making Choice B incorrect. Monocots typically have parallel-veined leaves while dicots have network-veined (or reticulate-veined) leaves, making Choice C incorrect. In both roots and stems, vascular tissues are arranged differently in monocots and dicots, making E incorrect.

34. **C.** A type III survivorship curve indicates an organism that produces many offspring, many of which do not survive over time. A type II curve represents organisms that produce several offspring, a decent proportion of which survive over time. A type I curve represents an organism that produces very few offspring, most of which survive over time.

35. **A.** Commensalism is a relationship between organisms that has no negative effects on one party but has great benefit for another. An example is moss that grows on trees: the moss obtains a nutrient-rich habitat

and can access sunlight, while the tree's function is unaffected by the presence of the moss.

36. **C.** Mitochondria are the least dense of the listed cellular organelles and will float to the topmost layer when cells undergo centrifugation.

37. **C.** Deoxygenated blood enters the heart from the rest of the body via the anterior vena cava and then enters the right atrium. From there, blood is pumped into the right ventricle and into the lungs to become reoxygenated. Reoxygenated blood is then pumped into the left atrium from the lungs and into the left ventricle, where it is then pumped out into the rest of the body via the aorta.

38. **A.** A hypertonic solution has a higher osmotic pressure, meaning it has a higher concentration of dissolved solutes. A blood cell in this environment will lose water into the solution and shrivel because there is a pressure gradient across the cell membrane.

39. **D.** Polyploidy is the term given to organisms with more than two sets of homologous chromosomes where one set is inherited from each parent. In triticale, the offspring possess six sets of chromosomes, making them hexaploid ($6n$).

40. **D.** Genetic engineering is the only listed technique that allows for the combination of genetic information between unrelated organisms. Selective breeding and artificial selection are changes made to a single species. Cloning will also only involve genes present in parents and not enable the integration of a gene from an alternate species. Sexual recombination, again, can also only occur within the same or closely related species.

41. **A.** Both parents must be homozygous recessive, thus rendering them incapable of producing a dark-haired baby displaying the dominant trait. In Choice B, if both parents are heterozygous, they can display dark hair but still produce a light-haired baby. In Choice C we know that the mother is homozygous recessive, but we do not know whether the paternal genotype is homozygous dominant or heterozygous. If the father is

heterozygous, it is possible that the couple could produce a light-haired child, making this an incorrect answer. Choice D is the same scenario as Choice C, but with the parents' genotypes reversed. In Choice E, no matter the woman's genotype, the couple may produce a dark-haired baby.

42. **D.** Genetic information is stored in the form of DNA. DNA is composed of nucleotide base pairs, which are read as codons. Several codons compose one gene. Multiple genes are organized onto one chromosome.

43. **C.** The phyla Mollusca and Arthropoda do not exhibit radial symmetry; they are bilaterally symmetrical. Phylum Porifera demonstrates an asymmetrical body plan. Phylum Cnidaria does exhibit radial symmetry; however, this group lacks any skeletal form, leaving the only possible correct answer to be Echinodermata.

44. **A.** Convergent evolution occurs when two unrelated species over time adapt the same structure. This is the reverse of what has occurred with tails in lobsters and crabs. An unused evolutionary relic can be termed a vestigial structure and also a homologous structure. This is an example of divergent evolution, where close relatives have begun to adapt differently from one another.

45. **B.** A disorder that is only found in males must be Y linked. An X-linked trait would occur in a small proportion of females.

46. **B.** Because ions carry a charge, they cannot cross the hydrophobic cell membrane and so must be transported by facilitated diffusion via ion channels.

47. **E.** Selection for an extreme phenotype would shift the mean for the population in the direction of that extreme. This is known as directional selection. It is not disruptive selection because only one extreme is selected for.

48. **B.** The large intestine eliminates digestive wastes rather than metabolic wastes.

49. **A.** When more than one gene affects a trait but only one is expressed, this is called *epistasis* because one gene "stands over" another.

50. **E.** A test cross is when an individual reproduces with another whose genotype is known to be homozygous recessive. If the parent with unknown genotype is heterozygous, 50% of offspring will exhibit the dominant trait.

51. **D.** Hemoglobin is a protein associated with iron ions. Iron deficiency can be a cause of anemia, or poor red blood cell function.

52. **E.** Time A on the associated graph depicts a steep curve of population increase over a short amount of time, which is characteristic of exponential population growth.

53. **C.** Because this graph demonstrates population growth for only one population, the answer cannot be Choice B or D. Climax communities are a product of succession, which is not being discussed in this question, making Choice A incorrect. Population growth is influenced by more than just predation rates, making both Choices D and E incorrect.

54. **E.** Because carrying capacities are shaped by so many ecological factors, a fluctuation of just one cannot exact such extreme change on them; only an extreme environmental change such as a natural disaster could drastically decrease a population's carrying capacity.

55. **E.** Drug 2 is most highly concentrated within two hours after injection. The graph shows that Drug 2, not Drug 1, is faster acting and at a higher concentration upon injection. It cannot be determined from the graph which drug is longer lasting. After four hours, Drug 1 is more highly concentrated than Drug 2.

56. **B.** If the drug effectively mimics insulin, it will decrease the patient's blood glucose, which becomes elevated after a meal. Insulin works by allowing glucose in the blood to enter muscle and other cells, increasing the amount of glucose in these cells.

57. **A.** Because Drug 2 peaks soon after injection, it is more likely than Drug 1 to cause blood glucose to drop too low after a meal. Drug 2 mimics the effects of insulin, which allows blood glucose to enter the cells of the body, decreasing the amount of glucose in the blood.

58. **C.** The individual indicated exhibits the trait, but neither of her parents do. This indicates that the trait is due to recessive alleles and that the daughter must have inherited two copies of this allele.

59. **B.** Individual II-4 does not exhibit the trait but has offspring who do. This means that he passed the allele for the trait to his offspring, with a likelihood of 100%, expressed as 1.0. Similar evidence is not available for the other individuals, making the likelihood that they are carriers less than 1.0.

60. **C.** The man in generation I (I-1) must be heterozygous in order for his offspring to exhibit the trait. The affected offspring inherit only one allele from their mother, who is affected. Therefore, they must have inherited the second allele from their father.

Biology-E Test Practice Test 1 Answers and Explanations

Answer Key

61. C	71. A
62. C	72. D
63. D	73. B
64. A	74. A
65. A	75. E
66. D	76. D
67. D	77. D
68. B	78. B
69. C	79. C
70. E	80. B

Answer Explanations

61. **C.** A tundra is a dry biome with a climate cool enough to maintain a permanently frozen region of soil known as permafrost. Both taiga and

temperate deciduous forests can be found in northern regions of the northern hemisphere, but both lack the permanent layer of frozen soil known as permafrost. Desert biomes are characterized by their lack of precipitation, and they distinctly lack permafrost. A savannah is a grassland characterized by an open canopy and seasonal rainfall.

62. **C.** While hyenas often feed on carrion, they are not considered decomposers. Decomposers convert molecules into substrates that may be used by producers to create organic compounds.

63. **D.** In order for there to be interspecific competition, each organism must occupy the same niche to some degree. Of all the listed examples, a deer and a hare are most likely to share food resources and habitat space, which would create competition between them.

64. **A.** Competition is a direct result of niche occupation. Two organisms that attempt to fill the same niche will inevitably compete, likely resulting in the removal of the less competitive species.

65. **A.** Because its evolutionary history is elsewhere, milfoil has adapted to an environment that lacks the natural predators and pathogens of North America, making it less susceptible to them and therefore more competitive than native plants in North America.

66. **D.** A secondary consumer is a consumer that obtains its energy from primary consumers that obtain their energy from primary producers.

67. **D.** A biotic factor is a living ecological influence that can shape a population's demographics. Intraspecific competition refers to competition between living organisms and thus is considered a biotic factor. Predation is the effect a living predator has on a prey species and is also considered a biotic factor. Nutrient availability refers to the nonliving materials an organism can gain from its environment and is considered an abiotic factor, making only I and II correct answers.

68. **B.** Algae are photosynthetic organisms that thrive in conditions of abundant nutrients such as nitrogen. A eutrophic lake is one that contains an overabundance of nutrients.

69. **C.** In a trophic pyramid, primary producers form the base, creating all the energy that will travel up through the pyramid. Just above the producers are primary consumers, which are herbivores that obtain all their energy directly from producers. To obtain that energy also requires energy, and so the amount of energy created by producers is not the same amount that moves up. Approximately 10% of energy is lost for every move up the pyramid, so in this example for the 800,000 kJ of energy produced, only 80,000 kJ will be present for primary consumers, the next level. Secondary consumers are the next level up, feeding on primary consumers, so another 10% of that level's energy will be lost, putting 8,000 kJ at this trophic level.

70. **E.** A common mutualism between plants and bacteria occurs in root systems, which host microorganisms that make limiting nutrients, such as nitrogen, available to the plants.

71. **A.** Plants that inhabit arid environments have adaptations that prevent photorespiration and allow them to close their stomata during the day, preventing the loss of water. One adaptation, found in C4 and CAM plants, converts carbon dioxide to a four-carbon compound as a preliminary step to photosynthesis.

72. **D.** Phosphorus is a limiting nutrient, as evidenced by the fact that when phosphorus was added, plant growth increased. Nitrogen is not a limiting nutrient; addition of nitrogen has no effect on vegetation.

73. **B.** Only two ecosystem types, tropical rain forest (white triangle) and temperate forest (black triangle), have a higher rate of evapotranspiration than grassland (white circle).

74. **A.** The net primary production of temperate forest is approximately 1,200 grams per square meter per year. This is the amount of plant biomass added. The amount of biomass added in one month, or one-twelfth of this value, is 100 grams.

75. **E.** Examination of the graph reveals that precipitation leads to a higher rate of net primary production. Biodiversity may be correlated to NPP but cannot cause it.

76. **D.** Solar energy increases net primary production but cannot do so unless water is available for use in photosynthesis. Therefore, deserts have lower rates of primary production than tropical rain forests.

77. **D.** Compared to net primary production, gross primary production is higher, because it includes energy used (and lost) in cellular respiration. Tundra, with a net primary production of approximately 250 g/m²/year, could potentially have a gross primary production of 500 g/m²/year.

78. **B.** Over time, this plant community shifts from one dominated by mosses to one with many tree species and an overall higher diversity. This shift indicates a forest undergoing succession or progression towards a stable climax community.

79. **C.** The data show a significant decrease in diversity for all three plant types between 1850 and 1900, suggesting some catastrophic event (for example, forest fire).

80. **B.** Because these data continue to change every time they are collected, one can infer that this community has yet to reach its climax. If numbers were to remain the same between two data collection periods, this would suggest a climax had been reached.

Biology-M Test Practice Test 1 Answers and Explanations
Answer Key

81. D	89. E
82. C	90. A
83. C	91. A
84. D	92. B
85. C	93. C
86. D	94. E
87. E	95. B
88. D	96. E

97. A   99. D

98. A   100. D

Answer Explanations

81. **D.** When homologous chromosomes fail to segregate during meiosis, the resulting gametes either lack that chromosome or possess an extra copy. This phenomenon is known as nondisjunction.

82. **C.** Enzymes lower the activation energy of biochemical reactions they catalyze. The activation energy is represented by point 2.

83. **C.** An aneuploid cell is one with an abnormal number of chromosomes. A trisomatic cell has an additional chromosome. A polyploid cell is one that contains an extra set of genetic material. All of these terms may apply to the gamete that inherits an extra chromosome due to nondisjunction. A monosomic cell is a diploid cell that is missing a single chromosome.

84. **D.** Blood recipients that lack the A antibody cannot receive blood from donors with the A antibody (blood types A and AB). Positive and negative blood types refer to Rh system (specifically, the D antibody). Recipients that lack this antibody (negative) cannot receive blood from positive donors. Therefore, the only safe recipients of A-positive blood are A positive and AB positive.

85. **C.** Muscle tissue is composed of two proteins: actin and myosin. Actin forms long chains, while myosin is arranged in bundles. These two proteins are arranged to form sarcomeres. If this mutation does not affect the linear structure of actin proteins, then sarcomere structure will be unaffected.

86. **D.** A hybrid of two species with differing chromosomal numbers will be incapable of forming its own gametes and thus is considered sterile. In order to form a zygote, homologous chromosomes or each gamete must pair. Because zebra gametes will only possess the haploid number of 23 chromosomes and a horse's gamete a haploid number of 32, the resulting zygote will have 54 chromosomes.

87. **E.** A stop codon terminates amino acid translation. If this occurs before the true end of a protein-coding sequence, the protein up to that point will be formed normally but then be truncated as an incomplete protein.

88. **D.** Nucleic acids are formed from mononucleotide polymers. A mononucleotide is one unit that is composed of three components: a sugar; a phosphate, which binds to the sugar in order to create the phosphodiester bond that unites nucleotides into a nucleic acid chain; and a nitrogen base, which pairs with other bases to form a readable sequence.

89. **E.** Reverse transcriptase is an enzyme used to transcribe RNA sequences to DNA sequences. Its function is the reverse of the transcriptase that produces mRNA from DNA.

90. **A.** A neuron contains both sodium and potassium ion channels. Potassium ion channels are referred to as "leak channels" because they are always open, under which condition the neuron continues to function normally.

91. **A.** The primary structure of a protein refers to its amino acid sequence. This can only be altered by a genetic mutation. Changes in pH or temperature may alter the secondary or higher-level structure of the protein.

92. **B.** Helicase separates the complementary strands of DNA, which are attached by hydrogen bond interactions between purines and pyrimidines.

93. **C.** According to Chargoff's rule, equal amounts of adenine and thymine, and of guanine and cytosine, will be present in a DNA sample. Therefore, the amount of cytosine will be equal to the amount of guanine, 32%. The percentages of adenine and thymine will total 36%, or 18% each.

94. **E.** Sister chromatids line up at the metaphase plate, and spindle fibers attach to kinetochore proteins at the centromeres. All sister chromatids must be present and attached to spindle fibers in order to prevent nondisjunction during anaphase. An unattached kinetochore protein generates a signal that prevents the transition from metaphase to anaphase.

95. **B.** In the diagram, it is implied that time moves from left to right. The most closely related groups will be on branches that diverge from a common point farthest to the right on the diagram, or most recently in time. The genera *Pletholax* branched from a common point shared by *Aprasia* (and *Ophidiocephalus*) more recently than any other genus.

96. **E.** Because noncoding DNA differences do not affect phenotype, they accumulate at a constant rate over time. The longer two groups have evolved independently, the more noncoding differences there will be between them. The genera *Lialis* and *Delma* diverged from a common ancestor farthest back in time and would therefore be expected to have the greatest number of DNA differences.

97. **A.** The diminished-ear phenotype is present in the genera *Aprasia*, *Ophidiocephalus*, and *Pletholax*. The mutation leading to this phenotype must therefore have occurred before these branches diverged from a common ancestor but after they diverged from other groups.

98. **A.** Larger DNA fragments travel through an agarose gel at a slower rate than smaller fragments. Fragment 1 is closest to the wells where the DNA was originally inserted. It has traveled the shortest distance and is therefore the largest.

99. **D.** Fragments 3 and 5 are not present in the mother's DNA. Therefore, the infant must have received the genetic information leading to these fragments from its father.

100. **D.** Male 1 lacks band 1, band 3, and the band just beneath band 2 in the infant's lane. Since the infant must have received the corresponding DNA from its father, this allows Male 1 to be ruled out. The lane for Male 2 contains these bands, so Male 2 could possibly be the father.

This book contains two practice tests. Visit mymaxscore.com to download your free third practice test with answers and explanations.

SAT Biology E/M Subject Test Practice Test 2

SAT Biology E/M Subject Test

Time—60 minutes

80 questions

Directions: The set of lettered choices below refers to the numbered questions or statements immediately following it. Select the one lettered choice that best fits each statement. A choice may be used once, more than once, or not at all in the set.

Questions 1–3 refer to the following cell membrane diagram.

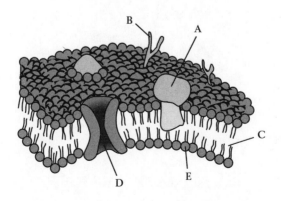

1.   This molecular structure is composed of lipid chains.

2. This structure is involved in facilitated diffusion.

3. This molecular structure is hydrophilic.

Questions 4–6 refer to the following.

    A. DNA
    B. mRNA
    C. rRNA
    D. snRNA
    E. tRNA

4. This nucleic acid carries genetic information to the site of translation.

5. This nucleic acid contains an anticodon.

6. This nucleic acid is associated with histone proteins.

Questions 7–9 refer to the following leaf diagram.

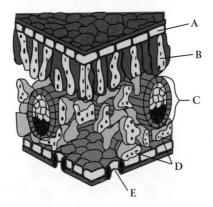

7. Photosynthesis primarily occurs in this tissue.

8. These cells regulate gas exchange in the leaf.

9. This tissue is composed of xylem.

Questions <u>10–13</u> refer to the following.

    A. B cell
    B. Fibrinogen
    C. Pathogen
    D. Phagocyte
    E. T cell

10. This lymphocyte matures in the thymus gland.

11. This produces antibodies specific to an infecting agent.

12. This produces antigens in the body.

13. This cell type is involved in nonspecific immunity.

Questions <u>14–16</u> refer to the following diagram.

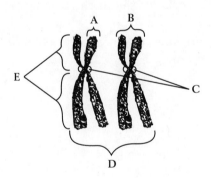

14. A single chromosome

15. A pair of sister chromatids

16. Crossing over occurs between this pair.

<u>Questions 17–19</u> refer to the following.

    A. Founder effect

    B. Heterozygote advantage

    C. Population bottleneck

    D. Random mating

    E. Reproductive isolation

17. This can result in stabilizing selection in a population.

18. This is a characteristic of a population in Hardy-Weinberg equilibrium.

19. This is required for speciation to occur.

Directions: Each of the questions or incomplete statements below is followed by five suggested answers or completions. Some questions pertain to a set that refers to a laboratory or experimental situation. For each question, select the one choice that is the best answer to the question.

20. Which muscle type lines the interior walls of hollow organs?

    I.   Cardiac

    II. Smooth

    III. Striated

    A. I only

    B. II only

    C. III only

    D. I and II

    E. II and III

21. The diagram shows the muscles involved in extending the arm.
    Which actions result in this movement?

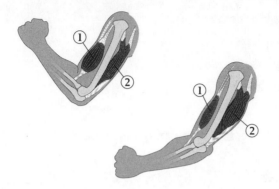

   A.   Muscle 1 relaxes while muscle 2 contracts.

   B.   Muscle 1 contracts while muscle 2 relaxes.

   C.   Muscle 1 contracts, and then both muscles relax.

   D.   Muscle 1 and muscle 2 both relax the same time.

   E.   Muscle 1 and muscle 2 both contract at the same time.

22. Which cellular process is responsible for the change shown below?

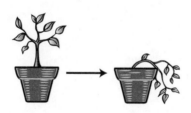

   A.   Closing of stomata

   B.   Slowing of photosynthesis

   C.   Reduction in protein synthesis

   D.   Degradation of the cytoskeleton

   E.   Decreased pressure in the vacuole

23. During which phase of mitosis do the centromeres split?

    A. Anaphase
    B. Cytokinesis
    C. Metaphase
    D. Prophase
    E. Telophase

24. Which of the following plays an important role in the human immune system?

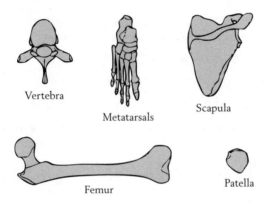

Vertebra

Metatarsals

Scapula

Femur

Patella

    A. Femur
    B. Metatarsals
    C. Patella
    D. Scapula
    E. Vertebra

25. How do enzymes help to carry out biochemical reactions?

    A. By decreasing the energy of the reactants
    B. By increasing the activation energy of the reaction
    C. By decreasing the activation energy of the reaction
    D. By increasing the energy of the products of the reaction
    E. By decreasing the energy of the products of the reaction

26. In which plants is the haploid gametophyte generation dominant?

    I.   Angiosperms

    II. Gymnosperms

    III. Horsetails, ferns, club mosses (lycophytes and pterophytes)

    IV. True mosses, liverworts, and hornworts (bryophtyes)

    A. I only

    B. I and II

    C. I, II, and III

    D. III and IV

    E. IV only

27. Which of the following uses a countercurrent exchange system?

    I.   Gills

    II. Kidneys

    III. Intestines

    IV. Lungs

    A. I and III only

    B. II and IV only

    C. I, II, and III

    D. I, II, and IV

    E. I, II, III, and IV

28. Which describes the cause of eutrophication in lakes?

    A. A lack of oxygen

    B. A lack of sunlight

    C. A lack of nutrients

    D. An excess of oxygen

    E. An excess of nutrients

29. Two parents with dimples have a child with no dimples. The allele *D* for dimples is dominant. What are the possible genotypes of the parents?

    I.   *DD* and *Dd*
    II. *Dd* and *Dd*
    III. *DD* and *dd*

    A. I only
    B. II only
    C. I or II
    D. II or III
    E. I, II, or III

30. Which of these are relationships in which one species benefits at the expense of another?

    I.   Commensalism
    II. Competition
    III. Parasitism
    IV. Predation

    A. III only
    B. III and IV
    C. I, II, and III
    D. II, III, and IV
    E. I, II, III, and IV

31. What is the most likely role of zooplankton in an aquatic ecosystem?

    A. Producer
    B. Primary consumer
    C. Secondary consumer
    D. Tertiary consumer
    E. Decomposer

32. Which refers to the degree to which a phenotype is determined by genetic variation in a population?

   A. Fitness

   B. Heritability

   C. Limited environmental resources

   D. Overproduction of offspring

   E. Phenotypic variation

33. Which of the following is the smallest unit that can evolve through natural selection?

   A. Cell

   B. Clade

   C. Organism

   D. Population

   E. Species

34. Which of the following leads to a replacement of the plant community in an ecosystem undergoing succession?

   A. Pollution

   B. Herbivory

   C. Parasitism

   D. Abiotic factors

   E. Intraspecific competition

35. Which of the following describes a possible path of a carbon atom among atmospheric carbon dioxide, the tissues of a consumer, and the tissues of a producer?

    A. Consumer ↔ producer ↔ atmosphere ↔ producer
    B. Producer ↔ consumer ↔ atmosphere ↔ consumer
    C. Producer ↔ atmosphere ↔ consumer ↔ atmosphere
    D. Atmosphere ↔ producer ↔ atmosphere ↔ consumer
    E. Consumer ↔ atmosphere ↔ producer ↔ atmosphere

36. Which of the following includes organisms that are able to utilize nitrogen in the form of nitrogen gas (N_2)?

    A. Producers
    B. Primary consumers
    C. Secondary consumers
    D. Tertiary consumers
    E. Decomposers

37. The graph shows the body size distribution in a population. Which statement describes the effects of stabilizing selection on the distribution?

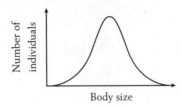

A. The mean shifts, and the curve remains the same.
B. The mean shifts, and the curve becomes narrower.
C. The mean remains the same, and the curve becomes wider.
D. The mean remains the same, and the curve becomes narrower.
E. The mean shifts to both the left and the right, and two new curves form.

38. Which of the following characteristics are present in monocots?

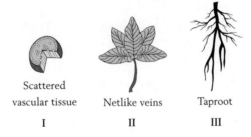

Scattered
vascular tissue   Netlike veins   Taproot

I   II   III

A. I only
B. II only
C. I and II
D. I and III
E. II and III

39. Identify the organism shown using the following dichotomous key.

1a	Abdomen has distinct segments	go to 2
1b	Abdomen lacks distinct segments	go to 3
2a	Pedipalps (large "pincers") in front of shorter legs	go to 4
2b	Long and slender legs, no pedipalps	Opiliones
3a	Body is divided into two main parts	Araneae
3b	Body is not divided into two parts and is oval in shape	Acari
4a	No stinger is present at the end of the abdomen	Pseudoscorpiones
4b	A stinger is present at the end of the abdomen	Scorpiones

    A.   Acari

    B.   Araneae

    C.   Opiliones

    D.   Scorpiones

    E.   Pseudoscorpiones

40. Within the animal lineage leading to humans, which of the following structures evolved first?

    A. Bone
    B. Cranium
    C. Jaws
    D. Notochord
    E. Vertebrae

41. In which structure does double fertilization occur?

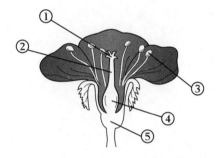

    A. 1
    B. 2
    C. 3
    D. 4
    E. 5

42. Mammals and sharks produce a compound called urea. What is the function of urea?

    A. It raises the pH level of the blood.
    B. It sends signals from cells that produce it to other organs.
    C. It provides energy to some cells and tissues.
    D. It prevents ammonia from building up in the body.
    E. It eliminates water from the bloodstream.

43. Deoxygenated blood is pumped to the lungs through which parts of the heart?

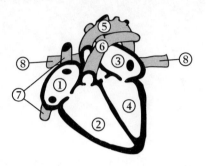

   A. 1, 2, and 6

   B. 1, 2, and 7

   C. 2, 4, and 6

   D. 3, 4, and 5

   E. 3, 4, and 8

44. Which of the following characteristics of an allele is required for it to increase in a population through natural selection?

   A. Individuals with the allele are better able to find food.

   B. Individuals with the allele are better able to resist disease.

   C. Individuals with the allele have an increased ability to find and retain mates.

   D. Individuals with the allele produce more offspring that reach adulthood.

   E. Individuals with the allele have a longer lifespan than those without it.

45. Which of the following do animals and fungi have in common?

    I.   Autotrophic mode of nutrition
    II. Extracellular digestion
    III. Lack of cell walls
    IV. Membrane-bound organelles

    A. I and III
    B. I and IV
    C. II and III
    D. II and IV
    E. IV only

46. Which structure releases hormones that signal the tissue lining the uterus to thicken?

    A. Corpus luteum
    B. Developing follicle
    C. Fallopian tube
    D. Hypothalamus
    E. Pituitary

47. In what order did the following types of organisms appear in the history of life on Earth?

   I.   Eukaryotes
   II.   Heterotrophic organisms
   III. Metazoa
   IV.   Photosynthetic organisms

   A. II, I, IV, III
   B. II, I, III, IV
   C. II, IV, I, III
   D. IV, I, II, III
   E. IV, II, I, III

48. Which of the following is required for speciation to take place?

   A. Increased genetic variation
   B. Random mating
   C. Reduced gene flow
   D. Geographic isolation
   E. Mutation

49. Which structure allows photosynthesis to begin in a germinating dicot plant?

   A. Cotyledon
   B. Endosperm
   C. Embryonic root
   D. Apical meristem
   E. Lateral meristem

50. Pepsinogen is secreted by the cells lining the stomach. In a low-pH solution, it is converted to an active enzyme, called pepsin. The purpose of producing pepsinogen instead of pepsin is to

   A. preserve the active site

   B. protect the secreting cells

   C. raise the pH of the liquid inside the stomach

   D. ensure that the enzyme is active when food is present

   E. prevent the enzyme from breaking down carbohydrate

51. The diagram shows a seed. What is the function of the structures indicated by the arrows?

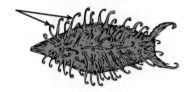

   A. Defense

   B. Dispersal

   C. Camouflage

   D. Water intake

   E. Photosynthesis

<u>Questions 52–55</u> refer to the following.

Scientists examined the effects of adding nutrients to waters off the Eastern coast of the United States. The graph shows the nutrient added and the resulting algae counts at six locations. No nutrients were added in the control condition.

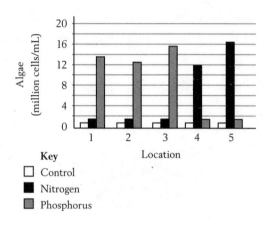

Key

☐ Control
■ Nitrogen
▨ Phosphorus

52. Which location experienced the greatest increase in algae in response to the addition of phosphorus?

   A. 1
   B. 2
   C. 3
   D. 4
   E. 5

53. At which locations was a sufficient supply of phosphorus present before the experiment was conducted?

    A. 1 only
    B. 1 and 2
    C. 1, 2, and 3
    D. 4 and 5
    E. 5 only

54. At which locations was nitrogen a limiting factor on algae growth?

    A. 1 only
    B. 1 and 2
    C. 1, 2, and 3
    D. 4 and 5
    E. 5 only

55. Algae incorporate nitrogen and phosphorus compounds in the environment into which of the following macromolecules?

    I.   Carbohydrates
    II. DNA
    III. Protein

    A. I and II
    B. I and III
    C. III only
    D. II and III
    E. I, II, and III

Questions 56–60 refer to the following.

In fruit flies, normal-sized, solid-colored body and red eyes are wild-type (normal) traits. Flies can be assumed to have these traits unless otherwise stated. A geneticist crosses fruit flies from a strain with purple eyes and with fruit flies from a strain with dwarf bodies. The results of the F1 cross are shown below. The scientist then crosses F1 flies together. Results from the F2 generation are included in the table.

GENERATION	NORMAL SIZE, PURPLE EYE	NORMAL SIZE, RED EYE	DWARF, PURPLE EYE	DWARF, RED EYE	TOTAL
F1	0	742	0	0	742
F2	102	318	33	95	548

The allele resulting in purple eyes is located near an allele resulting in streaks across the body, on the same chromosome. The streaked body phenotype is recessive. Crosses are performed with flies from purebred lines, which are wild type for all other traits.

56. Approximately what proportion of the F2 flies has the dwarf, red-eyed phenotype?

A. 1 in 3
B. 1 in 4
C. 1 in 16
D. 3 in 16
E. 9 in 16

57. Based on the results of the parent cross, which of the following phenotypes are recessive?

    I.   Red eyes
    II.   Purple eyes
    III. Dwarf body
    IV. Normal body

    A.   I and III
    B.   I and IV
    C.   II and III
    D.   II and IV
    E.   III only

58. Two flies from the F2 generation are crossed. One has a dwarf body
and red eyes, and the other has a dwarf body and purple eyes. Based
on the results shown, which combinations of traits could result in
the offspring?

    I.   Dwarf body, red eyes
    II.   Dwarf body, purple eyes
    III. Normal body, red eyes
    IV. Normal body, purple eyes

    A.   I only
    B.   II only
    C.   I and II
    D.   II and IV
    E.   III and IV

59. A purple-eyed fly is crossed with a streaked fly. The F1 flies are then crossed with each other. In the F2 generation, which phenotype will occur less often than expected?

I.   Streaked body, red eyes
II. Streaked body, purple eyes
III. Normal body, red eyes
IV. Normal body, purple eyes

A. I and II
B. I and III
C. I and IV
D. II and III
E. III and IV

60. In fruit flies, the normal or wild-type allele of a gene is indicated with a plus (+) sign. The diagrams below show the locations of the streak and purple eye genes on simplified chromosomes. Which diagram shows the correct haplotypes of the F1 flies resulting from a cross between a streaked parent and a purple-eyed parent?

A.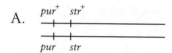
pur^+ str^+

pur str

B.
pur^+ str

pur^+ str

C.
pur^+ str^+

pur^+ str^+

D.
pur str

pur str

E.
pur^+ str

pur str^+

**IF YOU ARE TAKING THE BIOLOGY-E TEST,
CONTINUE WITH QUESTIONS 61–80.
IF YOU ARE TAKING THE BIOLOGY-M TEST, GO TO
QUESTION 81 NOW.**

SAT Biology E/M Subject Test
BIOLOGY-E TEST

Directions: Each of the questions or incomplete statements below is followed by five suggested answers or completions. Some questions pertain to a set that refers to a laboratory or experimental situation. For each question, select the one choice that is the best answer to the question.

61. Which describes a common difference between terrestrial and aquatic ecosystems?

   A. Organisms in terrestrial ecosystems are dependent on oxygen, while those in aquatic ecosystems are not.

   B. Nutrients are a limiting factor for populations in aquatic ecosystems but not for terrestrial populations.

   C. Producers make up the greatest amount of biomass in terrestrial ecosystems, while in aquatic ecosystems they do not.

   D. Sunlight is a limiting factor for populations in terrestrial ecosystems but not for populations in aquatic ecosystems.

   E. Energy in aquatic ecosystem is transferred from lower to higher trophic levels, but it moves in the opposite direction in aquatic ecosystems.

62. Which of the following are documented effects of increasing average global temperature on fish populations?

   I.   Movement from saline to fresh waters

   II.   Movement to deeper waters

   III. Movement to higher latitudes

   A.   I only

   B.   II only

   C.   III only

   D.   I and II

   E.   II and III

63. Which of the following remove nitrogen from the atmosphere?

   I.   Denitrifying bacteria

   II.   Industrial fertilizer production

   III. Lightning

   IV. Nitrogen-fixing bacteria

   A.   I and II only

   B.   I and III only

   C.   I, II, and III

   D.   II, III, and IV

   E.   I, II, III, and IV

64. At which time point in the graph below does the size of the population reach the carrying capacity for the ecosystem?

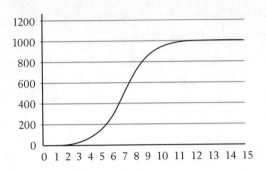

A. 3
B. 4
C. 6
D. 9
E. 12

65. An invasive species is likely to encounter fewer of which of the following in its new ecosystem?

I.   Ecological niches
II.   Predators
III. Suitable food sources

A. I only
B. II only
C. III only
D. I and III
E. II and III

66. Semelparous species produce a large number of offspring once in their life spans. Iteroparous species produce a small number of off-spring repeatedly throughout their lives. Which ecological condition will most likely select for a semelparous strategy?

    A. A surplus of nutrients or food sources
    B. A lack of competition from other species
    C. The availability of multiple ecological niches
    D. Persistent limiting factors in the environment
    E. A lack of consistency of environmental conditions

67. The first terrestrial forests depended on the evolution of which plant structure?

    A. Flowers
    B. Naked seeds
    C. Covered seeds
    D. Vascular tissue
    E. Deciduous leaves

68. The field of ecology that studies how species are distributed over the Earth is called

    A. ethology
    B. paleontology
    C. biogeography
    D. community ecology
    E. conservation ecology

69. Which of the following is a biotic factor that limits the growth of a
    population in aquatic ecosystems?

    A. Depth
    B. Competition
    C. Light penetration
    D. Nutrient availability
    E. Dissolved oxygen level

70. How does the concept of inclusive fitness explain altruistic behavior
    in animals?

    A. Altruism is the result of learning and occurs in most social species.
    B. Altruism results in the production of a greater number of offspring.
    C. Altruism lowers stress in altruistic individuals, which increases
        fitness.
    D. Altruism results in other individuals performing altruistic acts
        in return.
    E. Altruism increases the number of young of genetically similar
        individuals.

71. The diagrams show three dispersion patterns. Which species characteristic results in pattern 2?

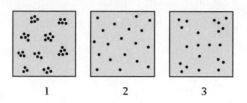

1   2   3

A. Sociability
B. Territoriality
C. Random distribution
D. *r*-selection
E. *K*-selection

72. Which type of population growth is represented by the graph below?

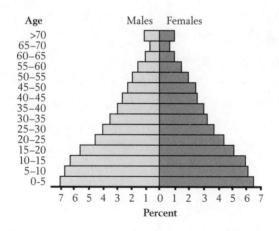

A. No growth
B. Slow growth
C. Slow decrease
D. Rapid increase
E. Rapid decrease

73. Which of the following is positively associated with biodiversity?

    I.   Diversity of ecosystems
    II. Genetic variation within species
    III. Species diversity within communities

    A. III only
    B. I and II only
    C. I and III only
    D. II and III only
    E. I, II, and III

74. Some rocks feature red bands or streaks made up of iron oxides, formed when iron reacts with oxygen. These originated from dissolved iron in the oceans, which formed oxides and settled to the ocean bottom. What allowed this chemical and physical process to occur?

    A. Early reducing atmosphere of Earth
    B. Evolution of cyanobacteria
    C. Symbiosis of photosynthetic bacteria and protists
    D. Adaptation of plants to terrestrial environments
    E. Metabolic activity of the first heterotrophs

75. Which statement BEST describes the Allee effect?

    A. Population growth increases as population density increases, below a certain density.

    B. Population growth increases as population density increases, above a certain density.

    C. Population growth decreases as population density increases, above a certain density.

    D. Population growth increases as population density increases, causing density to then decrease.

    E. Population growth decreases as population density increases, causing density to then decrease.

<u>Questions 76–78</u> refer to the following.

Ecologists surveyed the composition of three different forest plots. They measured the frequency of occurrence of 13 different tree species and the basal area of each species. The basal area is calculated by measuring tree circumference at breast height and calculating the area occupied by a particular species in square meters per hectare.

COMMON NAME	SPECIES	PLOT 1 BASAL AREA (m^2/ha)	FREQUENCY	PLOT 2 BASAL AREA (m^2/ha)	FREQUENCY	PLOT 3 BASAL AREA (m^2/ha)	FREQUENCY
Sugar maple	Acer saccharum	12.12	0.96	6.15	0.72	1.29	0.20
Red maple	Acer rubrum	1.38	0.28	2.11	0.44	5.42	0.76
Paper birch	Betula papyrifera	1.65	0.36	7.99	0.84	4.78	0.68
Yellow birch	Betula alleghaniensis	0.92	0.20	1.93	0.28		
Black ash	Fraxinus nigra			0.09	0.04		
White spruce	Picea glauca	0.09	0.04			0.18	0.04
Strobe pine	Pinus strobus	0.92	0.12	1.93	0.44	9.00	0.52
Red pine	Pinus resinosa			0.09	0.04	5.51	0.60
Quaking aspen	Populus tremuloides	1.93	0.20	4.68	0.48	3.03	0.36
Balsam poplar	Populus balsamifera	0.09	0.04				
Bur oak	Quercus macrocarpa	0.37	0.12	1.19	0.32	0.73	0.20
Red oak	Quercus rubra	4.13	0.60	0.09	0.04	2.39	0.40
American elm	Ulmus americana	0.09	0.04				

Data from: Host, G. and J. Pastor. 1998. Modeling forest succession among ecological land units in northern Minnesota. *Conservation Ecology* 2(2): 15.
Available at: http://www.consecol.org/vol2/iss2/art15/

76. Which is the most common tree species in Plot 3?

    A.   Red pine
    B.   Red maple
    C.   Strobe pine
    D.   Paper birch
    E.   Sugar maple

77. Which two species are most closely related?

    A.   Red pine and red oak
    B.   Red oak and red maple
    C.   Red oak and American elm
    D.   White spruce and strobe pine
    E.   Quaking aspen and balsam poplar

78. The data shows a negative, or inverse, correlation between which
    two tree species?

    A.   Strobe pine and paper birch
    B.   Red maple and sugar maple
    C.   Paper birch and yellow birch
    D.   Quaking aspen and paper birch
    E.   White spruce and American elm

Questions 79–80 refer to the following.

The graph on the left shows the average monthly temperature and pre-cipitation in Taiyuan, China. Taiyuan's average annual temperature is 10.3°C, and its average annual precipitation is 381 mm, or 38.1 cm. The graph on the right depicts the classification of biomes according to precipitation and temperature.

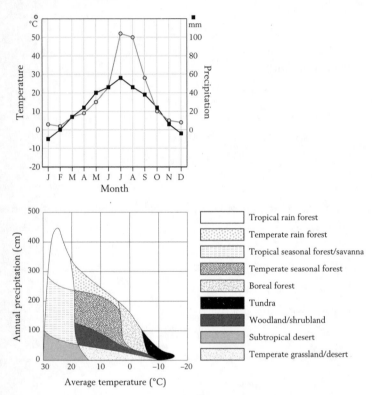

79. In which month does Taiyuan, China, experience the LEAST precipitation?

A. April
B. December
C. February
D. January
E. July

80. According to the graphs, in which type of biome is Taiyuan, China, located?

   A. Subtropical desert
   B. Tropical rain forest
   C. Temperate grassland
   D. Temperate rain forest
   E. Temperate seasonal forest

**IF YOU ARE TAKING THE BIOLOGY-M TEST,
CONTINUE WITH QUESTIONS 81–100.**

SAT Biology E/M Subject Test
BIOLOGY-M TEST

Directions: Each of the questions or incomplete statements below is followed by five suggested answers or completions. Some questions pertain to a set that refers to a laboratory or experimental situation. For each question, select the one choice that is the best answer to the question.

81. The table shows the restriction enzyme recognition sites present on a circular piece of DNA 4.0 kilobases (1 kb = 1,000 bases) long.

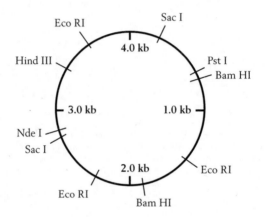

Which pair of restriction enzymes, used together, would produce a band that travels the farthest on an electropheresis gel?

A. Nde I and Pst I
B. Nde I and Eco RI
C. Sac I and Bam HI
D. Eco RI and Hind III
E. Bam HI and Hind III

82. Which of the following is generally identical in all the somatic cells of an organism?

I.   DNA sequences
II. Protein structures
III. RNA sequences

A. I only
B. II only
C. III only
D. I and II
E. I and III

83. Red blood cells placed in a hypotonic solution will

A. shrink due to osmotic water loss
B. rupture due to the influx of water
C. maintain their shape due to the cell wall
D. swell but avoid rupturing due to the cell wall
E. pump out excess water with the contractile vacuole

84. Animals store energy in which of the following molecular forms?

I.   Glucose
II. Glycogen
III. Lipid
IV. Protein

A. I and II
B. II and III
C. I, II, and III
D. II, III, and IV
E. I, II, III, and IV

85. In which phase of the cell cycle does DNA replication take place?

    A. G0
    B. G1
    C. G2
    D. M
    E. S

86. In eukaryotic cells, chromosomes and ribosomes share which of the following characteristics?

    I.   They consist of nucleic acid.
    II. They consist of protein.
    III. They are in the nucleus.

    A. I only
    B. II only
    C. III only
    D. I and II
    E. I and III

87. Which of the following is a macromolecule composed of amino acid subunits?

    A. Amylase
    B. Glycogen
    C. Phospholipid
    D. Polysaccharide
    E. Ribonucleic acid

88. The diagram depicts the movement of an amoeba. Which cellular structure is responsible for the amoeba's movement?

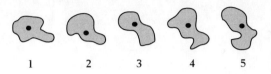

1   2   3   4   5

A. Cilia
B. Flagella
C. Cell wall
D. Cytoskeleton
E. Cell membrane

89. Where do the reactions of the Calvin cycle take place?

A. Stroma
B. Cytoplasm
C. Thylakoid membrane
D. Mitochondrial matrix
E. Mitochondrial membrane

90. The net equation for photosynthesis is

A. $C_6H_{12}O_6 + 6O_2 \rightarrow 6CO_2 + 6H_2O$
B. $6CO_2 + 6H_2O \rightarrow C_6H_{12}O_6 + 6O_2$
C. $C_6H_{12}O_6 + 6H_2O \rightarrow 6CO_2 + 6O_2H$
D. $6CO_2 + 6O_2 \rightarrow C_6H_{12}O_6 + 6H_2O$
E. $6CO_2 + C_6H_{12}O_6 \rightarrow + 6O_2 + 6H_2O$

91. A codon on the coding strand of a gene is shown below. Which anti-codon sequence will bind to the transcribed codon?

5'–ACT–3'

A. 3'–ACU–5'
B. 3'–TGA–5'
C. 3'–UGA–5'
D. 5'–ACU–3'
E. 5'–UGA–3'

92. Which statement describes one difference between hormones and neurotransmitters?

A. Hormones modify cellular activity.
B. Hormones are secreted into the bloodstream.
C. Hormones produce a change in animal behavior.
D. Hormones attach to receptors on the cell surface.
E. Hormones are released in response to external stimuli.

93. The antibiotic tetracycline works by binding to rRNA in prokary-
    otes. Which cellular activity does tetracycline directly disrupt?

    A. Translation
    B. Respiration
    C. Transcription
    D. DNA replication
    E. Active transport

94. In cellular respiration, the role of $FADH_2$ and NADH is to

    A. catalyze the breakdown of glucose to three-carbon sugars
    B. carry electrons to the cytochrome membrane proteins
    C. catalyze the addition of a phosphate group to ADP
    D. act as final electron acceptors in the electron transport chain
    E. transport hydrogen ions across the inner mitochondrial membrane

Questions 95–97 refer to the following.

Scientists grew *E. coli* bacteria in a nutrient solution containing a heavy, stable isotope of nitrogen, ^{15}N. They then transferred them to a medium with the more common light isotope of nitrogen. Periodically, DNA from the cells was extracted and subjected to density centrifugation. The strain of *E. coli* used divides once every 20 minutes. The results are illustrated below.

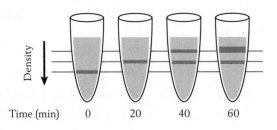

95. At which time point(s) is the heaviest DNA extracted from the cells?

    A. 0 minutes
    B. 20 minutes
    C. 40 minutes
    D. 60 minutes
    E. 40 and 60 minutes

96. After two cell divisions, what types of chains make up the DNA of the cells?

   I.   Two light-nitrogen chains
   II. Two heavy-nitrogen chains
   III. One light-nitrogen chain and one heavy-nitrogen chain

   A. I only
   B. II only
   C. III only
   D. I and II
   E. I and III

97. If the scientists were to continue extracting and centrifuging DNA every 20 minutes, which result would describe the DNA bands in the test tubes?

   A. The top band would move lower, while the middle band would disappear.
   B. The top band would grow thinner, while the middle band would grow thicker.
   C. The top and middle bands would both grow thicker and move lower in the tube.
   D. The top and middle bands would both grow thicker but remain at the same level.
   E. The top band would grow thicker, while the middle band would remain the same.

<u>Questions 98–100</u> refer to the following.

Scientists sequenced a portion of the aspartate transaminase enzyme from different species. The amino acid sequences are shown in the table. Each letter stands for an amino acid. Differences from the human sequence are indicated by bold letters. Missing amino acids are indicated by a dash (–).

ORGANISM	AMINO ACID SEQUENCE
Human	P F F D S A Y Q G F A S G N L E R D A W A I R Y F
Horse	P F F D S A Y Q G F A S G N L **D** R D A W A **V** R Y F
Rat	P F F D S A Y Q G F A S G **D** L E **K** D A W A I R Y F
Pig	P F F D S A Y Q G F A S G N L E **K** D A W A I R Y F
Chicken	P F F D S A Y Q G F A S G **S L D K** D A W A **V** R Y F
Yeast	P F F D S A Y Q G F A **T** G S L **D K** D A **Y** A V R **X X**
Alfalfa	P F F D S A Y Q G F A S G **S L D A D** A **Q P V** R L F
Bacteria	P **L** F D **F** A Y Q G F A **R** G – L E E D A **E G L** R A F

ORGANISM	AMINO ACID SEQUENCE (CONTINUED)
Human	**V S E G F E F F C A Q S F S K N F G L Y**
Horse	V S E G F E **L** F C A Q S F S K N F G L Y
Rat	V S E G F E **L** F C **P** Q S F S K N F G L Y
Pig	V S E G F E **L** F C A Q S F S K N F G L Y
Chicken	V S E G F E **L** F C A Q S F S K N F G L Y
Yeast	**L S T V S P V F V C** Q S F S K N **A G M** Y
Alfalfa	V **A D G G E L L V** A Q S **Y A** K N M G L Y
Bacteria	**A A M H K** E L **I** V A S S **Y** S K N F G L Y

98. Which pair of organisms is most similar in terms of the amino acid sequence shown?

    A. Pig and horse
    B. Chicken and rat
    C. Human and pig
    D. Alfalfa and yeast
    E. Bacteria and yeast

99. All of the following types of mutations could have resulted in the amino acid differences shown EXCEPT

    A. a deletion
    B. an insertion
    C. a missense mutation
    D. a silent mutation
    E. a substitution

100. Which genetic mutation occurred farthest back in time?

    A. Insertion of a codon for serine (S)
    B. Deletion of a codon for asparagine (N)
    C. Conversion of a codon for lysine (K) to one for arginine (R)
    D. Conversion of a codon for alanine (A) to one for cysteine (C)
    E. Conversion of a codon for leucine (L) to one for methionine (M)

END OF PRACTICE TEST 2

Practice Test 2 Answers and Explanations

Answer Key

1. C	25. C
2. D	26. E
3. E	27. D
4. B	28. E
5. E	29. B
6. A	30. D
7. B	31. B
8. E	32. B
9. C	33. D
10. E	34. D
11. A	35. E
12. C	36. E
13. D	37. A
14. B	38. A
15. B	39. E
16. D	40. D
17. B	41. D
18. D	42. D
19. E	43. A
20. B	44. D
21. A	45. D
22. E	46. A
23. A	47. C
24. A	48. C

49. A   55. D

50. B   56. D

51. B   57. C

52. C   58. A

53. C   59. D

54. C   60. E

Answer Explanations

1. **C.** The cell membrane is composed of a bilayer of phospholipids. Hydrophobic lipid chains of each layer sit adjacent to each other in the center of the cell membrane.

2. **D.** Protein channels spanning the cell membrane facilitate diffusion of certain molecules, such as ions, across the membrane.

3. **E.** The cell membrane is composed of a bilayer of phospholipids. The hydrophilic potions of the molecules making up each layer form the outer layers of the cell membrane.

4. **B.** The nucleic acid in mRNA carries genetic information from the nucleus to the ribosomes in the cytoplasm, where it is translated into a polypeptide.

5. **E.** The nucleic acid in tRNA contains an anticodon, which binds to the exposed codon in the mRNA-ribosome translation complex. Each tRNA molecule carries an amino acid to the site of translation.

6. **A.** In eukaryotic chromosomes, DNA is tightly coiled and wound around histone proteins to form chromosomes.

7. **B.** The cells of the palisade layer contain the highest concentration of chloroplasts and make up the primary site of photosynthesis.

8. **E.** Pairs of guard cells regulate gas exchange by opening or closing a stoma, or opening, in the leaf. Guard cells close to prevent water loss.

9. **C.** Veins of vascular tissue run through the leaf, transporting water

and nutrients throughout the plant. Xylem, phloem, and bundle sheaf cells make up these veins.

10. **E**. T cells are lymphocytes originating in the bone marrow. They migrate to the thymus, where they mature.

11. **A**. B cells produce antibodies specific to the pathogens of infecting agents, such as viruses. B cells are responsible for acquired immunity.

12. **C**. Antigens are produced by pathogens and are recognized by immune system lymphocytes.

13. **D**. Phagocytes engulf and destroy both foreign cells and damaged or nonfunctional cells in the blood. They do not specifically target an infecting agent.

14. **B**. A single chromosome, which has replicated its DNA, consists of two sister chromatids joined at the centromere. Although it has replicated, it is still considered a single chromosome.

15. **B**. A pair of sister chromatids makes up the two halves of a chromosome that has replicated its DNA. The sister chromatids are joined at the centromere. Although it has replicated, it is still considered a single chromosome.

16. **D**. Crossing over, the exchange of homologous DNA segments, occurs between homologous chromosomes in prophase of meiosis I. Homologous chromosomes are separate chromosomes with highly similar, but not identical, DNA sequences.

17. **B**. Heterozygote advantage confers a fitness advantage on heterozygous individuals. The amount of variance for the phenotype will decrease, though the mean will stay the same. On a graph of frequency vs. phenotype, this is depicted as a narrowing of the curve.

18. **D**. Random mating is one of the requirements for a population in Hardy-Weinberg equilibrium.

19. **E**. Speciation requires that two populations be reproductively isolated from each other, allowing natural selection to act independently on each.

20. **B.** Smooth muscle, which is not under voluntary control, lines the interior walls of organs such as the stomach, intestines, and blood vessels.

21. **A.** Voluntary muscle movements are carried out by the contraction and relaxation of opposing muscles. To carry out the movement shown, the triceps muscle (2) must contract while the biceps (1) relaxes.

22. **E.** Wilting of plants is caused by decreased turgor pressure due to a lack of water in the central vacuole. Uptake of water by the vacuole causes it to expand and exert pressure on the cell wall.

23. **A.** The centromeres joining sister chromatids split in anaphase. The chromosomes are then pulled to opposite poles.

24. **A.** B cells and immature T cells are produced in the marrow of the long bones, such as the femur or thigh bone.

25. **C.** Enzymes decrease the activation energy required for a chemical reaction to take place, allowing a reaction to proceed without a large energy input and thereby greatly increasing the reaction rate.

26. **E.** Only in bryophytes is the haploid gametophyte the dominant generation.

27. **D.** Gills, kidneys, and lungs all rely on countercurrent exchange for the intake of oxygen and/or release of waste compounds. The intestines do not feature countercurrent exchange.

28. **E.** Eutrophication, or the growth of algae, is caused by an excess of dissolved nutrients. The source of these nutrients is often agricultural or residential runoff.

29. **B.** Both parents have the dominant phenotype (dimples), but their child does not. The child must have the recessive genotype *dd*. The child must have inherited one recessive allele *d* from each parent. Therefore, both parents must be heterozygotes (*Dd*).

30. **D.** In competition, parasitism, and predation, one species benefits at the expense of the other. Commensalism is an ecological relationship in which one species benefits while the other is neither helped nor harmed.

31. **B.** Zooplankton are minuscule organisms that feed on algae or phytoplankton. While some zooplankton organisms feed on other zooplankton, the most common role for zooplankton is primary consumption.

32. **B.** The extent to which a phenotype is determined by differences in alleles in a population is referred to as heritability. Natural hair color is a highly heritable trait, whereas the number of legs has almost no heritability because there is little genetic variation for this phenotype in the population.

33. **D.** Natural selection changes the frequency of alleles within populations. A population is the smallest unit that can be affected by natural selection. An individual organism cannot be changed, within its lifetime, through natural selection.

34. **D.** In ecological succession, a plant community is replaced by a subsequent plant community. This occurs because the plants in the original community alter abiotic factors, such as shade and soil nutrients, making the ecosystem more suitable for the seeds of different plant species.

35. **E.** A carbon atom in the tissues of a consumer may be broken down via cellular respiration and released into the atmosphere. There, it may be taken up by a producer and converted to glucose through photosynthesis. The producer may subsequently break down the glucose for energy, once again releasing the carbon into the air. Carbon cannot pass directly from the tissues of a consumer to those of a producer.

36. **E.** Only certain soil bacteria are able to utilize nitrogen in the form of nitrogen gas from the atmosphere. Other organisms require nitrogen-fixing bacteria to convert nitrogen gas to other usable compounds (such as ammonia).

37. **A.** Directional selection results in a shift in the mean value for a continuous trait, such as body size, with no change in the variation among individuals. The curve shifts to the left or right without changing shape.

38. **A.** Monocots have scattered vascular tissue within their stems, leaves with parallel venation, and fibrous roots. Netlike veins and taproots are features of dicots.

39. **E.** The organism shown has distinct body segments (1a) and large pincers, or pedipalps (2a), and lacks a stinger at the end of the abdomen (4a). It is therefore Pseudoscorpiones.

40. **D.** Within chordates, the notochord evolved first and is shared, in some form, by all members of this group. In humans, the notochord evolved to form the gelatinous disks that cushion the spinal vertebrae.

41. **D.** Double fertilization, leading to the triploid endosperm tissue that makes up fruit, occurs in the ovary of the flower.

42. **D.** The production of urea serves to chemically join ammonia and carbon dioxide, thereby converting it to a relatively harmless compound. This prevents ammonia, which is toxic, from accumulating in the bloodstream and allows it to be eliminated without releasing large quantities of water.

43. **A.** Deoxygenated blood enters the right atrium of the heart (1) through each vena cava (7). From these, it is pumped to the right ventricle and through the pulmonary arteries, to the lungs.

44. **D.** In order for an allele to be acted on by natural selection, it must result in an increase in fitness. Fitness is defined as the ability to pass traits on to offspring. Therefore, individuals that produce the greatest number of offspring that grow to become fertile adults have the greatest fitness.

45. **D.** Like all eukaryotes, the cells of animals and fungi feature membrane-bound organelles. They are also capable of digestion outside of the cell, accomplished by secreting digestive enzymes and absorbing nutrients into the cell.

46. **A.** The corpus luteum, which forms after an egg is released from a follicle in the ovary, secretes estrogen and progesterone. These hormones cause the uterine lining to thicken. If a fertilized egg does not implant, the corpus luteum shrivels and the uterine lining is shed.

47. **C.** The first organisms were heterotrophic prokaryotes. The evolution of photosynthetic prokaryotes (cyanobacteria) led to an increase in Earth's atmospheric oxygen level. Eukaryotes and metazoa (animals) then evolved.

48. **C.** Only a reduction in gene flow is absolutely required for speciation to take place. Populations cannot evolve independently if their gene pools are shared.

49. **A.** The cotyledons of a dicot seed form the first "leaves" of the germinating plant. These are not true leaves, but they are capable of photosynthesis.

50. **B.** Pepsin is an enzyme that digests protein in the stomach. It is produced by cells as an inactive precursor to avoid damaging the proteins within the cells.

51. **B.** The structures on the cocklebur seed are able to attach to animal fur. They aid in seed dispersal.

52. **C.** Location 3 exhibited the greatest increase in algal growth in response to the addition of phosphorus (gray bars).

53. **C.** If the addition of phosphorus does not result in increased growth, this indicates that phosphorus was not a limiting nutrient. Algae at locations 4 and 5 did not exhibit growth in response to the addition of phosphorus.

54. **C.** The growth of algae in response to the addition of nitrogen indicates that this nutrient was a limiting factor. Algae at locations 4 and 5 exhibited growth in response to fertilization with nitrogen.

55. **D.** Nitrogen and phosphorus are incorporated into nucleic acids, such as DNA, which feature a phosphate group in the backbone, and protein, which is composed of amino acids containing nitrogen atoms.

56. **D.** In the F2 generation, 95 of a total of 548 flies have the dwarf, red eye. This corresponds to a ratio of approximately 3 in 16 flies.

57. **C.** The parent cross resulted in an F1 generation with normal-sized bodies and red eyes only. This indicates that these traits are dominant and that a dwarf body and purple eyes are recessive traits.

58. **A.** It is not known whether the F2 fly with red eyes is homozygous or heterozygous for this trait. Therefore, the offspring may exhibit either red or purple eyes. Because both parents have a dwarf body, a recessive trait, all offspring must also exhibit this trait.

59. **D.** Because the allele resulting in purple eyes is located close to the allele resulting in streaks, these traits are expected to be genetically linked. The combination of alleles present in the parents will be inherited together more often than expected, because the genes do not assort, or move into gametes, independently. The combinations of streaked body with purple eyes and normal body with red eyes will occur less often than expected in the F2 flies.

60. **E.** The streaked parent will be homozygous for the recessive streaked allele. It will have a *str* allele next to a wild-type allele for eye color, *pur*⁺. A purple-eyed parent will be homozygous for the recessive purple-eye allele. It will have a *pur* allele next to a wild-type allele for body color, *str*⁺. Each F2 fly will have one of each type of chromosome.

Biology-E Test Practice Test 2 Answers and Explanations

Answer Key

61. C	71. B
62. E	72. D
63. D	73. E
64. E	74. B
65. B	75. A
66. E	76. B
67. D	77. E
68. C	78. B
69. B	79. C
70. E	80. C

Answer Explanations

61. **C.** Producers in aquatic ecosystems, commonly phytoplankton, do not always make up the greatest amount of biomass. The phytoplankton may be very productive yet consist of a limited number of organisms at any given time.

62. **E.** One effect of the increase in global temperature due to carbon dioxide emissions is the movement of fish ranges to cooler locations, including deeper waters and higher latitudes.

63. **D.** Industrial fertilizer production, lightning, and nitrogen fixation by soil bacteria all convert atmospheric nitrogen gas to nitrogen compounds. Denitrifying bacteria return nitrogen compounds in the soil to the atmosphere.

64. **E.** When a population reaches the carrying capacity of its ecosystem, its growth curve levels off, and the population size no longer increases. This occurs at time point 12.

65. **B.** An invasive species thrives in an ecosystem because it lacks predators. It will have suitable food sources and ecological niches to exploit.

66. **E.** A lack of consistency in environmental conditions will favor semelparity. The offspring's genetic variation ensures that at least some will survive the changing conditions.

67. **D.** Terrestrial forests, the first of which developed in the Devonian period, are characterized by plants that grow to great height. Vascular tissues transport water and minerals from the roots to the leaves, enabling plants to grow tall.

68. **C.** Biogeography is the study of the distribution of species over the globe.

69. **B.** Competition, which involves the use of resources by other species, is a biotic factor that limits population growth. The remaining answer choices are abiotic factors.

70. **E.** The concept of inclusive fitness states that altruism can increase

an individual's fitness by increasing the number of offspring produced by genetically similar individuals, such as siblings or parents. Alarm calls and care for the offspring of others are examples of altruistic acts.

71. **B.** Pattern 2 shows uniform dispersion. Territorial species create this pattern as each individual maintains and protects an area of land around it, excluding others.

72. **D.** The diagram represents a rapidly increasing population. Most of the individuals in the population are young (20 and under).

73. **E.** Biodiversity includes ecosystem diversity, genetic diversity, and species diversity.

74. **B.** The evolution of cyanobacteria, the first oxygen-releasing photosynthetic organisms, led to the accumulation of oxygen in Earth's surface waters and atmosphere. The oxygen reacted with dissolved iron, creating the oxides found in rocks.

75. **A.** The Allee effect occurs when population are at low densities, and growth rate is low because individuals have difficulty locating mates. As a result, population growth is positively correlated with population density.

76. **B.** The frequency measures how often a particular tree species occurred in a plot. The tree with the highest frequency in plot 3 is *Acer rubum*, or red maple, with a frequency of 0.76.

77. **E.** Quaking aspen (*Populus tremuloides*) and balsam poplar (*Populus balsamifera*) are the most closely related species. They belong to the same genus, *Populus*.

78. **B.** Red maple and sugar maple are inversely correlated in the forest area studied. In plots where red maple occurs more frequently, sugar maple occurs less frequently, and vice versa.

79. **C.** The least amount of precipitation, about 3 mm, occurs in February.

80. **C.** According to the graphs, Taiyuan, China, is a temperate grassland. Its average annual temperature is 10.3°C, and its average annual precipitation is 381 mm, or 38.1 cm.

Biology-M Test Practice Test 2 Answers and Explanations

Answer Key

81. D	91. C
82. A	92. B
83. B	93. A
84. B	94. B
85. E	95. A
86. D	96. E
87. A	97. E
88. D	98. C
89. A	99. D
90. B	100. A

Answer Explanations

81. **D.** Digesting the plasmid with Eco RI and Hind III produces DNA fragments of approximately 0.3, 1.8, 1.0, and 0.7 kb in length. The 0.3 kb fragment is the shortest resulting from any of the answer choices, and smaller DNA fragments travel farther in gel electrophoresis.

82. **A.** Nearly all the somatic cells of an individual share the same DNA, carrying the same genetic information. Because different genes are expressed in different cell types, different RNA sequences and proteins are produced.

83. **B.** Animal cells placed in a hypotonic solution will rupture as water enters the cell through osmosis. A hypotonic solution has a lower concentration of solutes than the cell.

84. **B.** Glycogen and lipids are produced for the purpose of energy storage. Glycogen is composed of glucose molecules and is stored in the liver and muscles.

85. **E.** In a eukaryotic cell, DNA is replicated in the S phase. The cell enters the G2 and M phases, having completed DNA replication. However, the cell is still diploid, as sister chromatids are still bound at the centromere.

86. **D.** Ribosomes consist of rRNA and protein. Eukaryotic chromosomes consist of DNA wrapped around histone proteins.

87. **A.** Amylase, an enzyme found in saliva, is a protein. It is therefore composed of amino acids.

88. **D.** The amoeba moves by cytoplasmic streaming, which forms extensions called pseudopods. By extending these "false feet," an amoeba cell achieves locomotion. Streaming is due to the action of the cytoskeleton.

89. **A.** The Calvin cycle, or the dark reactions of photosynthesis, takes place in the stroma of the chloroplast.

90. **B.** Photosynthesis produces glucose and oxygen from carbon dioxide and water.

91. **C.** The complimentary codon on the template strand of DNA is transcribed to mRNA, resulting in a similar nucleotide sequence (5'–ACU–3'). The complimentary tRNA anticodon that binds to this mRNA sequence is 3'–UGA–5'.

92. **B.** Hormones are secreted into the bloodstream, while neurotransmitters are released into the synapses between neurons.

93. **A.** The ribosome, which is involved in translation of mRNA to protein, is composed of rRNA. Binding rRNA disrupts translation.

94. **B.** $FADH_2$ and NADH are formed by reduction of FAD and NAD^+ in the Krebs cycle. These reduced compounds carry electrons to the cytochrome proteins of the mitochondrial membrane.

95. **A.** The heaviest DNA, signified by the bottom band, is obtained at the 0-minute extraction.

96. **E.** After one cell division, the heavy chains have separated and formed double strands by pairing with light-isotope bases. After two cell divisions, the light chains have also paired with light-isotope chains.

97. **E.** As the bacteria continued to replicate, they would incorporate the light isotope of nitrogen into newly formed DNA. The top band would grow thicker as more DNA accrued. The heavy-isotope DNA strands would continue to separate and form new double strands of DNA, but no further heavy isotope would be incorporated. The middle band, formed by heavy and light chains, would remain the same.

98. **C.** Humans and pigs have identical amino acids at all positions except two. All other pairs of species shown differ at three or more positions.

99. **D.** A silent mutation is a point substitution resulting in a codon that specifies the same amino acid as the original codon. It does not result in an amino acid difference.

100. **A.** Bacteria lack a codon, present in alfalfa, yeast, and chicken, that codes for serine (S). Because bacteria are the most distantly related to all the other species in the table, this insertion most likely occurred first in the common ancestor of plants and animals.

Glossary

Acid: A substance that releases hydrogen ions in an aqueous solution, resulting in a pH of less than 7.0.

Acquired immunity: A state of the immune system that retains a "memory" of previously encountered antigens via B and T cells; when the same pathogens are later encountered, the immune system is able to mount an immediate, specific response.

Action potential: A signal that moves along a neuron from its dendrites to the axon terminals; a change in the electrical potential inside and outside the cell, produced by the opening and closing of ion channels.

Activation energy: The energy required for a chemical reaction to proceed; the quantity of energy affected by an enzyme.

Active site: The part of an enzyme that binds the substrate and catalyzes its reaction.

Active transport: A process in which energy is expended by a cell to move a substance against a concentration gradient, often across a cell membrane.

Adaptive radiation: Rapid speciation, leading to the formation of multiple, closely related species, that occurs when new niches become available (for example, Darwin's finches).

Adhesion: The property of water that refers to its ability to attract other surfaces and substances; important for water's capillary action.

ADP: Adenosine diphosphate; the lower-energy molecule formed when a phosphate group is removed from ATP; the molecule that is phosphorylated to form ATP.

Agarose gel electrophoresis: See *electrophoresis, gel.*

Allele: One of two or more versions of the same gene, which may be dominant or recessive to other alleles.

Alpha helix: A secondary structure of a protein in which the amino acid chain twists to form a tight spiral.

Amino acid: A simple compound that, when linked in a chain, makes up a polypeptide or protein; a molecule specified by one of twenty different R groups or side groups.

Amniotic fluid: The protective fluid that surrounds the fetus.

Amoeba: A single-celled heterotrophic protist that moves using cytoplasmic extensions (pseudopodia).

Anaphase: The third phase of mitosis, in which the sister chromatids separate at the centromeres and migrate to the opposite sides of the cell.

Antibiotic: A material, usually of microbial origin, that can kill or control bacteria.

Antibody: A Y-shaped protein produced by B cells in response to exposure to an antigen, which binds specifically to that antigen.

Anticodon: The series of three bases on a tRNA molecule that is complementary to one or several specific mRNA codons.

Artery: A large, thick-walled tube that carries blood from the heart toward the body tissues or lungs and branches into smaller arterioles.

Asexual reproduction: A form of reproduction that does not involve the fusion of nuclei and results in offspring that are genetically identical to the parent.

ATP: Adenosine triphosphate; a small molecule containing three phosphate groups, that is produced by cellular respiration and used as a source of energy in biochemical reactions.

Base: A solution with a pH greater than 7.0; an alkaline solution.

Base, nitrogen: See *nucleotide.*

Bilateral symmetry: The body plan of an organism that can be divided into two mirror halves through a central axis.

Biochemical reaction: A chemical reaction carried out within the cells or bodies of living organisms, often catalyzed by enzymes.

Blastocyst: The ball of cells that forms from the zygote.

Blood: The fluid connective tissue that flows through the circulatory system and transports needed materials and wastes to and from cells.

Bone: Hard, calcium-storing tissue that forms the vertebrate endoskeleton.

Capillary: Small vessels, with walls the width of a single cell, that carry blood through body tissues and facilitate gas exchange.

Carbon cycle: The biogeochemical cycle of carbon as it changes form (organic or inorganic) and location (ocean sediments, water, atmosphere, biosphere).

Cell: The smallest and most basic unit of life, consisting of at least a genome, membrane, and ribosomes.

Cell membrane: The cell structure, composed of a phospholipid bilayer and proteins, that surrounds the cytosol of a cell and regulates the flow of materials in and out of the cell.

Cell wall: The structure that surrounds the cell membranes of some prokaryotic and eukaryotic cells, providing structure and protection.

Cellular respiration: A biochemical process that produces ATP from the oxidation of glucose or other molecules; in eukaryotes, this process is carried out in the mitochondria.

Cellulose: A polymer of glucose that makes up plant cell walls.

Centriole: A cell structure associated with the formation of spindle proteins in mitosis and meiosis.

Chloroplast: The eukaryotic organelle in which photosynthesis takes place.

Chromosome: A circular or large, linear segment of DNA (and, in eukaryotes, histones) that contains genetic information.

Citric acid cycle (Krebs Cycle, TCA Cycle): A series of enzyme-catalyzed reactions in the mitochondria that break down pyruvate, providing energy and electrons to reduce NAD^+ to NADH and FAD to $FADH_2$, synthesizing two molecules of ATP, and producing carbon dioxide.

Codominance: The expression of both alleles of a gene if present together in an organism.

Codon: A sequence of three adjacent bases in a strand of DNA or mRNA that codes for (represents) a specific amino acid.

Cohesion: A property of water; the hydrogen bonding interactions between water molecules that result in their "sticking together," which leads to high surface tension.

Cytoplasm: The interior of a eukaryotic cell, which consists of the cytoskeleton, cytosol, and organelles and excludes the interior of the nucleus.

Cytoskeleton: The protein network inside a eukaryotic cell that provides the cell structure and shape.

Denature: To change an enzyme's tertiary structure in a way that disrupts its active site; denaturation may be due to changes in temperature, pH, or other conditions and may be temporary or permanent.

Dendrite: A short cellular extension from the neuron cell body, which connects to and receives signals from many other adjacent neurons.

Differentiation: The process, important in embryonic development and maintenance of the organism, by which an original parent cell forms populations of specialized daughter cells; the result of differences in gene expression.

DNA: Deoxyribonucleic acid; a double-stranded polymer of nucleotides in which alternating deoxyribose sugar and phosphate groups make up the backbones and paired nitrogenous bases make up the inside "rungs"; usually has a double helix configuration.

Dominant trait: A trait that is expressed when only a single allele for it is inherited.

Ecosystem: A system consisting of the biological and physical factors in an area, and their interactions.

Electrophoresis, gel: A DNA-analysis technique in which a charge difference causes DNA or protein to move through a porous medium; results in the separation of DNA fragments or proteins.

Embryo: The structure formed by a mitotically dividing zygote; in mammals, the structure that forms the fetus.

Emigration: The movement of organisms out of a population.

Endoplasmic reticulum (ER): A network of membranes, contiguous with the nuclear envelope, in which newly synthesized proteins are modified.

Endosymbiotic theory: The explanation of the origin of eukaryotic organelles (for example, mitochondria, chloroplasts) from a mutually beneficial symbiotic relationship between a larger cell and prokaryotic cells.

Endothermic: A chemical reaction that absorbs or requires energy because the products contain more energy than the reactants.

Energy: In physics, the ability to do work (such as carry out a chemical reaction, transport material, or move cells and tissues).

Enzyme: A protein that catalyzes a specific biochemical reaction by lowering the reaction's activation energy, greatly increasing the rate at which it occurs.

Eukaryote: A cell containing a nucleus and other membrane-bound organelles. Eukaryotic organisms may be unicellular or multicellular.

Evolution: Any change in the allele frequency of a population over time; the descent of species from common ancestors via speciation.

Exothermic: A chemical reaction that releases or produces energy because the products contain less energy than the reactants; exothermic reactions can provide energy to drive other endothermic reactions.

Facilitated diffusion: Passive transport through a membrane protein channel.

Fertilization: The process whereby the nucleus of a haploid ovum merges with that of a haploid sperm cell to produce a genetically unique, diploid zygote.

Follicle stimulating hormone (FSH): The pituitary hormone with multiple functions in both males and females, including driving the follicular phase of the menstrual cycle.

Frameshift mutation: A DNA insertion or deletion that changes the reading frame of the gene, usually resulting in a string of missense (amino acid substitutions) followed by a nonsense mutation (a stop codon, leading to a truncated protein).

Gametes: Haploid cells produced by meiosis for sexual reproduction; sperm and egg cells.

Gene: A sequence of chromosomal DNA that is transcribed and translated into a protein.

Gene expression: The synthesis of a protein and its resulting phenotype, from the information in a gene.

Gene linkage: The tendency of alleles of different genes to be inherited together due to the gene loci being close together on the chromosome.

Genetic code: The correspondence between codons in DNA and mRNA and specific amino acids in the resulting polypeptide; multiple codons may code for a single amino acid.

Genetic drift: Changes in the relative frequencies of alleles that occur due to chance events; observed in population bottlenecks and founder effects.

Genome: The complete set of genetic information contained in an organism's DNA.

Genotype: For a particular gene, the combination of alleles present in an organism's genome.

Gland: An organ that secretes hormones, such as those of the endocrine system.

Glucose: A biologically important six-carbon sugar (hexose) with a structural formula of $C_6H_{12}O_6$.

Golgi body: In eukaryotic cells, a network of membranes separate from the ER in which proteins are further modified and packaged for transport in vesicles that "bud" from the Golgi membranes. Also called *Golgi apparatus.*

Habitat: The type of environment that provides a species with the resources needed to survive.

Haploid: Having one copy or homolog of each chromosome, or $1n$; the most common state for gametes.

Hemoglobin: A large, iron-containing protein found in red blood cells, which binds and transports oxygen to cells.

Heterozygous: A genotype that involves different alleles on the homologous chromosomes.

Homeostasis: The process of maintaining a fairly consistent environment within a cell or organism.

Homologous pair: In a diploid organism, chromosomes containing the same genes, one originating from the mother and one from the father.

Homologous structures: Anatomic features that share similarities due to both species having evolved from a common ancestor, for example, the forearms of primates and the front fins of dolphins.

Homozygous: A genotype that involves having the same allele on both homologous chromosomes in a pair.

Hormone: A chemical substance that is secreted by a gland and that travels through the bloodstream; hormones affect only those body tissues with the appropriate receptors.

Human growth hormone (HGH): A pituitary hormone that stimulates growth and maintenance of body tissues.

Hydrophilic: Literally, "water loving" or water attracting.

Hydrophobic: Literally, "water fearing" or water repelling.

Immigration: The movement of organisms into a population.

Immune system: The body system that protects multicellular organisms from infection; consists of innate and acquired components.

Inheritance: The passing of genotypes and phenotypes from one generation to the next.

Innate immunity: The nonspecific barriers and responses to infectious agents (pathogens); includes the skin, mucous membranes, macrophages, and complement proteins.

Ionic bond: Type of bond in which one atom donates electrons to another; the compounds often form ions when dissolved in water.

Insertion (DNA): A small-scale mutation in which one or several base pairs are added to a DNA sequence, possibly resulting in a frameshift.

Interspecific competition: Competition for resources between individuals of different species.

Intraspecific competition: Competition for resources between individuals of the same species.

Ion: A charged atom or molecule.

Keystone species: A species that helps to maintain biodiversity in an ecosystem through predation and other community interactions.

Krebs cycle: See *citric acid cycle*.

Law of dominance: Mendel's observation that, when different alleles of the same gene are inherited, the phenotype associated with one allele may mask or override the expression of the other allele.

Law of independent assortment: Mendel's observation that the alleles for one gene are inherited in a way that is not influenced by the inheritance of the alleles for any other gene; this law is violated in gene linkage.

Law of segregation: Mendel's observation that each parent passes one allele of a gene to an offspring, which, in combination with the allele from the other parent, results in a new or different genotype.

Luteinizing hormone (LH): A pituitary hormone that in females triggers ovulation and in males stimulates the production of testosterone.

Meiosis: The two-step process by which a eukaryotic cell separates the pairs of homologous chromosomes in its nucleus, forming haploid cells that contain one homolog from each pair (gametes); homologs separate in meiosis I.

Messenger RNA (mRNA): The form of RNA that is transcribed, by RNA polymerase, from genetic information in nuclear DNA.

Metabolism: The entire set of chemical reactions and processes in a cell or organism.

Metaphase: The second phase of mitosis, in which the replicated chromosomes align in the central plane of the cell.

Mitochondria: In eukaryotic cells, the organelle with a highly folded internal membrane, responsible for converting the energy in glucose and other molecules to ATP via respiration.

Mitosis: The process by which the eukaryotic nucleus replicates, allowing cell division.

Molecular biology: The study of the molecular interactions and processes within the cell (for example, cell cycle regulation, DNA replication, protein synthesis).

Mutation: Any change in the DNA sequence or chromosomal structure of an organism; may be passed on to offspring.

Natural selection: A mechanism for evolutionary change in which alleles that confer greater fitness become more common in a population.

Nerve: A bundle of neurons.

Neuron: A cell of the nervous system capable of conducting an action potential; a neuron consists of dendrites, a cell body (soma), and a long axon that transmits a signal to the terminal branches.

Neurotransmitter: Any of a number of chemical messengers that affect adjacent neurons and are released by neurons helping to transmit signals through the nervous system.

Neutral: In chemistry, a solution that has a pH of about 7.0 and is neither acidic nor basic.

Nucleic acid: A polymer of nucleotides; DNA or RNA.

Nucleotide: A monomer composed of a nitrogenous base, five-carbon sugar, and phosphate group; the building block of DNA and RNA.

Nucleus: A membrane-bound structure of eukaryotic cells; contains the chromosomes (genetic material).

Organ: An organized group of tissues, which forms a structure that performs some function.

Organ system: A collection of organs that carry out a bodily function in a coordinated fashion.

Osmosis: The diffusion of water (the solvent) from an area of lower total solute concentration to an area of higher total solute concentration.

Passive transport: A mechanism whereby no energy is expended by a cell to move a substance across a membrane (for example, diffusion down a concentration gradient).

Pathogen: An agent that causes infectious disease, such as a bacterium or a virus.

pH: The "power of hydrogen," a logarithmic value of the number of hydrogen ions (H^+) in a solution.

Phospholipid bilayer: A main component of the cell membrane and internal membranes, consisting of two sheets of phospholipid molecules, arranged with their hydrophilic "heads" on the surfaces and their hydrophobic "tails" in the interior layer.

Photorespiration: In plants, an inefficient and unnecessary process caused by low carbon dioxide and high oxygen levels.

Photosynthesis: The biochemical process that harvests the energy in sunlight and converts it to chemical energy in the form of glucose. Photosynthesis takes place in two stages: the light reactions and the Calvin cycle, or dark reactions.

Phototropism: The directional growth of a plant toward a source of light.

Phylogeny: A grouping of organisms based on descent from common ancestors, using both molecular and morphologic information.

Plant: A multicellular, photosynthetic autotroph with complex, differentiated tissues and cells that contain chloroplasts.

Point mutation: A change in a single base of an organism's DNA.

Polymerase chain reaction (PCR): A technique for creating multiple copies of a piece of DNA from a small sample, using the enzyme DNA polymerase, sequence-specific DNA primers, and free nucleotides, in a solution that is cycled through different temperatures.

Population: Members of the same species that share an ecosystem.

Primary structure: The sequence of amino acids in a protein.

Producer: An autotrophic organism, which is able to provide organic materials to heterotrophs or consumers.

Product: In chemistry, the substance or substances that result from the chemical reaction (chemical change) of one or more reactants.

Prokaryote: A simple, single-celled organism lacking a nucleus and membrane-bound organelles; eubacteria or archaea.

Prolactin: A hormone that stimulates lactation.

Promoter: A region of DNA that regulates the transcription of a nearby gene.

Prophase: The first phase of mitosis, in which the indistinct chromatin condenses into readily identifiable chromosomes and the nuclear envelope disappears.

Protein: A large polymer of amino acid subunits made up of one or more polypeptides.

Punnett square: A graphical presentation used to determine the probabilities of offspring genotypes by showing the possible gamete combinations from parents.

Qualitative trait: A trait that cannot be measured and often occurs in two or more distinct forms in a population (for example, eye color). (Compare to *quantitative trait.*)

Quaternary structure: Describes how the polypeptide proteins associate with one another in their final configurations.

Quantitative trait: A trait that can be measured and is found along a continuum in a population, such as size or length, and is usually influenced by many genes. (See *qualitative trait.*)

Reactant: The chemical substance or substances that enter into a reaction and are altered to create a product or products.

Receptor: A molecule on a cell surface that binds to specific hormones or other compounds.

Recessive trait: A trait that is expressed only when the dominant allele is not present; a trait usually requiring the inheritance of two recessive alleles (homozygous recessive genotype).

Red blood cell: A disk-shaped blood cell, lacking a nucleus, that contains hemoglobin and is responsible for binding and transporting oxygen.

Replication (of DNA): The semiconservative copying of a cell's genome, carried out by "unzipping" of DNA strands, complementary base pairing of free nucleotides, and creation of a new strand by DNA polymerase.

Reproductive isolation: A condition in which two previously interbreeding gene pools become separate due to geographic, behavioral, or physiologic reasons; often leads to speciation.

Restriction enzyme: An enzyme that cleaves double-stranded DNA at a very specific sequence, called the recognition site.

Ribonucleic acid (RNA): A normally single-stranded polymer of nucleotides containing a backbone of alternating ribose sugar and phosphate, and a sequence of nitrogenous bases.

Ribosomal RNA (rRNA): The RNA that, along with ribosomal proteins, makes up the ribosomes.

Ribosome: A structure composed of rRNA and protein that is found in multiple copies in all cells and that translates mRNA to synthesize protein.

Secondary structure: The shapes formed by the initial coiling or folding of a polypeptide, such as alpha helices and beta pleated sheets.

Semipermeable: Permitting some substances to pass while disallowing others.

Sequencing, gene: Determining the order of nitrogenous bases that make up a gene.

Sex chromosomes: In mammals, the X and Y chromosomes.

Sex-linked gene: A gene that is located on either the X or Y chromosome and that does not follow Mendelian patterns of inheritance.

Sex-linked trait: A trait influenced by a gene that is located on either the X or Y chromosome.

Sexual reproduction: A form of reproduction that involves combining the haploid genomes of two parents to form genetically unique, diploid offspring.

Sexual selection: Selection that occurs when individuals with phenotypes that make them more likely to mate have greater fitness.

Skeleton: A rigid internal (endoskeleton) or external (exoskeleton) framework that provides structure and support.

Skin: The constantly shedding epithelial tissue that surrounds and protects an animal's body.

Skull: The set of fused bones that encases and protects the brain.

Smooth muscle: Nonstriated muscle tissue that is under involuntary control.

Solute: The material dissolved in a solvent.

Solvent: A liquid or gas that dissolves a solute.

Somatic cell: Any cell within the body that is not a germ cell (gamete).

Speciation: An evolutionary process in which two new, separate non-interbreeding genetic pools arise from one progenitor population.

Species: The most restrictive taxonomic category; often defined as a group of organisms that normally breed to produce fertile offspring.

Stabilizing selection: Natural selection due to increased fitness of individuals with average or mean phenotypes in a population (for example, average size, length, or degree of pigmentation); leads to a reduction in genetic variation.

Substitution: The simplest type of DNA mutation, which involves a change from one nitrogen base to another, resulting in a missense or nonsense codon.

Synapse: The tiny gap between neurons, into which neurotransmitters are released.

T cell: The type of lymphocyte produced in the thymus that is responsible for the destruction of cells infected with viruses and the activation of B cells.

Territoriality: An animal behavior centered on the control of access to a geographical resource (for example, defending a territory or nest from intruders).

Tertiary structure: The final, three-dimensional structure of a protein after folding.

Testosterone: A hormone produced in both the testes and ovaries that is associated with development of male secondary sex characteristics.

Thyroid: Endocrine gland located in the neck that secretes the hormones that regulate metabolism.

Thyroid-stimulating hormone (TSH): A pituitary hormone that stimulates the thyroid gland to secrete thyroid hormones.

Tissue: A group of cells from a common origin that carry out the same function.

Transcription: The process of producing a complementary messenger RNA strand from a DNA template by copying the genetic information needed for translation of the protein. A protein, hormone, or other compound that affects the transcription and expression of a gene is a transcription factor.

Transfer RNA (tRNA): A form of RNA that attaches to an amino acid and carries it to the ribosome for protein assembly.

Transpiration: The evaporation of water in the leaves and stems of a plant, which serves to pull up more water from the roots.

Tricarboxylic acid cycle: See *citric acid cycle*.

Trophic level: In an ecosystem community, the feeding level of a population (for example, producer, primary consumer, secondary consumer).

Tropism: Response toward or away from a stimulus.

Uric acid: The nitrogen-containing molecule that is produced in order to contain nitrogen compounds safely and dispose of them with minimal water loss.

Vaccination: A process in which safe viral and bacterial products are introduced into the body, so that when the agents are later encountered, the immune system is able to mount an immediate, specific response.

Vacuole: A vesicle that stores food, water, or other substances in the cell; the large, central vacuole of a plant cell stores water and pigments.

Vascular tissue: In plants, responsible for conducting water and sap in tubes (for example, xylem and phloem).

Vein: In animals, a large tube with valves that carries the blood from the smaller venules to the heart; in plants, a tube consisting of xylem and phloem.

Vena cava: One of the two very large-diameter veins that empty into the right atrium of the heart.

Vertebrate: Organism characterized by the presence of a backbone in which the hollow dorsal nerve cord is enclosed in bony vertebrae that are cushioned by disks derived from the notochord.

Vestigial structure: A structure that is no longer useful or serves a different, less essential function than that for which it originally evolved.

Virus: A nonliving molecular parasite of cells that use host cellular mechanisms (for example, ribosomes, polymerases) in order to replicate.

Water cycle: The worldwide biogeochemical cycle of water, involving evaporation, transpiration, condensation, precipitation, runoff, and groundwater accumulation.

White blood cell: An immune system cell of the blood, which does not carry hemoglobin; also called a *leukocyte*.

X chromosome: The large sex chromosome, of which females have two; genes on the X chromosome are sex linked.

Y chromosome: In mammals, the sex chromosome that contains the male-determining gene; genes on the Y chromosome are sex linked.

Zygote: The single diploid cell that results from the fusion of a sperm cell's haploid nucleus with that of an egg cell.

About the Author

Maria Malzone holds a bachelor's degree in biology from the State University of New York at Stony Brook and a master's degree in technical communication from the University of Washington in Seattle. She is a certified biology teacher in the state of New York and has nearly a decade of experience writing and editing instructional material. Maria has written live assessment items, classroom lesson plans, and a wide range of test-prep materials for many different scientific exams. Maria is a senior assessment editor for Northeast Editing, Inc., a full-service educational publisher based in Northeastern Pennsylvania.

Also Available

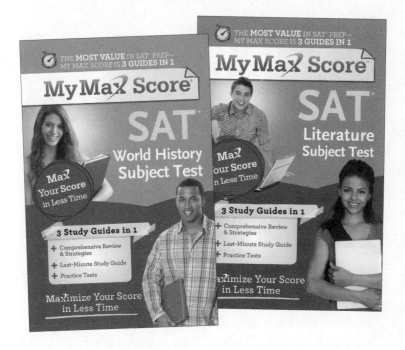

Also Available

My Max Score AP Biology
by Dr. Robert S. Stewart Jr. • 978-1-4022-4315-8

My Max Score AP Calculus AB/BC
by Carolyn Wheater • 978-1-4022-4313-4

My Max Score AP English Language and Composition
by Jocelyn Sisson • 978-1-4022-4312-7

My Max Score AP English Literature and Composition
by Tony Armstrong • 978-1-4022-4311-0

My Max Score AP European History
by Ira Shull and Mark Dziak • 978-1-4022-4318-9

My Max Score AP Statistics
by Amanda Ross, PhD, and Anne Collins • 978-1-4022-7286-8

My Max Score AP U.S. Government and Politics
by Del Franz • 978-1-4022-4314-1

My Max Score AP U.S. History
by Michael Romano • 978-1-4022-4310-3

My Max Score AP World History
by Kirby Whitehead • 978-1-4022-4317-2

$14.99 U.S./$17.99 CAN/£9.99 UK

To download additional AP, SAT, and ACT practice tests and
learn more about My Max Score, visit mymaxscore.com.

My Max Score
AP* Study Guide Apps
Maximize Your Score in Less Time

**Our bestselling
AP Study Guides
are now interactive
and available in
the App Store.**

These iPad and iPhone
compatible apps contain
everything you need to
prepare for your AP exam.

The MyMaxScore AP Study Guide apps:

✔ Provide an interactive way to study for AP exams
✔ Allow you to track your time spent on each question
✔ Give you the opportunity to make notations and mark questions for
  further study
✔ Give you a personalized progress report
✔ Help you stay organized

It's never too early to start a complete review, but it's also never too late
for a score-boosting crash session.

Download these valuable AP test prep apps today:

✔ AP Calculus AB/BC
✔ AP U.S. History
✔ AP English Language and Composition
✔ AP English Literature and Composition
✔ AP U.S. Government and Politics

Go to MyMaxScore.com today to learn
more about how you can max your score!

Essentials from
Dr. Gary Gruber
and the creators of My Max Score

*"Gruber can ring the bell on any number
of standardized exams."*
—*Chicago Tribune*

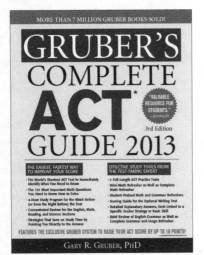

$19.99 U.S./£14.99 UK
978-1-4022-7301-8

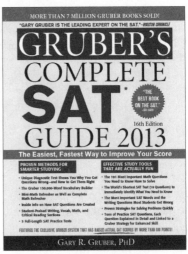

$19.99 U.S./£14.99 UK
978-1-4022-6492-4

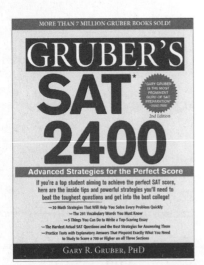

$16.99 U.S./$19.99 CAN/£11.99 UK
978-1-4022-4308-0

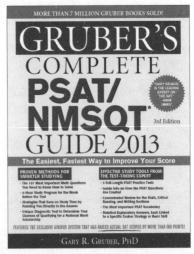

$13.99 U.S./£9.99 UK
978-1-4022-6495-5

"Gruber's methods make the questions
seem amazingly simple to solve."
—*Library Journal*

"Gary Gruber is the leading expert on the SAT."
—*Houston Chronicle*

$16.99 U.S./£11.99 UK
978-1-4022-5337-9

$14.99 U.S./£9.99 UK
978-1-4022-5340-9

$14.99 U.S./£9.99 UK
978-1-4022-5343-0

$12.99 U.S./£8.99 UK
978-1-4022-6072-8

Notes

Notes

Notes

Notes

Notes